Fodor's
BEIJING

WELCOME TO BEIJING

China's capital city is a vibrant jumble of neighborhoods and districts. Home to such historic treasures as the Forbidden City and the Summer Palace, Beijing is constantly transforming itself with a building boom that never seems to end. Colorful markets stand toe-to-toe with ritzy shopping malls, and lively old *hutong* (alleyway neighborhoods) stand in the shadow of glittering towers that dwarf their surroundings. Given the country's spectacular economic growth, spending time in Beijing is at once the exploration of an ancient civilization and the discovery of a modern world power.

TOP REASONS TO GO

★ **Forbidden City:** The world's most well-preserved palace housed Emperors for centuries.

★ **Modern Architecture:** The world's top architects are reshaping Beijing.

★ **Great Wall:** Mankind's most impressive fortification is just a short drive away.

★ **Real Chinese Food:** Flavors from all over the country are here for the tasting.

★ **Unique Markets:** Everything from kitsch to curio, cheap handbags to grade-A pearls.

★ **Tiananmen Square:** The country's political heart is also a spectacular public square.

Fodor's BEIJING

Publisher: Amanda D'Acierno, *Senior Vice President*

Editorial: Arabella Bowen, *Executive Editorial Director*; Linda Cabasin, *Editorial Director*

Design: Fabrizio La Rocca, *Vice President, Creative Director*; Tina Malaney, *Associate Art Director*; Chie Ushio, *Senior Designer*; Ann McBride, *Production Designer*

Photography: Melanie Marin, *Associate Director of Photography*; Jessica Parkhill and Jennifer Romains, *Researchers*

Maps: Rebecca Baer, *Map Editor*; David Lindroth; Mark Stroud, Moon Street Cartography, *Cartographers*

Production: Linda Schmidt, *Managing Editor*; Evangelos Vasilakis, *Associate Managing Editor*; Angela L. McLean, *Senior Production Manager*

Sales: Jacqueline Lebow, *Sales Director*

Marketing & Publicity: Heather Dalton, *Marketing Director*; Katherine Fleming, *Senior Publicist*

Business & Operations: Susan Livingston, *Vice President, Strategic Business Planning*; Sue Daulton, *Vice President, Operations*

Fodors.com: Megan Bell, *Executive Director, Revenue & Business Development*; Yasmin Marinaro, *Senior Director, Marketing & Partnerships*

Copyright © 2014 by Fodor's Travel, a division of Random House, Inc.

Editors: Robert Fisher and Margaret Kelly

Editorial Contributors: Sky Canaves, Gareth Clark, Julius Honnor, Ami Li, Adrian Standiford

Production Editor: Elyse Rozelle

4th Edition

ISBN 978-0-7704-3245-4

ISSN 1934-5518

All details in this book are based on information supplied to us at press time. Always confirm information when it matters, especially if you're making a detour to visit a specific place. Fodor's expressly disclaims any liability, loss, or risk, personal or otherwise, that is incurred as a consequence of the use of any of the contents of this book.

SPECIAL SALES

This book is available at special discounts for bulk purchases for sales promotions or premiums. For more information, e-mail specialmarkets@randomhouse.com

PRINTED IN COLOMBIA

10 9 8 7 6 5 4 3 2 1

CONTENTS

Fodor's Features

ABOUT
THIS GUIDE

Fodor's Recommendations

Everything in this guide is worth doing—we don't cover what isn't—but exceptional sights, hotels, and restaurants are recognized with additional accolades. **Fodor's**Choice★ indicates our top recommendations; and **Best Bets** call attention to notable hotels and restaurants in various categories. Care to nominate a new place? Visit Fodors.com/contact-us.

Trip Costs

We list prices wherever possible to help you budget well. Hotel and restaurant price categories from $ to $$$$ are noted alongside each recommendation. For hotels, we include the lowest cost of a standard double room in high season. For restaurants, we cite the average price of a main course at dinner or, if dinner isn't served, at lunch. For attractions, we always list adult admission fees; discounts are usually available for children, students, and senior citizens.

Hotels

Our local writers vet every hotel to recommend the best overnights in each price category, from budget to expensive. Unless otherwise specified, you can expect private bath, phone, and TV in your room. For expanded hotel reviews, facilities, and deals visit Fodors.com.

Restaurants

Unless we state otherwise, restaurants are open for lunch and dinner daily. We mention dress code only when there's a specific requirement and reservations only when they're essential or not accepted. To make restaurant reservations, visit Fodors.com.

Credit Cards

The hotels and restaurants in this guide typically accept credit cards. If not, we'll say so.

Top Picks	Hotels &
★ **Fodor's**Choice	**Restaurants**
	⬚ Hotel
Listings	↵ Number of rooms
✉ Address	
✉ Branch address	⎙ Meal plans
☎ Telephone	✗ Restaurant
🖷 Fax	⬠ Reservations
⊕ Website	🏛 Dress code
✉ E-mail	⊟ No credit cards
📧 Admission fee	$ Price
☉ Open/closed times	
Ⓜ Subway	**Other**
⊹ Directions or Map coordinates	⇨ See also
	☞ Take note
	🏌 Golf facilities

EXPERIENCE BEIJING

The Heart of the Dragon

WHAT'S WHERE

1 Dongcheng District.
You'll only be able to truly say you've seen Beijing after wandering through Dongcheng, which is packed with the city's top must-see attractions. Tiananmen Square and the Forbidden City top anyone's list of things to do, but don't forget to explore the *hutong* (alleyway) neighborhoods that surround the Drum and Bell towers and the Buddhist grandeur of the Lama Temple. In the summer of 2010, the former district of Chongwen, situated to the southeast of the imperial palace, was subsumed into Dongcheng. Once upon a time, this area teemed with the activity of markets, gambling parlors, and less savory establishments. A historically accurate (but sanitized) re-creation of old Qianmen Street recaptures some of that lost glory. The Temple of Heaven features some of China's most impressive imperial-era architecture.

2 Xicheng District.
Along with Dongcheng, Xicheng encompasses the historically significant areas of Beijing that once lay safe inside the city walls. Together the two districts make up the capital's old inner core with the Forbidden City, home to the ruling imperial family, sitting proudly in the center. Six small lakes west of that key landmark lie at the heart of the district, which was once an imperial playground and is now home to China's top leaders. Farther west, fashionable young Beijingers spend their hard-earned cash in the side-by-side shopping malls at Xidan. Tea lovers won't want to miss Maliandao Tea Street.

3 Chaoyang District.
This unwieldy district wraps around many of the areas forming new Beijing. With the skyline-altering Central Business District in the south, the nightlife of Sanlitun in the middle, and the 798 Art District (aka Dashanzi) and Olympic Park in the north, Chaoyang represents today's China: lots of flash, with very little or no connection to the country's 5,000 years of history, but plenty of action.

4 Haidian District.
The nation's brightest minds study at prestigious Tsinghua and Peking universities in Beijing's northwestern Haidian District. China's own budding Silicon Valley, Zhongguancun, is also located here. Need to stretch your legs and get some fresh air? Head for one of the former imperial retreats at the Summer Palace, Fragrant Hills Park, or the Beijing Botanical Garden.

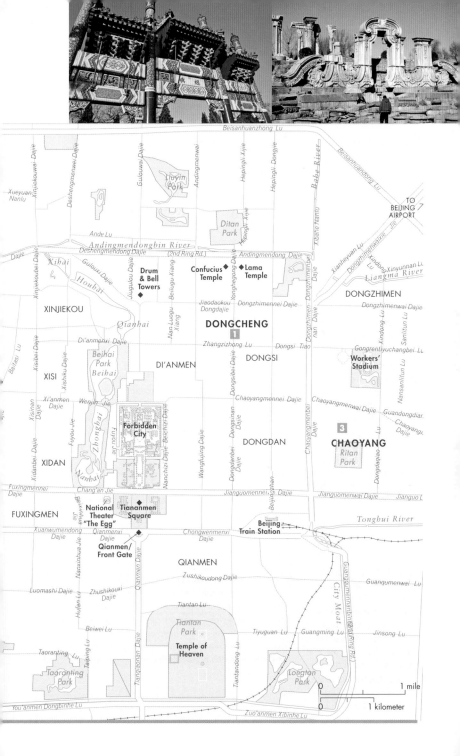

Beisanhuanzhong Lu

TO
BEIJING
AIRPORT

Liangma River

DONGZHIMEN

Xueyuan
Nanlu

Luyin
Park

Ditan
Park

Drum
& Bell
Towers

Confucius
Temple

Lama
Temple

XINJIEKOU

Qianhai

DONGCHENG
1

Beihai
Park
Beihai

DI'ANMEN

Zhangzizhong Lu

Dongsi Tiao

DONGSI

Workers'
Stadium

XISI

Forbidden
City

DONGDAN

CHAOYANG
3

Ritan
Park

XIDAN

Chang'an Jie

Jianguomennei Dajie

Jianguomenwai Dajie

Jianguo L

FUXINGMEN

National
Theater
"The Egg"

Tiananmen
Square

Beijing
Train Station

Tonghui River

Qianmen/
Front Gate

QIANMEN

Zushikoudong Dajie

Guanqumenwai Lu

Luomashi Dajie

Zhushikouxi
Dajie

Tiantan Lu

Tiantan
Park

Temple of
Heaven

Tiyuguan Lu

Guangming Lu

Jinsong Lu

Taoranting

Taoranting
Park

Longtan
Park

0   1 mile

0   1 kilometer

You'anmen Dongbinhe Lu

Zuo'anmen Xibinhe Lu

WELCOME TO BEIJING

When to Go

The best time to visit Beijing is spring or early fall; the weather is better and crowds are a bit smaller. Book at least one month in advance during these times of year. In winter Beijing's Forbidden City and Summer Palace can look fantastical and majestic, especially when traditional tiled roofs are covered with a light dusting of snow and there are few tourists.

The weather in Beijing is at its best in September and October, with a good chance of sunny days and mild temperatures. Winters are very cold, but it seldom snows. Some restaurants may be poorly heated, so be prepared with a warm sweater. Late April through June is lovely. In July the days are hot and excruciatingly humid with a good chance of rain. Spring is also the time of year for Beijing's famous dust storms. Pollution is an issue year-round.

Avoid travel during Chinese New Year and National Day. Millions of Chinese travel during these weeks, making it difficult to book hotels, tours, and transportation. If you must visit during Chinese New Year, be sure to check out the traditional temple fairs that take place at religious sites around the city.

Getting Around

On Foot: Though traffic and modernization have put a bit of a cramp in Beijing's walking style, meandering remains one of the best ways to experience the capital—especially the old hutong.

By Bike: The proliferation of cars (some 1,000 new automobiles take to the streets of the capital every day, bringing the total to more than 5 million vehicles) has made biking less pleasant and more dangerous. Fortunately, most streets have wide, well-defined bike lanes often separated from other traffic by an island. Bikes can be rented at many hotels and next to some subway stations.

By Subway: The subway is the best way to avoid Beijing's frequent traffic jams. With the opening of new lines, Beijing's subway service is increasingly convenient. The metropolitan area is currently served by 14 lines as well as an express line to the airport. The subway runs from about 5 am to midnight daily, depending on the station. Fares are Y2 per ride for any distance and transfers are free. Stations are marked in both Chinese and English, and stops are also announced in both languages. Subways are best avoided during rush hours, when severe overcrowding is unavoidable.

By Taxi: The taxi experience in Beijing has improved significantly as the city's taxi companies gradually shift to cleaner, more comfortable new cars. In the daytime, flag-fall for taxis is Y10 for the first 3 km (2 miles) and Y2 per kilometer thereafter. The rate rises to Y3 per kilometer on trips over 15 km (8 miles) and after 11 pm, when the flag-fall also increases to Y11. At present, there's also a Y1 gas surcharge for any rides exceeding 3 km (2 miles). ⚠ Be sure to check that the meter has been engaged to avoid fare negotiations at your destination. Taxis are easy to hail during the day, but can be difficult during evening rush hour, especially when it's raining. If you're having difficulty, go to the closest hotel and wait in line there. Few taxi drivers speak English, so ask your hotel concierge to write down your destination in Chinese.

Getting Oriented

At the heart of Beijing sits the Forbidden City, home of the emperors of old, which is adjacent to the secretive and off-limits Zhongnanhai, home of China's current leadership. The rest of the city revolves around this core area, with a series of concentric rings roads reaching out into the suburbs, and most major arteries running north–south and east–west. As you explore Beijing, you'll find that taxis are often the best way to get around. However, if the recently expanded subway system goes where you're headed, it's often a faster option than dealing with traffic, which has become increasingly congested in recent years with the rise of private automobiles.

The city is divided into 18 municipal and suburban districts (*qu*). Only four of these districts are the central stomping grounds for most visitors; our coverage focuses on those districts. **Dongcheng** ("east district") encompasses the Forbidden City, Tiananmen Square, Wangfujing (a major shopping street), the Lama Temple, and many other historical sites dating back to imperial times. **Xicheng** ("west district"), directly west of Dongcheng, is a lovely lake district that includes Beihai Park, former playground of the imperial family, and a series of connected lakes bordered by willow trees, courtyard-lined hutong, and lively bars. **Chaoyang** is the biggest and busiest district, occupying the areas north, east, and south of the eastern Second Ring Road. As it lies outside the Second Ring Road, which marked the eastern demarcation of the old city wall, there's little of historical interest here, though it boasts many of the city's top hotels, restaurants, and shops. Chaoyang is also home to the foreign embassies, multinational companies, the Central Business District, and the Olympic Park. **Haidian,** the district that's home to China's top universities and technology companies, is northwest of the Third Ring Road; it's packed with shops selling electronics and students cramming for their next exam.

Etiquette

It's respectful to dress modestly at religious sites: cover your shoulders and don't wear short skirts or shorts. Keep in mind that authorities are very sensitive about public behavior in Tiananmen Square, which teems with plainclothes state security officers at all times.

Street Vocabulary

Here are some terms you'll see over and over again. These words will appear on maps and street signs, and they're part of the name of just about every place you go:

Dong is east, **xi** is west, **nan** is south, **bei** is north, and **zhong** means middle. **Jie** and **lu** mean street and road respectively, and **da** means big, so dajie equals avenue.

Gongyuan means park. Jingshan Park is also called Jingshan Gongyuan.

Nei means inside and **wai** means outside. You will often come across these terms on streets that used to pass through a gate of the old city wall. Andingmen Neidajie, for example, is the section of the street located inside the Second Ring Road (where the gate used to be), whereas Andingmen Waidajie is the section outside the gate.

Qiao, or bridge, is part of the place name at just about every entrance and exit on the ring roads.

Men, meaning door or gate, indicates a street that once passed through an entrance in the old wall that surrounded the city until it was mostly torn down in the 1960s. The entrances to parks and some other places are also referred to as *men*.

BEIJING
TOP ATTRACTIONS

Forbidden City

(A) The Forbidden City has been home to a long line of emperors, beginning with Yongle, in 1420, and ending with Puyi (made famous by Bernardo Bertolucci's film *The Last Emperor*), who was forced out of the complex by a warlord in 1924. The Forbidden City is the largest palace in the world, as well as the best preserved, and offers the most complete collection of imperial architecture in China.

Magnificent Markets

(B) It's hard to resist: so much to bargain for, so little time! Visit outdoor Panjiayuan (aka the Dirt Market), where some 3,000 vendors sell antiques, Cultural Revolution memorabilia, and handicrafts from across China. Looking for knockoffs? The Silk Alley Market is popular with tourists, but local expats prefer the Yashow Market, which has better prices.

Lama Temple

(C) The sweet smell of incense permeates one of the few functioning Buddhist temples in Beijing. When Emperor Yongzheng took the throne in 1723, his former residence was converted into this temple. During the Qianlong Period (1736–95) it became a center of the Yellow Hat sect of Tibetan Buddhism. At its high point, 1,500 lamas lived here. The Hall of Celestial Kings houses a statue of Maitreya, and the Wanfu Pavilion has a 75½-foot Buddha carved from one piece of sandalwood.

Summer Palace

(D) This garden complex dates back eight centuries to when the first emperor of the Jin Dynasty built the Gold Mountain Palace on Longevity Hill. Notable sights are the Long Corridor (a covered wooden walkway) and the Hall of Benevolent Longevity. At the west end of the lake is the famous Marble Boat that Cixi built with

money intended to create a Chinese navy. The palace, which served as an imperial summer retreat, was ransacked by British and French soldiers in 1860 and burned in 1900 by Western soldiers seeking revenge for the Boxer Rebellion.

Confucius Temple
(E) This temple, with its towering cypress and pine trees, offers a serene escape from the crowds at nearby Lama Temple. This is the second-largest Confucian temple in China, after that in Qufu, the master's hometown in Shandong Province. First built in the 14th century, the Confucius Temple was renovated in the 18th century.

Temple of Heaven
(F) The Temple of Heaven is one of the best examples of religious architecture in China. Construction began in the early 15th century under the orders of Emperor Yongle. The complex took 14 years to complete; it contains three main buildings where the emperor, as the "Son of Heaven," offered semiannual prayers. The sprawling, tree-filled complex is a pleasant place for wandering: watch locals practicing martial arts, playing traditional instruments, and enjoying ballroom dancing on the grass.

Tiananmen Square
(G) Walking beneath the red flags of Tiananmen Square is a quintessential Beijing experience. The political heart of modern China, the square covers 100 acres, making it the world's largest public square. It was here, from the Gate of Heavenly Peace, that Mao Zedong proclaimed the founding of the People's Republic of China in 1949, and it is here he remains, embalmed for eternity in a mausoleum constructed in the square's center. Many Westerners think only of the massive student demonstrations here in the 1980s, but it has been the site of protests, rallies, and marches for close to 100 years.

GREAT ITINERARIES

The Italian priest Matteo Ricci arrived in Beijing in 1598. His efforts to understand the capital led him to stay for another 12 years. You, on the other hand, have to get back home before the week's out. But while you may not have the luxury of time on your side, you do have the advantage of something Ricci could only dream of: our handy guide to the best one-, three- and five-day tours. Hit the best; forget the rest.

Beijing in . . . ONE DAY

It's impossible to see everything Beijing has to offer in a single day. Still, if that's all you've got, you can cover a lot of the key sights if you go full steam. The geographical center of **Tiananmen Square** is on most people's must-do list. Fundamentally, however, it's just a big square. Make the trip worthwhile by being first in line for the **Mao Memorial Hall** at 8 am (early birds may want to take in the pomp of the flag-raising ceremony held each dawn, which takes place around 7 am during winter months). Within this stern-looking building (closed on Monday), which dominates the center of the square, you'll find the Chairman's embalmed remains. Remember to take your passport (and deposit any bags at the designated storage facility before queuing).

Follow this curious experience by heading to the north side of the square to the **Gate of Heavenly Peace**, which marks the entrance to the **Forbidden City**, a sight that needs no introduction. This may be the home of the emperors, but the mark of Mao remains. You'll have to pass under his portrait to make your way in. Exploring this imperial palace takes hours. The peripheral courtyards provide a welcome escape if the crowds become too trying. Save some energy for the gentle hike to the top of the hill in **Jingshan Park** opposite the north exit of the Forbidden City. Too many run out of gas and skip the stunning views.

Reward yourself with a cracking good lunch deal at **Temple Restaurant Beijing**: fine dining in a 600-year-old temple. Take it easy in the afternoon with a stroll around Beihai Park—a former imperial garden—before renting a boat for a lazy time on its large lake. It's then a half-hour walk (or short cab ride) to the tourist mecca of **Wangfujing** shopping street. The snack stalls here are particularly fun, especially if you're brave enough to try the likes of scorpion on a stick.

Ride the subway two stops from Wangfujing to Tiananmen West to round off the night with some world-class classical music at the architectural wonder that is **The Egg**.

Beijing in . . . THREE DAYS

Start with our one-day tour as above. But then what to do with your other two days? Well, it'd be foolish to come all the way to China and not visit the **Great Wall**. There's no getting around the fact, however, that this requires a full day. The Badaling section is closest; the wall at Mutianyu is better—both are somewhat "touristy." If that bothers you then you may want to hike one of the "wilder" sections of the Great Wall. It's possible, although not recommended, to do this independently. You're better off hiring a guide. Our favorite is Tony Chen at Stretch-a-leg Travel (⊕ *www.stretchalegtravel*). Dine on Peking duck for dinner. Take your pick from **Da Dong**, **Made in China**, or **Duck de Chine**—three of the best places in town to try Beijing's signature dish.

For your final day get ready to explore the capital's historical hutongs—the fast-disappearing network of ancient alleyways that were the lifeblood of old Peking. Start at the atmospheric **Lama Temple** (easily reached via Line 2). This is the most important functioning Buddhist temple in Beijing and remains full of life. Drop by the nearby **Confucius Temple**, dedicated to China's great sage, before wandering through the area's cute hutongs—Wudaoying and Guozijian are of particular interest. Wind your way through the area's alleys en route to the **Drum** and **Bell towers**, which provided the city's official means of timekeeping up until 1924. It should be a half-hour walk. But don't worry if you get lost in the lanes, as that's all part of the adventure. Climb the tower for a fabulous view. You'll see the nearby **Houhai** lakes to the west—a good spot to rent a boat in summer or go ice-skating in winter. If you want to explore the area on foot then head to the **Silver Ingot Bridge** instead, before finishing your day in the buzzing hutong around Nanluoguxiang (1 km [½ mile] east of Houhai), packed with boutiques, bars, and restaurants.

Beijing in . . . FIVE DAYS

Lucky enough to have five days in the capital? Follow our three-day tour, then spend your remaining time taking in Beijing's glorious mix of old and new, from temples and palaces to contemporary art and shopping galore. Kick off day four with an early start down south at the beautiful **Temple of Heaven**. This is where the emperors used to pray for prosperity. Today you'll find it populated with the city's pensioners practicing *taiji* (tai chi) or singing songs.

Once done with this impressive imperial sight, hop into a cab for the 5-km (3-mile) journey east to the **Panjiayuan dirt market**. A great place to pick up presents and mementos, the traders here sell everything from Chinese chess sets and delicate porcelain to Mao alarm clocks and traditional instruments. Another cab will take you to the **798 Art District** up in the northeast part of the city (a half-hour drive in good traffic; an hour in bad), which is a wonderful way to spend an afternoon—avoid Monday, however, when most things here are shut. Formerly a factory complex, the area is now a thriving arts hub. The best gallery to visit is the UCCA, but the proliferation of little shops, cafés, and bars make this a great place to hang out even if you're not into art.

Head back to downtown **Sanlitun** for sundown. Shopaholics can squeeze in some last-minute spending at **Yashow**, an indoor market full of cheap clothes, bags, and such; bargain harder than you ever have before. Spend the evening soaking up Sanlitun's bustling nightlife. Avoid the main "bar street" and check out the watering holes and eateries in **The Village** instead. Get out of the city on your final day. Spend the morning back in imperial China at the striking **Summer Palace** up in Beijing's northwest corner. Combine the trip with the ruins of the nearby **Old Summer Palace**. You may want to spend the afternoon at the **Fragrant Hills**—popular among residents escaping the urban grind—or the **Botanical Garden**. Both are even farther west than the Summer Palace and visiting just one will take the rest of the day.

TOP EXPERIENCES

Tour de Beijing
Four wheels may be good for getting around, but two wheels are better. The capital demands to be discovered by bicycle. Unlock a different perspective on the city by renting a bike from Serk (⊕ *www.serk.cc*) and spending a day in the saddle. Or take a tour with Bike Beijing (⊕ *www.bikebeijing.com*).

Dance the night away
Beijing's pensioners love to dance wherever they can set up a sound system: parks, squares, streets, and underpasses. One of the best places to join in is outside Saint Joseph's Cathedral on Wangfujing. Hundreds of movers and groovers gather here every night. Get yourself down there and sway along to the sounds.

Train in Taiji (Tai Chi)
You'll see plenty of folk practicing this gentle Chinese martial art throughout town. Our favorite way to train is with Bespoke Beijing (⊕ *www.bespoke-beijing.com*), who can arrange a private hour-long class among the trees of the Temple of Heaven. Even better, it's led by a taiji master who trained at the Shaolin Temple as a child.

Eat scary snacks
There's some wonderful food to be had here. There are also some truly terrifying dishes to try if you're feeling brave. The likes of scorpions on a stick are served up at Wangfujing snack street. To be safer, choose carts with a high turnover.

Go for gold at the Water Cube
The site of Michael Phelps's extraordinary eight golds at the Beijing Olympics has now been turned into a thrilling water park. Little ones will enjoy the lazy river and gentle slides. Grown-ups will feel like big kids when taking on the crazier rides, including one with a trapdoor that swings open to send you hurtling down the chute.

Meditate with monks
If a visit to the downtown Lama Temple awakens your spiritual side, then a weekend away staying with monks at Chaoyang Temple—an hour or two outside the city in Huairou District—may be the key to reaching real enlightenment. A crash course in Zen Buddhism awaits the curious (⊕ *www.90percenttravel.com*).

Enjoy a night at the opera
Peking opera is regarded as one of the country's cultural treasures. If you want to check out this unique form of traditional Chinese theater then you won't get a better opportunity than in its birthplace (⇨ *see Chapter 6 for more*). Be warned: the sonic style may not be music to all ears. Still, when in Rome—or, indeed, Peking . . .

Hike the Great Wall
There's more than one way to see the world's most famous wall. Abandon the tourist trail and escape the crowds with Beijing Hikers (⊕ *www.beijinghikers.com*). This walking group runs regular trips to some of the more interesting areas of the Great Wall. Join them to explore unrestored sections most tourists don't even know exist.

Rock out
Beijing is the beating heart of China's burgeoning rock scene. Join the city's hipsters and rock kids at one of the many gigs on the local circuit. MAO Live House (⊕ *www.maolive.com*) and Yugong Yishan (⊕ *www.yugongyishan.com*)are two of the best venues to crash if you're out cool hunting.

Have a Beijing tea party

Fans of a nice cup of cha won't want to miss Maliandao—the largest tea market in north China. For a more personal experience you should head to Fangjia Hutong where you'll find Tranquil Tuesdays (⊕ *www.tranquiltuesdays.com*), a local social enterprise dedicated to China's tea culture. Its founder, Charlene Wang, personally sources the nation's best natural leaves for sale. Call ahead for an appointment.

Check out the stunning stunts

China's acrobats train harder than any others. The results, as seen in many of the shows across town, are guaranteed to elicit oohs and aahs of amazement. Take your pick of the bunch listed in Chapter 6, although the show at the Chaoyang Theater is the most conveniently located, and has an excellent Japanese whisky bar attached.

Soak it up

Yes, Beijing is one of China's biggest cities, but life here isn't just about the urban grind. A number of serene hot springs surround the capital's fringes and make a welcome escape. Our favorite is Chun Hui Yuan (☎ *010/6945–4433*) in the suburb of Shunyi. Let go of it all as you blissfully sink into one of the warm outdoor pools.

Take a sideways look down the lanes

The capital's ancient alleys are there for all to explore. Walk or cycle, it's up to you. But for a completely different view of things we recommend booking a tour with Beijing Sideways (⊕ *www.beijingsideways.com*) who will whiz you off to hard-to-find places deep in the hutong network while riding aboard the sidecar of a vintage motorbike.

Let the games begin

Basketball is so popular in China that it's practically the national sport. Cheer on the Beijing Ducks (led to their first title in 2012 by ex-NBA star Stephon Marbury) at their nest in Shijingshan District. It is, however, quite the trek. For an easier sporting fix, go support the soccer team, Beijing Guoan, at the Workers' Stadium in Sanlitun.

Delve into the bizarre

Weird can be wonderful. And when it comes to bizarre museums in which to while away an afternoon, Beijing has to be up there. Where else in the world could you go to a eunuch's tomb and exhibit (☎ *010/8872–4148*) in the morning and then an entire museum dedicated to the history of tap water (☎ *010/6465–0787*) in the afternoon? Exactly.

Get suited up

London's got Savile Row. Beijing's got top tailoring for a fraction of the dough. Where you go depends on how much cash you want to splash, but you can't go wrong at Wendy's (on the third floor of Yashow Market). There's no way you'll get made-to-measure shirts of this quality for such a low price back home.

Become a master chef

If you dine right (with our help, we hope), you'll eat so well that you'll want to take the secrets of these tasty Chinese treats home. Hurry down to The Hutong (⊕ *www.thehutongkitchen.com*) for its packed calendar of cooking classes, which cover everything from making dumplings to creating sizzling Sichuanese dishes.

BEIJING THEN AND NOW

In the Beginning

Since the birth of Chinese civilization, different towns of varying size and import have stood at or near the site where Beijing is now. For example, the popular local beer, Yanjing, refers to a city-kingdom based here 3,000 years ago. With this in mind, it's not unreasonable to describe Beijing's modern history as beginning with the Jin Dynasty, approximately 800 years ago. Led by nine generations of the Jurchen tribe, the Jin Dynasty eventually fell into a war against the Mongol hordes.

The Mongols

Few armies had been able to withstand the wild onslaught of the armed Mongol cavalry under the command of the legendary warrior Genghis Khan. The Jurchen tribe proved no exception, and the magnificent city of the Jin was almost completely destroyed. A few decades later, in 1260, when Kublai Khan, the grandson of Genghis Khan, returned to use the city as an operational base for his conquest of southern China, reconstruction was the order of the day. By 1271 Kublai Khan had achieved his goal, declaring himself emperor of China under the Yuan Dynasty (1271–1368), with Beijing (or Dadu, as it was then known) as its capital.

The new capital was built on a scale befitting the world's then superpower. Its palaces were founded around Zhonghai and Beihai lakes. Beijing's current layout still reflects the Mongolian design.

The Mings

About 100 years after the Mongolians settled Beijing they suffered a devastating attack by rebels from the south. The southern roots of the quickly unified Ming Dynasty (1368–1644) deprived Beijing of its capital status for half a century. But in 1405, the third Ming emperor, Yongle, began construction on a magnificent new palace in Beijing: an enormous maze of interlinking halls, gates, and courtyard homes, known as the Forbidden City.

The Ming also contributed mightily to China's grandest public works project: the Great Wall. The Ming Great Wall linked or reinforced several existing walls, especially near the capital, and traversed seemingly impassable mountains. The majority of the most spectacular stretches of the wall that can be visited near Beijing were built during the Ming Dynasty. But wall building drained Ming coffers and, in the end, failed to prevent Manchu horsemen from taking the capital—and China—in 1644.

And finally, the Qings

This foreign dynasty, the Qing, inherited the Ming palaces, built their own retreats (most notably, the "old" and "new" summer palaces), and perpetuated feudalism in China for another 267 years. In its decline, the Qing proved impotent to stop humiliating foreign encroachment. It lost the first Opium War to Great Britain in 1842 and was forced to cede Hong Kong "in perpetuity" as a result. In 1860 a combined British and French force stormed Beijing and razed the Old Summer Palace.

Mao takes the reins

After the Qing crumbled in 1911, its successor, Sun Yat-sen's Nationalist Party, struggled to consolidate power. Beijing became a cauldron of social activism. On May 4, 1919, students marched on Tiananmen Square to protest humiliations in Versailles, where Allied commanders negotiating an end to World War I gave Germany's extraterritorial holdings in

China to Japan. Patriotism intensified, and in 1937 Japanese imperial armies stormed across Beijing's Marco Polo Bridge to launch a brutal eight-year occupation. Civil war followed close on the heels of Tokyo's 1945 surrender and raged until the Communist victory. Chairman Mao himself declared the founding of a new nation from the rostrum atop the Gate of Heavenly Peace on October 1, 1949.

Like Emperor Yongle, Mao built a capital that conformed to his own vision. Soviet-inspired structures rose up around Tiananmen Square. Beijing's historic city wall was demolished to make way for a ring road. Temples and churches were torn down, closed, or turned into factories during the upheaval of the 1966–76 Cultural Revolution.

Economic growth and the city

In more recent years the city has suffered most, ironically, from prosperity. Many ancient neighborhoods have been bulldozed to make room for glitzy commercial developments. A growing commitment to preservation has very slowly begun to take hold, but *chai* (to pull down) and *qian* (to move elsewhere) remain common threats across the capital.

Today Beijing's some 20 million residents—including 7 million migrant workers—enjoy a fascinating mix of old and new. Early morning *taiji* enthusiasts, ballroom and disco dancers, old men with caged songbirds, and amateur Beijing opera crooners frequent the city's many parks. Cyclists clog the roadways, competing with cars on the city's thoroughfares. Beijing traffic has gone from nonexistent to nightmarish in less than a decade; there are now more than 5 million cars on the road (with around 2,000 more joining that number each day).

As the seat of China's immense national bureaucracy, Beijing carries a political charge. The Communist Party, whose self-described goal is "a dictatorship of the proletariat," has yet to relinquish its political monopoly.

Communism Today

In 1989 student protesters in Tiananmen Square dared to challenge the party. The government's brutal response remains etched in global memory, although younger Chinese people are likely never to have heard of that seismic moment due to the taboo nature of the subject and the country's strict censorship laws. More than 20 years later, secret police still mingle with tourists on the square. Mao-style propaganda persists. Slogans that preach unity among China's national minorities and patriotism still festoon the city on occasion. Yet as Beijing's robust economy—now the second largest in the world—is boosted even further by the government's continuing embrace of "a socialist market economy" (read state-sanctioned capitalism) and the massive influx of foreign investment, such campaigns appear increasingly out of touch with the iPhone-wielding generation. And so there is now a more modern side to the city to consider, one perhaps best encapsulated by the drastic changes made to both skyline and streets as Beijing readied itself for the 2008 Olympics, its very own debutante ball. The result is an incongruous mixture of new prosperity and throwback politics: socialist slogans adorn shopping centers selling everything from Big Macs to Louis Vuitton. Beijing is truly a land of opposites where the ancient and the sparkling new collide.

A CITY IN TRANSITION

The 2008 Summer Olympics changed the look of the Chinese capital like never before. Whole city blocks were razed to make way for modern buildings, new hotels, and state-of-the-art sports facilities. The subway system has expanded from just 2 to 16 lines, with 4 more under construction. Just about everywhere you look you'll find signs of that feverish development boom continuing where the games left off. But the focus has switched from iconic Olympic venues and government-initiated state buildings—such as the extraordinary headquarters for the state-run TV network—to more commercially minded projects looking to mix architectural innovation with functional office space and money-making shopping malls. Yes, China is rightly proud of its 5,000 years of history, but in terms of looking forward and not back, Beijing's 21st-century projects—many designed by top international architects—are impressive to say the least.

Beijing Capital International Airport, Terminal 3

With its lantern-red roof shaped like a dragon, Beijing's airport expansion embraces traditional Chinese motifs with a 21st-century twist: its architect calls it "the world's largest and most advanced airport building." This single terminal contains more floor space than all the terminals at London's Heathrow Airport combined. Construction started in 2004 with a team of 50,000 workers and was completed a few months before the Olympic Games. ⊠ *Beijing Capital International Airport.*

Architect: Norman Foster, the preeminent British architect responsible for global icons such as Hong Kong's widely respected airport, London's "Gherkin" skyscraper, and the Reichstag dome in Berlin.

Beijing Linked Hybrid

With 700 apartments in eight bridge-linked towers surrounding a plethora of shopping and cultural options, including Beijing's best art-house cinema, the Linked Hybrid has been applauded for parting from the sterility of typical Chinese housing. The elegant complex also features an impressive set of green credentials such as geothermal heating and a wastewater recycling system. ⊠ *Adjacent to the northeast corner of the 2nd Ring Rd.*

Architects: New York–based Steven Holl—who has won awards for his contemporary art museum in Helsinki, Finland and innovative "horizontal skyscraper" in Shenzhen—and Li Hu, who helped design China's first contemporary museum in Nanjing.

CCTV (China Central Television) Headquarters

The most remarkable of China's new structures, the new central television headquarters twists the idea of a skyscraper quite literally into a 40-story-tall gravity-defying loop. What some have called the world's most complex building is also, with a $1.3 billion price tag, one of the world's priciest. An accompanying building that was to include a hotel, a visitor center, and a public theater was seriously destroyed after it caught on fire during the Chinese New Year fireworks display in 2009. Due to the complex engineering involved the secondary building remains under reconstruction. ⊠ *32 Dong San Huanzhonglu (32 E. 3rd Ring Middle Rd).*

Architects: Rem Koolhaas (a Dutch mastermind known for his daring ideas and successful Seattle Public Library) and Ole Scheeren (Koolhaas's German protégé).

National Stadium ("the Bird's Nest")

Despite the heft of 42,000 tons of steel bending around its center, this 80,000-seat stadium somehow manages to appear delicate rather than clunky, with its exterior lattice structure resembling the twigs of an elegant nest—hence the nickname. Now home to events such as visiting soccer games and the occasional concert, it's an absolutely massive structure, and must be seen to be believed. ⊠ *Beijing Olympic Park at Bei Si Huanlu (N. 4th Ring Rd).*

Architects: Herzog and de Meuron of Switzerland, who won the prestigious Pritzker Prize for converting London's Bankside Power Station into the much-loved Tate Modern art gallery. The stadium also saw the involvement of leading Chinese creative Ai Weiwei as artistic consultant.

National Aquatics Center ("the Water Cube")

The translucent skin and hexagonal high-tech "pillows" that define this 17,000-seat indoor swimming stadium create the impression of a building fashioned entirely out of bubbles. The structure is based on the premise that bubbles are the most effective way to divide a three-dimensional space—and they help save energy and keep the building earthquake-proof. The center has now been turned into a public aquatics center and water park. ⊠ *Beijing Olympic Park.*

Architects: PTW, the Australian firm that cut its teeth on venues for the 2000 Olympic Games in Sydney.

National Center for the Performing Arts ("the Egg")

Located near Tiananmen Square, and completely surrounded by water, this bulbous opera house—a spectacular dome of titanium and glass known locally as "The Egg"—might cause passersby to think that some sort of spaceship has landed in the capital. Its close proximity to the Forbidden City, and its soaring costs (more than $400 million), earned it a hostile welcome among some Chinese architects, although it has now been embraced by the city thanks to its excellent program of classical music and refreshingly unconventional appearance. ⊠ *Xi Chang'anjie (just west of Tiananmen Sq.).*

Architect: French-born Paul Andreu, who designed the groundbreaking Terminal 1 of Paris's Charles de Gaulle airport in 1974, as well as working on the French capital's La Grande Arche.

Galaxy Soho

Consisting of four huge amorphous globes, wrapped in curved white panels and flowing glass curtain walls, this mixed-use complex from one of the country's largest property developers (Soho China) continues the futuristic theme of The Egg. Opened at the end of 2012, it's quite the statement: a bold continuation of the architectural ambition initiated by the Games, now transferred to the more functional world of office and retail space. Welcome to Beijing's next chapter. ⊠ *E. 2nd Ring Rd (next to Chaoyangmen subway station).*

Architect: Iraqi-British starchitect Zaha Hadid—the first woman to win the Pritzker Prize—who made a splash in China prior to this with her Guangzhou Opera House in Canton.

BEIJING TODAY

The air is dirty, the traffic is horrendous, and almost nobody speaks more than a word or two of English—so what makes Beijing one of the world's top destinations?

Today's Beijing . . .

. . . is old and new. The flat skyline of Beijing, punctuated only by imposing ceremonial towers and the massive gates of the city wall, is lost forever. But still, standing on Coal Hill and looking south across the Forbidden City—or listening to the strange echo of your voice atop an ancient altar at the Temple of Heaven—you can't help but feel the weight of thousands of years of history. It was here that Marco Polo dined with Kublai Khan and his Mongol hordes; that Ming and Qing emperors ruled over China from the largest and richest city in the world; and that Mao Zedong proclaimed the founding of the People's Republic in 1949. Much of Beijing's charm comes from the juxtaposition of old and new. When you're riding a taxi along the Third Ring Road it may seem that the high-rise apartments and postmodern office complexes stretch on forever. They do, but tucked in among the glass and steel are elaborate temples exuding wafts of incense, and tiny alleyways where old folks still gather in their pajamas every evening to play cards and drink warm beer. Savoring these small moments is the key to appreciating Beijing.

. . . lets you eat your heart out. If you really love General Tso's chicken back at your local Chinese take-out place, you may want to skip Beijing altogether. Many a returned visitor has complained of being unable to enjoy the bland stuff back home after experiencing the myriad flavors and textures of China's varied regional cuisines. From the mouth-numbing spices of Sichuan, to the delicate presentation of an imperial banquet, or the cumin-sprinkled kebabs of China's Muslim west, Beijing has it all. If you're looking for the ultimate in authenticity, dine at a restaurant attached to one of the city's provincial representative offices, where the chefs and ingredients are imported to satisfy the taste buds of bureaucrats working far from home. The crispy skin and tender flesh of the capital's signature dish, Peking duck, is on everyone's must-eat list. Don't worry if you tire of eating Chinese food three times a day. As Beijing has grown rich in recent years, Western and fusion cuisine offerings have improved greatly, with everything from French to

COOL FACTS ON THE CAPITAL CITY

With around 20 million residents, Beijing is vying with Shanghai to become the largest city in China.

The city has existed in various forms for 2,500 years, but *Homo erectus* fossils prove that humans have lived here for 250,000 years.

Beijing was once surrounded by a massive city wall constructed during the Ming Dynasty. Of the 16 original gates, only 3 remain standing. The wall was demolished in 1965 to make way for the Second Ring Road.

At 100 acres, Tiananmen Square is the largest urban square in the world; during the Cultural Revolution, as many as 1 million people were able to stand on numbered spaces for huge rallies with Chairman Mao.

Middle Eastern to Texas-style barbecue now available. If you're looking for a special—although somewhat expensive—night out, take your pick from Maison Boulud (set up by New York's three-Michelin-starred Daniel Boulud), which is to be found in the capital's old Legation Quarter, and serves faultless French food in what was once the American Embassy. Or, you could try Temple Restaurant Beijing, where east meets west in the grounds of a 600-year-old temple, which has been turned into a fine-dining destination dishing up contemporary European cuisine.

. . . is part of a new world order. Beijing's transformation hasn't only been limited to Olympic venues. Prestige projects such as the National Center for the Performing Arts ("The Egg"), the new CCTV building, and a massive subway expansion are meant to show that China is ready to play with the big boys. The Chinese are fiercely patriotic, and antiforeign demonstrations occasionally break out when the country's collective pride is insulted. The official version of Chinese history taught in schools emphasizes the nation's suffering at the hands of foreign colonial powers during the 19th and 20th centuries, and the subsequent Communist liberation. Still, you'll find Beijingers infinitely polite and curious about your life back home. People here aren't quite sure what to make of their new surroundings, and they're as interested in finding out about you as you are about them. So strike up a conversation (with your hands if necessary), but be sure to go easy on the politics.

. . . is the place to make it or break it. Newcomers could be forgiven for seeing bustling Shanghai as China's go-to place. But anyone who has spent a little time in the capital swears that it's the soul of the country. People from all over China are drawn here by the many opportunities the city offers, the cultural fervor, and the chance to reinvent themselves. There's an unusual freedom here that has made Beijing the creative center of the country, and this attracts the creative elite from all around the world. Art galleries have sprung up in hotels, courtyard houses, shut-down factories, and even an ancient watchtower. This is where serious musicians must come to make it or break it. Even no-nonsense businessmen see Beijing as a mecca because they believe the challenges—and rewards—are greater here.

Despite major efforts to improve Beijing's air quality, pollution levels in the city remain several times higher than World Health Organization limits. Adding to the problem, a single sandstorm (usually arriving in spring) can drop tens of thousands of tons of dust onto the city in mere hours.

Beijingers love to brew, and more than 1,000 tea shops can be found along Maliandao Tea Street in the city's southwest. Top-quality leaves can run as high as 5,000 yuan per pound.

The 798 Art District is home to China's red-hot modern art scene. An example: a Yue Minjun painting inspired by the 1989 crackdown in Tiananmen Square sold for $5,000 in 1994 and resold for $6.9 million in 2008.

BEIJING WITH KIDS

Education Without Yawns

Military Museum. A toy soldier–lover's dream come true, this museum contains endless collections of AK-47s, captured tanks, missile launchers, and other war toys. Your kids will love every minute of China's 5,000-year military history. Easy access by subway ensures they won't have to ask, "Are we there yet?"

Forbidden City. The largest surviving palace complex in the world, there are plenty of wide-open spaces here for kids to run amok. While you're appreciating the finest collection of imperial architecture in China, your little ones can imagine what it was like to have thousands of mandarins catering to their every whim. Sort of like having parents.

Blue Zoo Beijing. Not to be confused with an actual zoo, this is Asia's largest walk-through aquarium. Divers feed thousands of sea creatures, including sharks, twice a day. A visit here can be negotiated as a prize for letting you shop in peace at nearby Yashow Market.

China Science & Technology Museum. A paradise for curious kids, this museum features hands-on interactive displays with a strong focus on Chinese inventions like the compass, gunpowder, and paper. The on-site "Fundazzle" playground will keep your little one entertained even when the robot performance is finished.

Performances

Amazing Acrobats. Take the kids out for a night on the town to show them that hand-eye coordination doesn't only come from playing video games. To really inspire, look for a performance featuring child acrobats who dedicate every day to perfecting their awe-inspiring craft.

China Puppet Theater. Actors manipulate huge puppets through performances of Western classics like *The Nutcracker* and Chinese classics like *The Monkey King*. There's a playground, too, for kids who just won't sit still.

Activities

Go Fly a Kite. China's love affair with kites goes back nearly 3,000 years. Head for the open spaces of Tiananmen Square or the Temple of Heaven, where old folks with decades of flying experience will help send your child's kite soaring into the air.

Climb the Wall. Do we really have to convince you? After climbing hundreds (or thousands) of steps, your little one will sleep soundly while dreaming of turning back the marauding Mongol hordes.

A Trip Around the World. World Park offers a bizarre collection of 100 scaled-down tourist attractions from across the globe. Kids enjoy climbing on the pyramids; parents can marvel at the outdated and politically incorrect international stereotypes.

Fun in the Sun. Ritan Park (Altar of the Sun) is an altar of fun for children of all ages. Little tykes can ride the merry-go-round, older kids can try their luck on the climbing wall, and you can stop in for a drink at the outdoor Stone Boat, a particularly kid-friendly bar.

Set Sail. Cruise the imperial lakes at Houhai in a paddleboat, and take the family for a rectangular pie at Hutong Pizza when you get back to shore. In winter the lakes freeze over, and kids in ice chairs gleefully glide across the surface.

FREE (OR ALMOST FREE)

Although Beijing isn't as inexpensive as it once was, it's still a fabulous bargain compared to travel in Europe, North America, and more developed Asian nations such as Japan and South Korea. While expats have complained of rising prices—especially since the Olympics—visitors from Western countries are often overwhelmed by a feeling that life in the city is practically free. Bottled water, snacks, subway and bus rides, or some steamed dumplings from a street stall, will all cost well under the equivalent of 50 cents. Average-length cab rides, a dish at a decent restaurant, or museum admission tickets will set you back only two or three dollars. And the capital is filled with acceptable hotels for about 50 bucks per night. Little is free in Beijing, but there's also very little to make much of a dent in your wallet.

ART

The modern art scene in China has exploded onto the world stage over the past decade. Beijing's 798 Art District, located northeast of the city center along the road to the airport, is the country's artistic nucleus. The complex was built under East German supervision in the 1950s to house sprawling electronics factories, but artists took over after state subsidies dried up in the late 1990s. The district is now home to at least 100 top-notch galleries, and almost all of them are free.

* 798 Space * Art Bridge Gallery * Asia Art Center * Beyond Art Space * Boers-Li Gallery * CO2 United Creative Space * Contrasts Gallery * Faurschou Foundation * Galerie Urs Meile * Mulpa Space * Pace Beijing * Pekin Fine Arts * Red Gate Gallery * Red T Space * Taikang Space * Ullens Center for Contemporary Art (Y10; free on Thursday)

MUSEUMS

The city's most famous museums aren't exactly charging an arm and a leg for admission, while the smaller and quirkier museums listed here ask only for donations or charge less than Y10.

* Arthur M. Sackler Museum * Beijing Ancient Coins Exhibition Hall * Beijing Police Museum * Beijing Tap Water Museum * Cao Xueqin Former Residence * China Honey Bee Museum * Song Tang Zhai Museum of Traditional Chinese Folk Carving * Xu Beihong Museum

OFFBEAT EXPERIENCES

Beijing's urban sprawl is interrupted by a number of lovely parks designed in traditional Chinese style. Of particular historical significance are the four parks built around altars used for imperial sacrifice: the **Altar of the Sun** (Ritan), **Altar of Heaven** (Tiantan), **Altar of the Earth** (Ditan), and **Altar of the Moon** (Yuetan).

If you happen to be in Beijing for Spring Festival (Chinese New Year), you literally won't be able to avoid the party atmosphere that overtakes the city. You may have seen a display of fireworks before, but have you ever been *inside* a fireworks show? Just remember to bring earplugs, as the explosions go on at all hours for days on end.

Set aside some time for random wandering, especially through the hutong neighborhoods inside the Second Ring Road. Much of what makes Beijing special happens on a very small scale. Listen for the call of the local knife sharpener who rides by daily on his bicycle. See the old folks out and about in pajamas as they walk the block with their dogs.

FAQ

Do I need any special documents to get into the country?

Aside from a passport that's valid for at least six months after date of entry, and a valid visa, you don't need anything else to enter the country. You're required to have your passport with you at all times during your trip, but it's safer to carry a photocopy and store your passport in a safe at your hotel (if they have one).

How difficult is it to travel around the city?

It's extremely easy (traffic aside). Taxis are plentiful and cheap, and Beijing also has a good subway system that has expanded rapidly and now reaches more places. Stops are announced in both English and Chinese. Public buses can be a challenge because street signs are not often written in English and bus drivers are unlikely to be fluent in any foreign languages. Renting a car can be difficult and traffic and roads can be quite challenging, so driving on your own isn't recommended. However, hiring a car and driver isn't very expensive and is a good alternative for getting around. Beijing, with its many bike lanes, is a cycle lover's city, so consider renting some wheels for part of your stay.

Should I consider a package tour?

If the thought of traveling unescorted to Beijing absolutely terrifies you, then sign up for a tour. But Beijing is such an easy place to get around that there's really no need. Discovery is a big part of the fun—exploring an ancient temple, walking down a narrow hutong or alleyway, stumbling upon a great craft shop or small restaurant—and that's just not going to happen on a tour. If you're more comfortable with a package tour, pick one with a specific focus, like a pedicab hutong ride or an afternoon of food shopping and cooking, so that you're less likely to get a generic package.

Do I need a local guide?

Guides are really not necessary in a city like Beijing, where it's easy to get around by taxi and public transportation, and where most of the important tourist destinations are easy to reach. An added plus is that the local people are friendly and always willing to give a hand. It's much more gratifying to tell the folks back home that you discovered that wonderful backstreet or interesting restaurant all by yourself.

Will I have trouble if I don't speak Chinese?

Not really. Most people in businesses catering to travelers speak at least a little English. If you encounter someone who doesn't speak English, they'll probably point you to a coworker who does. Even if you're in a far-flung destination, locals will go out of their way to find somebody who speaks your language. Or you can make use of travel services such as Bespoke Beijing, which will arm you with a mobile phone, plus a stylish and personalized guide to the best sights, restaurants, bars and nightlife, as well as access to a Chinese translator or English-speaking expert (⊕ *www. bespoke-beijing.com*).

Can I drink the water?

No, you can't. All drinking water must be boiled. Bottled water is easily available all over the city and in outlying areas, such as the Great Wall. Most hotels provide two free bottles of drinking water each day. To be on the safe side, you may also want to avoid ice.

Are there any worries about the food?

China has suffered from some major national food scandals in recent years, from tainted milk to exploding watermelons, but there's no need to be afraid

in Beijing. Even the humblest roadside establishment is likely to be clean. If you have any doubts about a place, just move on to the next one. There's no problem enjoying fruit or other local products sold from street stands, but any fruit that can't be peeled should perhaps be cleaned with bottled water before eating.

Do I need to get any shots?

You probably don't have to get any special vaccinations or take any serious medications if you're not planning on venturing outside the capital. The U.S. Centers for Disease Control and Prevention warn that there's some concern about malaria in some of the rural provinces much farther south of Beijing, such as Anhui, Yunnan, and Hainan. Immunizations for Hepatitis A and B are recommended for all visitors to China.

Should I bring any medications?

It can be difficult to readily find some medications in Beijing, and while the city has several international clinics, prices for even over-the-counter remedies can be quite expensive. So yes, it's advisable to make sure you have all your medications with you.

Can I use my ATM card?

Most ATMs in Beijing accept both MasterCard and Visa cards, but each bank may charge a different fee for each transaction. There are Citibank ATM machines located at several places around the city. Check the exchange rate before you use an ATM for the first time so that you know exactly how much local currency you want to withdraw.

Do most places take credit cards?

Almost all traveler-oriented businesses accept credit cards. You may encounter smaller restaurants and hotels that don't accept them at all, but these are pretty rare. Some businesses don't like to accept credit cards because their banks charge them exorbitant fees for credit-card transactions. They will usually relent and charge you a small fee for the privilege.

What if I don't know how to use chopsticks?

Chopsticks are the utensils of choice but cutlery is available in many restaurants. That said, it's a good idea to brush up on your chopstick chops. The standard eating procedure is to hold the bowl close to your mouth and eat the food. Noisily slurping up soup and noodles is also the norm. It's considered bad manners to point or play with your chopsticks, or to place them on top of your rice bowl when you're finished eating (place the chopsticks horizontally on the table or plate). Don't leave your chopsticks standing up in a bowl of rice—it makes them look like the two incense sticks burned at funerals, and is seriously frowned upon.

How should I dress?

Most Chinese people dress for comfort and you can do the same. There's very little risk of offending people with your dress; Westerners tend to attract attention regardless of attire. Although miniskirts are best left at home, pretty much anything else goes.

Should I tip?

For a long time, tipping was officially forbidden by the government; as a result, locals simply don't do it. In general, you can follow their lead without any qualms. Nevertheless, the practice is now beginning to catch on, especially among tour guides. You don't need to tip in restaurants or in taxis.

A GOOD WALK

Check out the West's 19th-century fingerhold in Beijing. The Old Legation Quarter, a walled area where foreign businesses and government offices were once housed, was heavily vandalized during the Cultural Revolution and altered again during the '80s boom. That said, a surprising number of early 20th-century European structures can still be found here.

The Old Legation Quarter

This walk begins on Dong Jiao Min Xiang. It can easily be reached via the lobby of the Novotel Xinqiao hotel. Exit through the back door right to the street. We'll first take you down the north side of the street and then along its south side. The most prominent structure that remains of the quarter is **St. Michael's Catholic Church**. Built by French Vincentian priests in 1902, this Gothic church is still crowded during Mass every Sunday.

Foreign Emissaries

The red building opposite the church started out as the **Belgian Embassy** and later became the **Burmese Embassy** following Burma's liberation.

On the north side of the street at No. 15 is the former location of the **French Legation**. Former Cambodian leader Prince Sihanouk stayed here during his many visits to China. The old **French Post Office** is now a Sichuan restaurant. **Hongdu Tailors** (No. 28) was once tailor to the top Communist officials who came here to have their revolutionary Mao jackets custom-made.

At the northeast corner of Zhengyi Lu, formerly known as Rue Meiji, is a grand-looking building that was once the **Yokohama Specie Bank**; peek in for a look at the early 20th-century interior

and ceilings. The pleasant patch of greenery you see running down the center of Zhengyi Lu was created in 1925, when the old rice-transport canal was filled in with earth. Continue west on Dong Jiao Min Xiang. In the middle of the next block on your right are the gleaming headquarters of **China's Supreme People's Court** (27 Dong Jiao Min Xiang), which sits on the site of the former Russian Legation. A gate remains here from the original Russian complex.

Financial Street

Walking up the south side of the street, you'll see a building with thick Roman columns; this was first the **Russia Asiatic Bank**, and afterwards the **National City Bank of New York**—the fading letters NCB can still be seen in a concrete shield at the top of the building. This is now the **Beijing Police Museum**. Down a bit farther on the north side of the street, just before Tiananmen Square, is the old **French Hospital**. Opposite the hospital is the former **American Legation** (this is the last complex just before the steps leading to Tiananmen Square). It was rebuilt in 1901 after being destroyed by the Boxers. More than a century later, it has become home to some particularly high-end restaurants and retail spaces.

Highlights:	Excellent examples of the types of colonial buildings that served as Western legations, shops, and financial institutions around the turn of the 20th century
Where to Start:	Dong Jiao Min Xiang (east end)
Length:	One hour if you're walking at a leisurely pace (just over a mile)
Where to Stop:	At the former American Legation next to Tiananmen Square (or you can walk back down the street to where you started)
Best Time to Go:	Early morning or late afternoon when the weather is better
Worst Time to Go:	In the afternoon during the heat of the day
Good in the Hood:	Maison Boulud (⊕ www.danielnyc.com/maisonboulud.html)

FABULOUS FESTIVALS

The majority of China's holidays and festivals are calculated according to the lunar calendar and can vary by as much as a few weeks from year to year. Check a lunar calendar online for more specific dates. Travel should generally be avoided during China's major holidays.

Chinese New Year. Chinese New Year, China's most celebrated and important holiday, follows the lunar calendar and falls between mid-January and mid-February. Also called Spring Festival (*Chūnjié*), it gives the Chinese an official weeklong holiday to visit their relatives, eat special meals, and set off firecrackers to celebrate the New Year and its respective Chinese zodiac animal. Students and teachers get up to four weeks off, as do some factory workers. ⚠ **It's a particularly crowded—and very noisy—time to travel in China.** Most offices and services reduce their hours or close altogether. It's best to avoid visiting during Spring Festival as the city tends to shut down and many of the things you'll want to see may be shut.

Dragon Boat Festival. The Dragon Boat Festival, on the fifth day of the fifth moon (usually falling in June), celebrates the national hero Qu Yuan, who drowned himself during the Warring States Period of ancient China in protest against a corrupt emperor. Legend has it that fishermen, who unsuccessfully attempted to rescue him by boat, tried to distract fish from eating his body by throwing rice dumplings wrapped in bamboo leaves into the river. Today crews in narrow dragon boats race to the beat of heavy drums, and rice—wrapped in bamboo leaves—is consumed en masse.

Labor Day. Labor Day falls on May 1, and is another busy travel time. In 2008 the government reduced the length of this holiday from five days to two, but the length of the holiday now changes from year to year.

Mid-Autumn Festival. Mid-Autumn Festival is celebrated on the 15th day of the eighth moon, which generally falls between mid-September and early October. The Chinese spend this time gazing at the full moon and exchanging edible "mooncakes": moon-shape pastries filled with meat, red-bean paste, lotus paste, salted egg, date paste, and other delectable surprises.

National Day. On October 1, National Day celebrates the founding of the People's Republic of China back in 1949. Tiananmen Square fills up with a hefty crowd of visitors on this official holiday, which gives people the entire week off. Domestic tourists from around the country flock to the capital during this time. Steer clear of Beijing during national week if you don't like to battle endless crowds at all the main sights.

Qing Ming. Not so much a holiday as a day of worship, Qing Ming (literally, "clean and bright"), or Tomb Sweeping Day, gathers relatives at the graves of the deceased on the 15th day from the spring equinox—April 4, 5, or 6, depending on the year—to clean the surfaces and leave fresh flowers. In 1997, a law was passed stating that cremation is compulsory. As such, this festival has since lost much of its original meaning.

Spring Lantern Festival. The Spring Lantern Festival marks the end of the Chinese New Year on the 15th day of the first moon. Residents flock to local parks for a display of Chinese lanterns and fireworks.

Continued on page 40

Terracotta soldiers

THE AGE OF EMPIRES

When asked his opinion on the historical impact of the French Revolution, Chairman Mao quipped, "It's too early to tell." Though a bit tongue in cheek, China does measure its history in millennia, and in its grand timeline, interactions with the West have been mere blips.

According to historical records, Chinese civilization stretches back to the 15th century BC—markings found on turtle shells carbon dated to around 1500BC bear some similarity to modern Chinese script. China then resembled city-states rather than a unified nation. Iconic figures such as Lao Tzu (the father of Taoism), Sun Tzu (author of the Art of War), and Confucius lived during this period. Generally, 221BC is accepted as the beginning of Imperial China, when the city-states united under various banners.

Over the next 2,200 years (give or take a few), China alternated between periods of harmony and political upheaval. Its armies conquered new territory and were in turn conquered by external invaders (most of whom wound up themselves being assimilated).

By the early 18th century, the long, slow decline of the Qing—the last of China's Imperial dynasties—was already in progress, making the ancient nation ripe for exploitation by rising European powers. The Imperial era ended with the forced abdication of child Emperor Puyi (whose life is chronicled in Bernardo Bertolucci's The Last Emperor), and it's here that the history of modern China, first with the founding of the republic under Sun Yat-sen and then with the establishment of the People's Republic under Mao Zedong, truly begins.

Writing Appears

1500BC   1200BC   900BC

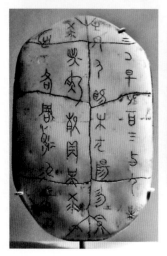

(left) Oracle shell with early Chinese characters. (top, right) The Great Wall stretches 4,163 miles from east to west. (bottom, right) Confucius, Lao-tzu, and a Buddhist Arhat.

circa 1500 BC
Writing Appears

The earliest accounts of Chinese history are still shrouded in myth and legend, and it wasn't until 1959 that stories were verified by archaeological findings. For millennia, people formed communities in the fertile lands of what is now central China. The first recorded Chinese characters are said to have been developed 3,500 years ago. Though sometimes referred to as the Shang Dynasty, this period was more of a precursor to modern Chinese dynasties than a truly unified kingdom.

722-475 BC
The Warring States Period

China was so far from unified that these centuries are collectively remembered as the Warring States Period. As befitting such a contentious time, military science progressed, iron replaced bronze, and weapons material improved. Some of China's greatest luminaries lived during this period, including the father of Taoism, Lao-tzu, Confucius, and Sun-Tzu, one of the greatest military tacticians and the author of the infamous *Art of War,* which is still studied in military academies around the world.

221-207 BC
The First Dynasty

The Qin Dynasty eventually defeated all of the other warring factions thanks to their cutting-edge military technology, namely the cavalry. The Qin were also called Ch'in, which may be where the word China first originated. The first Emperor, Qin Shi Huang, unified much of the lands and established a legal code and vast bureaucracy to hold it together. The Qin dynasty also standardized the written and spoken language and introduced a common currency.

(left) Terracotta
warrior.
(top right)
Temple of Xichan
in Fuzhou

In order to protect his newly unified country, Qin Shi Huang ordered the creation of the massive Great Wall of China, which was built and rebuilt over the next 1,000 years. He was also a sculpture enthusiast and commissioned a massive army of stone soldiers to follow him into the afterlife. Buried with him, these terra-cotta warriors would remain hidden from the eyes of the world for two thousand years, until they were found by a farmer digging in a field just outside of Xian. These warriors are among the most important archaeological finds of the 20th century.

Buddhism Arrives

220-265 BC

Emperor Qin's dreams of a unified China fell apart, and eventually the kingdom split into three warring factions. But what was bad for stability turned out to be good for literature. The Three Kingdoms Period is still remembered in song and story. *The Romance of the Three Kingdoms* is as popular among Asian book worms as the *Legend of King Arthur* is among Western readers. It's still widely read and has been translated into almost every language. Variations of the story have been adapted for manga, television series, and video games.

The Three Kingdoms period was filled with court intrigue, murder, and massive battles that, while exciting to read about centuries later, weren't much fun at the time. Armies ravaged the countryside, and most people lived and died in misery. Perhaps it was the carnage and disunity of the time that turned the country into a magnet for forces of harmony; it was during this period that Buddhism was first introduced into China, traveling over the Himalayas from India, via the Silk Road.

(left) Statue of Genghis Khan. (top right) Donguan Mosque in Xining, Qinghai. (bottom right) Empress Shengshen

Religion Diversifies

618-845

Chinese spiritual life continued to diversify. Nestorian Monks from Asia Minor arrived bearing news of Christianity, and Saad ibn Abi Waqqas (a companion of the Prophet Muhammad) supposedly visited the Middle Kingdom to spread the word of Islam. During this era, Wu Zetian, onetime concubine, seized power from the Tang Dynasty and became the first (and only) woman to assume the title of emperor. She ruled for 25 years through puppet emperors and finally, for 15 years as Emperor Shengshen.

Ghengis Invades

1271-1368

In Xanadu did Kublai Khan a stately pleasure dome decree...

Or so goes the famed Coleridge poem. But Kublai's grandfather Temujin (better known as Ghengis Khan) had bigger things in mind. One of the greatest war tacticians in history, he united the restive nomads of Mongolia's grassy plains and eventually sacked, looted, and pillaged much of the known west and most of the Chinese landmass. By the time Ghengis died in 1227, his grandson was well-tutored and ready to take on the rest of China.

By 1271, Kublai had established a capital in a land-locked city that would only much later become known as Beijing. This marks the beginning of the first (but not last) non-Han dynasty. Kublai Khan kept fighting southward and by 1279, Guangzhou fell to the Mongols, and Khan became the ultimate monarch of China. Though barbarians at heart, the Mongols must be credited for encouraging the arts and a number of early public works projects, including extending the highways and grand canals.

(left) Emperor Chengzu of the Ming Dynasty. (top right) Forbidden City in Beijing (bottom right) Child emperor Puyi.

Ming Dynasty

1368-1644

Many scholars believe that the Mongols' inability to relate with the Han is what ultimately pushed the Han to rise up and overthrow them. The reign of the Ming Dynasty was the last ethnically Han Dynasty to rule over a unified China. At its apex, the Bright Empire encompassed a landmass easily recognized as China, even by today's mapmakers. The Ming Emperors built a huge army and navy, refurbished the agricultural system, and printed many books using movable type long before Gutenberg. In the 13th century, Emperor Yongle began construction of the famous Forbidden City in Beijing, a veritable icon of China.

Also during the Ming Dynasty, China's best known explorer, Zheng He, plied the seven seas in massive treasure fleets that dwarfed in size and range the ships of Christopher Columbus. A giant both in stature and persona, Admiral Zheng (who was also a eunuch) spent two decades expanding China's knowledge of the world outside of its already impressive borders. He traveled as far as India, Africa, and (some say) even the coast of the New World.

Qing Dynasty

1644-1911

The final dynasty represented a serious case of minority rule. They were Manchus from the northeast. The early Qing dynasty was a brutal period as forces loyal to the new emperor crushed those loyal to the old. The Qing Dynasty peaked in the mid-to-late 18th century but soon after, its military powers began to wane. In the 19th century, Qing control weakened and prosperity diminished. By 1910 China was fractured, a baby sat on the Imperial throne, and the Qing Dynasty was on its deathbed.

(top left) A depiction of the Second Opium War. (bottom left) Chiang Kai-shek (top, right) Mao Zedong on December 6, 1944. (bottom, right) Sun Yat Sen.

The Opium Wars

1834-1860

European powers were hungry to open new territories up for trade, but the Qing weren't buying. The British East India Company, strapped for cash, realized they could sell opium in China at huge profits. The Chinese government quickly banned the nefarious trade and in response, a technologically superior Britain declared war. After a humiliating defeat in the first Opium War, China was forced to cede Hong Kong. Other foreign powers soon followed with territorial demands of their own.

Republican Era

1912-1949

China's Republican period was chaotic and unstable. The revolutionary Dr. Sun Yat-sen—revered by most Chinese as the father of modern China—was unable to build a cohesive government without the aid of regional warlords and urban gangsters. When he died of cancer in 1925, power passed to Chiang Kai-shek, who set about unifying China under the Kuomintang. What began as a unified group of both left- and right-wingers quickly deteriorated, and by the mid-1920s, civil war between the Communists

and Nationalists was brewing.

The '30s and '40s were bleak decades for the Chinese people, caught between a vicious war with Japan and periodic clashes between Kuomintang and Communist forces. After Japan's defeat in 1945, China's civil war kicked into high gear. Though the Kuomintang were armed with superior weapons and backed by American money, the majority of Chinese people rallied behind the Communists. Within four years, the Kuomintang were driven off the mainland to Taiwan, where the Republic of China exists to the present day,

(top left) 1950s
Chinese stamp with
Mao and Stalin.
(top right) Shenzhen
(bottom left) Poster of
Mao's slogans.

The People's Republic

1949-Present

On October 1, 1949, Mao Zedong declared from atop Beijing's Gate of Heavenly Peace that "The Chinese People have stood up." And so the People's Republic of China was born. The Communist party set out to overhaul China's ancient feudal system, emphasizing class struggle, redistribution of wealth, and elimination of foreign dominance. The next three decades would see a massive, often painful transformation of Chinese society from feudalism into the modern age.

The Great Leap Forward was a disaster—Chinese peasants were encouraged to cram 100 years of industrial development into as many weeks. Untenable decisions led to industrial and agricultural ruin, widespread famine, and an estimated 30 million deaths. The trauma of this period, however, pales in comparison to The Great Proletarian Cultural Revolution. From 1966–1976, fear and zealotry gripped the nation as young revolutionaries heeded Chairman Mao's call to root out class enemies. During this decade, millions died, millions were imprisoned, and much of China's accumulated religious,

historical, and cultural heritage literally went up in smoke.

Like a phoenix rising from its own ashes, China rose from its own self-inflicted destruction. In the early 1980s, Deng Xiao-ping took the first steps in reforming China's stagnant economy. With the maxim "To Get Rich is Glorious," Deng loosened central control on the economy and declared Special Economic Zones where the seeds of capitalism could be incubated. Three decades later, the nation is one of the world's most vibrant economic engines. Though China's history is measured in millennia, her brightest years may well have only just begun.

ENGLISH	PINYIN	CHINESE CHARACTERS
Beihai Park	Běihǎi gōngyuán	北海公园
Beijing Ancient Architecture Museum	Běijīng gǔdài jiànzhú bówùguǎn	北京古代建筑博物馆
Beijing Urban Planning Museum	Běijīng shì guīhuà zhǎnlǎnguǎn	北京市规划展览馆
Confucius Temple	Kǒngmiào	孔庙
Cultural Palace of Minorities	Mínzú wénhuàgōng	民族文化宫
Ditan Park (Altar of the Earth)	Dìtán gōngyuán	地坛公园
Forbidden City	Gùgōng	故宫
Great Hall of the People	Rénmín dàhuìtáng	人民大会堂
Houhai (Back Lake)	Hòuhǎi	后海
Jingshan Park (Coal Hill)	Jǐngshān gōngyuán	景山公园
Lama Temple	Yōnghégōng	雍和宫
Lu Xun House and Museum	Lǔxùn guǎn	鲁迅馆
Mao Zedong Memorial Hall	Máozhǔxí jìniàntáng	毛主席纪念堂
Museum of Antique Currency	Gǔdàiqiánbì bówùguǎn	古代钱币博物馆
Nanluoguxiang	Nánluógǔ xiàng	南锣鼓巷
Poly Art Museum	Bǎolì yìshù bówùguǎn	保利艺术博物馆
Qianhai (Front Lake)	Qiánhǎi	前海
Ritan Park (Altar of the Sun)	Rìtán gōngyuán	日坛公园
Silver Ingot Bridge	Yíndìng qiáo	银锭桥
Summer Palace	Yíhéyuán	颐和园
Taxi	chū zū chē	出租车
Temple of Heaven	Tiāntán	天坛
Tiananmen Square	Tiānānmén guǎngchǎng	天安门广场
Xiangshan Park (Fragrant Hills)	Xiāngshān gōngyuán	香山公园

EXPLORING

Updated by
Sky Canaves

Only one hour from downtown Beijing looms one of the great wonders of the world: The Great Wall of China. Built by the emperors of the Ming Dynasty to keep out the world, the vast brick structure offers a telling contrast to something that today casts a far larger shadow: the Great "Call" of China. The country's economic pheromones emanate most strongly from Beijing, capital of the world's second greatest economy and an ever-present conundrum for those who have Will-the-future-belong-to-China? questions on their minds.

Existing on a seemingly superhuman scale that matches its status as the capital city of the world's most populous nation, Beijing is laid out with vast expanses of wide avenues and roadways organized in an orderly pattern. Though the city's original grid layout has remained the same for many years (as has remnants of its past as the last capital of Imperial China), its infrastructure has undergone numerous transformations, most recently in preparation for the 2008 Summer Olympics. Despite all the changes necessitated by the proliferation of lacquered office towers, high-rise residences, and shopping centers, there are still plenty of world-class historic sites to be discovered, along with tranquil residential oases of a bygone time, most beloved of which are the rapidly disappearing style of alleyway neighborhoods called *hutong*.

Underlying Beijing's thrust toward modernity is an intriguing historic core. Scores of the city's imperial palaces, halls of power, mansions, and temples built under the Mongols during the Yuan Dynasty (1271–1368) were rebuilt during later Ming and Qing dynasties. Despite the ravages of time and the depredations of the Cultural Revolution, many of these refurbished sites are still in excellent condition including, to name a few, the Niujie Mosque, with Koranic verses curling around its arches, and Tiananmen Square, bold brainchild of Mao Zedong.

Continued on page 50

BEIJING'S SUBWAY

Although Beijing's subway system has grown to 16 lines, the original 2 lines provide access to the most popular areas of the capital. Line 1 runs east and west along Chang'an Jie past the China World Trade Center, Jianguomen (one of the embassy districts), the Wangfujing shopping area, Tiananmen Square and the Forbidden City, Xidan (another major shopping location), and the Military Museum, before heading out to the far western suburbs. Line 2 (the loop line) runs along a sort of circular route around the center of the city shadowing the Second Ring Road. Important destinations include the Drum and Bell towers, Lama Temple, Dongzhimen (with a connection to the airport express), Dongsishitiao (near Sanlitun and the Workers' Stadium), Beijing Train Station, and Qianmen (Front Gate), south of Tiananmen Square. Free transfers between Line 1 and 2 can be made at either Fuxingmen or Jianguomen stations. Line 10, which will eventually form a rough loop following the Third Ring Road, is currently operating on the northern and eastern stretches of the route, which runs through the Central Business District at Guomao station (where a transfer is possible to Line 1), up towards the Sanlitun area at Tuanjiehu, and connects with the airport express line at Sanyuanqiao.

If both you and your final destination are near the Second Ring Road, on Chang'an Jie, or on the northern or eastern sides of the Third Ring Road, the best way to get there is probably by subway. It stops just about every kilometer (half mile), and you'll easily spot the entrances (with blue subway logos) dotting the streets. Each stop is announced in both English and Chinese, and there are clearly marked signs in English or pinyin at each station. Transferring between lines is easy and free, with the standard Y2 ticket including travel between any two destinations.

Subway tickets can be purchased from electronic kiosks and ticket windows in every station. Start off by finding the button that says "English," insert your money, and press another button to print. Single-ride tickets cost Y2, and you'll want to pay with exact change; the machines don't accept Y1 bills, only Y1 coins. It's also possible to buy a stored-value subway card with a Y20 deposit and a purchase of Y10–Y100.

In the middle of each subway platform, you'll find a map of the Beijing subway system along with a local map showing the position of exits. Subway cars also have a simplified diagram of the line you're riding above the doors.

Trains can be very crowded, especially during rush hour, and it's not uncommon for people to push onto the train before exiting passengers can get off. Prepare to get off by making your way to the door before you arrive at your station. Be especially wary of pickpockets.

⚠ Unfortunately, the subway system is not convenient for disabled people. In some stations there are no escalators, and sometimes the only entrance or exit is via steep steps.

THE FORBIDDEN CITY

Undeniably sumptuous, the Forbidden City, once home to a long line of emperors, is Beijing's most enduring emblem. Magnificent halls, winding lanes, and stately courtyards await you—welcome to the world's largest palace complex.

As you gaze up at roofs of glazed-yellow tiles—a symbol of royalty—try to imagine a time when only the emperor ("the son of God") was permitted to enter this palace, accompanied by select family members, concubines, and eunuch-servants. Now, with its doors flung open, the Forbidden City's mysteries beckon.

The sheer grandeur of the site—with 800 buildings and more than 8,000 rooms—conveys the pomp and circumstance of Imperial China. The shady palaces, musty with age, recall life at court, where corrupt eunuchs and palace officials schemed and bored concubines gossiped.

BUILDING TO GLORY
Under the third Ming emperor, Yongle, 200,000 laborers built this complex over the course of 14 years, finishing in 1420. Yongle relocated the Ming capital to Beijing (from Nanjing in the south) to strengthen China's northern frontier. After Yongle, the palace was home to 23 Ming and Qing emperors, until the dynastic system crumbled in 1911.

In imperial times, no buildings were allowed to exceed the height of the palace. Moats and massive timber doors protected the emperor. Gleaming yellow roof tiles marked the vast complex as the royal court's exclusive dominion. Ornate interiors displayed China's most exquisite artisanship, including ceilings covered with turquoise-and-blue dragons, walls draped with priceless scrolls, intricate cloisonné screens, sandalwood thrones padded in delicate silks, and floors of golden-hued bricks. Miraculously, the palace survived fire, war, and imperial China's collapse.

MORE THAN FENG SHUI
The Forbidden City embodies Feng Shui, architectural principles used for thousands of years throughout China. Each main hall faces south, opening to a courtyard flanked by lesser buildings. This symmetry repeats itself along a north–south axis that bisects the imperial palace, with a broad walkway paved in marble. This path was reserved exclusively for the emperor's sedan chair.

The entire complex follows the principles of Feng Shui.

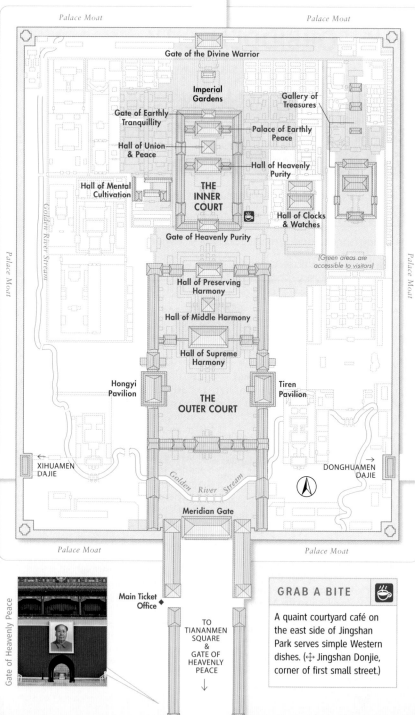

Palace Moat

Palace Moat

Gate of the Divine Warrior

Imperial Gardens

Gallery of Treasures

Gate of Earthly Tranquillity

Palace of Earthly Peace

Hall of Union & Peace

Hall of Heavenly Purity

Hall of Mental Cultivation

THE INNER COURT

Gate of Heavenly Purity

Hall of Clocks & Watches

Golden River Stream

Palace Moat

(Green areas are accessible to visitors)

Palace Moat

Hall of Preserving Harmony

Hall of Middle Harmony

Hall of Supreme Harmony

Hongyi Pavilion

Tiren Pavilion

THE OUTER COURT

← XIHUAMEN DAJIE

→ DONGHUAMEN DAJIE

Golden River Stream

Meridian Gate

Palace Moat

Palace Moat

Gate of Heavenly Peace

Main Ticket Office ◆

TO TIANANMEN SQUARE & GATE OF HEAVENLY PEACE ↓

GRAB A BITE

A quaint courtyard café on the east side of Jingshan Park serves simple Western dishes. (⟡ Jingshan Donjie, corner of first small street.)

WHAT TO SEE

The most impressive way to reach the Forbidden City is through the **Gate of Heavenly Peace** (Tiananmen), connected to Tiananmen Square. The Great Helmsman himself stood here to establish the People's Republic of China on October 1, 1949.

The **Meridian Gate** (Wumen), sometimes called Five Phoenix Tower, is the main southern entrance to the palace. Here, the emperor announced yearly planting schedules according to the lunar calendar; it's also where errant officials were flogged. The main ticket office and audio-guide rentals are just west of this gate.

The central entrance of the Meridian was reserved for the emperor. The one day the empress was allowed to walk through it was her wedding day.

THE OUTER COURT

The **Hall of Supreme Harmony** (Taihedian) was used for coronations, royal birthdays, and weddings. Bronze vats, once kept brimming with water to fight fires, ring this vast expanse. The hall sits atop three stone tiers with an elaborate drainage system with 1,000 carved dragons. On the top tier, bronze cranes symbolize longevity. Inside, cloisonné cranes flank the imperial throne, above which hangs a heavy bronze ball—placed there to crush any pretender to the throne.

Take a close look at the bronze vats and you'll see the telltale scratch marks of greedy foreign soldiers who scraped the gold with their bayonets.

Emperors greeted audiences in the **Hall of Middle Harmony** (Zhonghedian). It also housed the royal plow, with which the emperor would turn a furrow to commence spring planting.

The highest civil service examinations, which were personally conducted by the emperor, were once administered in the **Hall of Preserving Harmony** (Baohedian). Behind the hall, a 200-ton marble relief of dragons, the palace's most treasured stone carving, adorns the staircase.

A short jaunt to the right is **Hall of Clocks and Watches** (Zhongbiaoguan), where you'll find a collection of early timepieces. It's pure opulence: there's a plethora of jeweled, enameled, and lacquered timepieces (some astride elephants, others implanted in ceramic trees). Our favorites? Those crafted from red sandalwood. *(Admission: Y10)*

The Hall of Supreme Harmony was the site of many imperial weddings.

You'll see that lions in the palace live in pairs. A female lion playing with a cub symbolizes imperial fertility. A male lion, sitting majestically with a sphere beneath his paw, represents power.

Marble dragons will greet you behind the Hall of Preserving Harmony.

DID YOU KNOW?

- 24 emperors and two dynasties ruled from within these labyrinthine halls.

- The emperor was the only non-castrated male allowed in the eastern and western palaces. This served as proof that any pregnant concubine was carrying the royal one's baby.

- If you prepared for your trip by watching Bertolucci's *The Last Emperor*, you may recognize the passage outside the Hall of Mental Cultivation: this is where young Puyi rode his bike in the film.

- Women can enter the Forbidden City for half price on March 8, International Women's Day.

- When it was first built in the 15th century, the palace was called the Purple Forbidden City; today, its official name is the Ancient Palace Museum (Gugong Bowuguan); often it's shortened simply to Gugong.

Emperors Throne in the Palace of Heavenly Purity

THE INNER COURT

Now you're approaching the very core of the palace. Several emperors chose to live in the Inner Palace with their families. The **Hall of Heavenly Purity** (Qianqinggong) holds another imperial throne; the **Hall of Union and Peace** (Jiaotaidian) was the venue for the empress's annual birthday party; and the **Palace of Earthly Peace** (Kunninggong) was where royal couples consummated their marriages. The banner above the throne bizarrely reads DOING NOTHING.

On either side of the Inner Palace are six western and six eastern palaces—the former living quarters of concubines, eunuchs, and servants. The last building on the western side, the **Hall of Mental Cultivation** (Yangxindian), is the most important of these; starting with Emperor Yongzheng, all Qing Dynasty emperors attended to daily state business in this hall.

AN EMPEROR CHEAT SHEET

JIAJING (1507–1567)

Ming Emperor Jiajing was obsessed with Taoism, which he hoped would give him longevity, but which also led him to ignore state affairs for 25 years. His other fixation was the pursuit of girls: his 18 concubines conspired to strangle him in his sleep, but their plot was uncovered. Nearly all of the girls, and their families, were killed.

YONGZHENG (1678–1735)

The third emperor of the Qing Dynasty, Yongzheng was tyrannical but efficient. He became emperor amid rumors that he had forged his father's will. He appeased his brothers by promoting them, but then proceeded to murder and imprison anyone who posed a challenge, including his own brothers, two of whom died in prison.

Pagoda in the Imperial Garden

FAST FACTS

Address: The main entrance is just north of the Gate of Heavenly Peace, which faces Tiananmen Square on Chang'an Jie.

Phone: 010/8513-2255

Web site: www.dpm.org.cn

Admission: Y60

Hours: Oct. 16–Apr. 15, daily 8:30–4:30; Apr. 16–Oct. 15, daily 8:30–5

UNESCO Status: Declared a World Heritage Site in 1987. You must check your bags prior to entry and also pass through a metal detector.

The Gallery of Treasures (Zhenbaoguan), actually a series of halls, has breathtaking examples of imperial ornamentation. The first room displays candleholders, wine vessels, tea sets, and a golden pagoda commissioned by Qing emperor Qian Long in honor of his mother. A cabinet on one wall contains the 25 imperial seals. Jade bracelets, golden hair pins, and coral fill the second hall; carved jade landscapes a third. *(Admission: Y10)*

HEAD FOR THE GREEN

North of the Forbidden City's private palaces, beyond the **Gate of Earthly Tranquillity,** lie the most pleasant parts of the Forbidden City: the **Imperial Gardens** (Yuhuayuan), composed of ancient cypress trees and stone mosaic pathways. During festivals, palace inhabitants climbed the Hill of Accumulated Elegance. You can exit the palace at the back of the gardens through the park's **Gate of the Divine Warrior** (Shenwumen).

■ The palace is always packed with visitors, but it's impossibly crowded on national holidays.

■ Allow 2–4 hours to explore the palace. There are souvenir shops and restaurants inside.

■ You can hire automated audio guides at the Meridian Gate for Y40 and a Y100 returnable deposit.

CIXI (1835–1908)

The Empress Dowager served as de facto ruler of China from 1861 until 1908. She was a concubine at 16 and soon became Emperor Xianfeng's favorite. She gave birth to his only son to survive: the heir apparent. Ruthless and ambitious, she learned the workings of the imperial court and used every means to gain power.

PUYI (1906–1967)

Puyi, whose life was depicted in Bertolucci's classic *The Last Emperor,* took the throne at age two. The Qing dynasty's last emperor, he was forced to abdicate after the dynasty fell. During an attempted restoration in 1917, he held the throne for 12 days. Puyi was forced out of the Imperial City in 1924 by a warlord.

DONGCHENG DISTRICT 东城区

Sightseeing
★★★★☆

Dining
★★★☆☆

Lodging
★★★★☆

Shopping
★★★☆☆

Nightlife
★★★☆☆

A grave sense of China's awe-inspiring history is inevitable as you stand on the Avenue of Eternal Peace, Chang'an Jie, right at the crossroads of ancient and modern China. The pale expanse of Tiananmen Square, built by Mao Zedong to fit up to a million revolutionary souls, leaves even mobs of tourists looking tiny and scattered. The iconic portrait of Mao sits upon the scarlet wall of Tiananmen Gate, the serenity of his gaze belying the tumult of his reign. And beyond, the splendors of the Forbidden City await.

Start with the imposing majesty of Tiananmen Square and the Forbidden City for a view of official China at its peak, past and present. Nearby, witness the rise of China's middle class firsthand on Wangfujing, where you'll find familiar brands (McDonald's, Nike) amid a dwindling number of large stores that are relics from the days of central planning. Then take a detour deeper into the past-meets-present dichotomy with a visit to the hutong surrounding the Confucius Temple. Wudaoying Hutong and Fangjia Hutong currently feature the best array of restaurants, quirky boutiques, and cafés in the neighborhood. From the old men playing chess in the hutong to the sleek, chauffeured Audis driving down Chang'an Jie, to the colorful shopping on Wangfujing, the Dongcheng District offers visitors a thousand little tastes of what makes Beijing a fascinating city.

EXPLORING

TOP ATTRACTIONS

Fodor's Choice
★

Confucius Temple (孔庙 *Kǒngmiào*). This tranquil temple to China's great sage has endured close to eight centuries of additions and restorations. The Hall of Great Accomplishment in the temple houses Confucius's funeral tablet and shrine, flanked by copper-colored statues depicting China's wisest Confucian scholars. As in Buddhist and Taoist temples, worshippers can offer sacrifices (in this case to a mortal, not a deity). The 198 tablets lining the courtyard outside the Hall of Great Accomplishment contain 51,624 names belonging to advanced Confucian scholars from the Yuan, Ming, and Qing dynasties. Flanking the Gate of Great Accomplishment are two carved stone drums dating to the Qianlong period (1735–96). In the Hall of Great Perfection you'll find the central shrine to Confucius. Check out the huge collection of ancient musical instruments.

In the front and main courtyards of the temple you'll find a cemetery of stone tablets. These tablets, or stelae, stand like rows of creepy crypts. On the front stelae you can barely make out the names of thousands of scholars who passed imperial exams. Another batch of stelae, carved in the mid-1700s to record the *Thirteen Classics*, philosophical works attributed to Confucius, line the west side of the grounds.

▥ TIP➔ We recommend combining a tour of the Confucius Temple with the nearby Lama Temple. Access to both is convenient from the Yonghegong subway stop at the intersection of Line 2 and Line 5. You can also easily get to the Temple of Heaven by taking Line 5 south to Tiantandongmen.

The complex is now combined with the Imperial Academy (国子监, *Guózǐjiān*) next door, once the highest educational institution in the country. Established in 1306 as a rigorous training ground for high-level government officials, the academy was notorious, especially during the early Ming Dynasty era, for the harsh discipline imposed on scholars perfecting their knowledge of the Confucian classics. The Riyong Emperors Lecture Hall is surrounded by a circular moat (although the building is rectangular in shape). Emperors would come here to lecture on the classics. This ancient campus would be a glorious place to study today with its washed red walls, gold-tiled roofs, and towering cypresses (some as old as 700 years). ⊠ *13 Guozijian Lu, off Yonghegong Lu near Lama Temple, Dongcheng District* ☎ *010/8401–1977* ⊕ *www.kmgzj.com* ☞ *Y30* ⊙ *Daily 8:30–5* Ⓜ *Yonghegong.*

Dongbianmen Watch Tower (东便门角楼 *Dōngbiànmén jiǎolóu*). This is Beijing's last remaining Ming watchtower. Be sure to check out the Red Gate Gallery located inside, which shows works by well-known contemporary Chinese artists. The gallery was set up in 1991 by Brian Wallace, an Australian who studied art history at China's Central Academy of Fine Arts. The second and third floors are devoted to the history of the Dongcheng District. ⊠ *Dongbianmen Watchtower, Dongcheng District* ☎ *010/6525–1005* ⊕ *www.redgategallery.com* ☞ *Free* ⊙ *Daily 9–5.*

GETTING ORIENTED

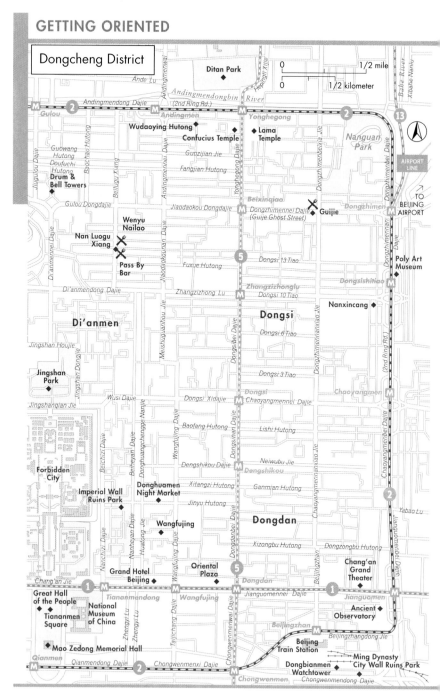

Dongcheng District

QUICK BITES

Wenyu Nailao. Have a cup of fresh yogurt at Wenyu Nailao, which makes its yogurt the traditional Chinese way. ⊠ *49 Nan Luogu Xiang, Dongcheng District* ☏ *010/6405–7621.*

Pass By Bar. The Pass By Bar offers good drinks, food, and wireless Internet access. ⊠ *108 Nan Luogu Xiang, Dongcheng District* ☏ *010/8403–8004.*

Guijie (簋街 *Guǐjiç***).** For a nighttime-munchies cure, head to Guijie, also known as Ghost Street, which is full of restaurants serving up Chinese specialties such as noodles, hotpot, and fried delights. One of the most popular dishes here is *malaxia,* or spicy crawfish. ⊠ *Dongzhimennei Dajie, Dongcheng District.*

NEIGHBORHOOD TOP 5

1. Explore the wonders of the **Forbidden City** and **Tiananmen Square.** Then climb the hill in **Jingshan Park** for a timeless view of the golden rooftops of the Forbidden City.

2. Visit the **Lama Temple,** Beijing's most famous Tibetan Buddhist temple, then the **Confucius Temple;** finally, stroll down nearby Wudaoying Hutong to take in the trendy shops and cafés.

3. Have dinner in the renovated courtyard of **The Source** (⇨ *Chapter 3*), then walk through **Nan Luogu Xiang,** the city's hippest hutong area.

4. Walk up **Wangfujing,** Beijing's premier shopping spot, and try some local delicacies (scorpion on a stick for the brave) from the vendors at Wangfujing Snack Street or at the Donghuamen Night Market.

5. Walk along the well-landscaped **Imperial Wall Ruins Park,** which begins one block north of Chang'an Jie on Nan Heyandajie.

GETTING HERE

Dongcheng is easily accessible by subway, with stops along most of its perimeter: Tiananmen East station to Jianguomen on Line 1 forms the south side of this district; Jianguomen to Gulou Dajie on Line 2 forms the district's north and east sides. Line 2 stops at the Lama Temple, the Ancient Observatory, Wangfujing, and Tiananmen Square. Taxi travel during peak hours (7 to 9 am and 5 to 8 pm) is difficult. At other times traveling by taxi is affordable, convenient, and the fastest option (especially at noon, when much of the city is at lunch, and after 10 pm). Renting a bike to see the sites is also a good option. Bus travel within the city is only Y1 for shorter distances and can be very convenient, but requires reading knowledge of Chinese to find the correct bus to take. Once on the bus, stops are announced in Chinese and English.

MAKING THE MOST OF YOUR TIME

Most of Dongcheng can be seen in a day, but it's best to set aside two, because the **Forbidden City** and **Tiananmen Square** will likely take the better part of one day. The climb up Coal Hill (also called Prospect Hill) in **Jingshan Park** will take about 30 minutes for an average walker. From there, take a taxi to the **Lama Temple,** which is worth a good two hours, then visit the nearby **Confucius Temple.**

2

Though many sights were damaged during the Cultural Revolution, Confucian temples can still be seen.

Jingshan Park (景山公园 *Jǐngshān gōngyuán*). This park, also known as Coal Hill Park, was built around a small peak formed from earth excavated for the Forbidden City's moats. Ming rulers ordered the hill's construction to improve the feng shui of their new palace to the south. You can climb a winding stone staircase past peach and apple trees to Wanchun Pavilion, the park's highest point. On a clear day it offers unparalleled views of the Forbidden City and the Bell and Drum towers. Chongzhen, the last Ming emperor, is said to have hanged himself at the foot of Coal Hill as his dynasty collapsed in 1644. ⊠ *Jingshanqian Dajie, opposite the north gate of the Forbidden City, Xicheng and Dongcheng districts* ☎ 010/6404–4071 🚇 *Y2* ⊙ *Daily 6 am–7 pm.*

Lama Temple (雍和宫 *Yōnghégōng*). Beijing's most-visited religious site and one of the most important functioning Buddhist temples in Beijing, this Tibetan Buddhist masterpiece has five main halls and numerous galleries hung with finely detailed *thangkhas* (Tibetan religious scroll paintings). The entire temple is decorated with Buddha images—all guarded by somber lamas dressed in brown robes. Originally a palace for Prince Yongzheng, it was transformed into a temple once he became the Qing's third emperor in 1723. The temple flourished under Emperor Qianlong, housing some 500 resident monks. This was once the official "embassy" of Tibetan Buddhism in Beijing but today only about two dozen monks live in this complex.

Don't miss **The Hall of Heavenly Kings**, with statues of Maitreya, the future Buddha, and Weitou, China's guardian of Buddhism. This hall is worth a slow stroll. In the courtyard beyond, a pond with a bronze mandala represents paradise. The Statues of Buddhas of the Past,

TIPS FOR TOURING WITH KIDS

Although incense-filled temples and ancient buildings do not, at first glance, seem child-friendly, Beijing's historic sites do offer some unique and special activities for the young. The Summer Palace is a great place for kids to run around and go splashing in paddleboats; the old Summer Palace has a fun maze; Tiananmen Square is a popular spot to fly kites; the Drum Tower holds percussion performances; and the Temple of Heaven's Echo Wall offers up some unusual acoustical fun. Budding astronomers might also be intrigued by the Ancient Observatory with its Ming Dynasty star map and early heaven-gazing devices built by early Jesuit missionaries who worked for the imperial court. Wherever you go, remember this: Chinese kids are generally allowed to run around and act like children, so don't worry that your own tyke's behavior will be viewed as inappropriate.

Present, and Future hold court in **The Hall of Harmony**. Look on the west wall where an exquisite silk thangkha of White Tara—the embodiment of compassion—hangs. Images of the Medicine and Longevity Buddhas line **The Hall of Eternal Blessing**. In **The Pavilion of Ten Thousand Fortunes** you see the breathtaking 85-foot Maitreya Buddha carved from a single sandalwood block.⊠ *12 Yonghegong Dajie, Beixingqiao, Dongcheng District* ☎ *010/6404–4499* 🎫 *Y25* ⊙ *Daily 9–4:30* Ⓜ *Yonghegong, Line 2.*

NEED A BREAK?   **Lao She Teahouse.** The area just south of Qianmen was once the nightlife hub of imperial China. Visit this old teahouse for a taste of Chinese performing arts along with your cuppa. ⊠ *3 Qianmen Xilu, Dongcheng District* ☎ *010/6303–7562.*

Ming Dynasty City Wall Ruins Park (明城墙遗址公园 *Míng chéngqiáng yízhǐ gōngyuán*). The new Ming Dynasty City Wall Ruins Park is a renovated section of Beijing's old inner-city wall. The structure was rebuilt using original bricks that had been snatched decades earlier after the city wall had been torn down. This rebuilt section of the wall is a nicely landscaped area with paths full of Chinese walking their dogs, flying kites, practicing martial arts, and playing with their children. At the eastern end of the park is the grand Dongbianmen Watch Tower, home to the popular Red Gate Gallery. ⊠ *Dongbianmen, Dongdajie St., Dongcheng District* 🎫 *Free* ⊙ *Daily, park open 24 hrs.*

National Museum of China (中國國家博物館 *Zhōngguó guójiā bówùguǎn*). Reopened in 2011 following a lengthy $400 million renovation, this monumental edifice on the eastern side of Tiananmen Square showcases 5,000 years of history in immaculate surroundings. With 2 million square feet of exhibition space, it's impossible to see everything, though the propaganda-heavy history sections are safely skipped. Focus instead on the ancient China section on the lower level, which houses magnificent displays of bronzes and jade artifacts. The museum also features strong shows of visiting works from abroad, such as Renaissance art from Florence and ceramics from the British Museum

and Victoria and Albert Museum. ✉ *16 Dong Chang Anjie, Dongcheng District* ☏ *010/6511–6400* ⊕ *en.chnmuseum.cn* ✉ *Free with passport* ☉ *Tues.–Sun. 9–5, ticket booth closes at 3:30* Ⓜ *Tiananmen East.*

Fodor's Choice
★

Tiananmen Square (天安门广场 *Tiānānmén guǎngchǎng*). The world's largest public square, and the very heart of modern China, Tiananmen Square owes little to grand imperial designs and everything to Mao Zedong. At the height of the Cultural Revolution, hundreds of thousands of Red Guards crowded the square; in June 1989 the square was the scene of tragedy when student demonstrators were killed.

Today the square is packed with sightseers, families, and undercover policemen. Although formidable, the square is a little bleak, with no shade, benches, or trees. Come here at night for an eerie experience—it's a little like being on a film set. Beijing's ancient central axis runs right through the center of Mao Zedong's mausoleum, the Forbidden City, the Drum and Bell towers, and the Olympic Green. The square is sandwiched between two grand gates: the Gate of Heavenly Peace (Tiananmen) to the north and the Front Gate (Qianmen) in the south. Along the western edge is the Great Hall of the People. The National Museum of China lies along the eastern side. The 125-foot granite obelisk you see is the Monument to the People's Heroes; it commemorates those who died for the revolutionary cause of the Chinese people. ✉ *Bounded by Chang'an Jie to the north and Qianmen Dajie to the south, Dongcheng District* ✉ *Free* ☉ *Daily 5 am–10 pm* Ⓜ *Tiananmen East.*

DID YOU
KNOW?

A network of tunnels lies beneath Tiananmen Square. Mao Zedong is said to have ordered them dug in the late 1960s after Sino-Soviet relations soured. They extend across Beijing and many have been sealed up or fallen into disrepair, though migrant workers inhabit some.

Wangfujing (王府井 *Wángfǔjǐng*). Wangfujing, one of the city's oldest and busiest shopping districts, is still lined with a handful of *laozihao*, or old brand-name shops, some dating back a century, and 1950s-era state-run stores. This short walking street is a pleasant place for window-shopping. Also on Wangfujing is the gleaming Oriental Plaza, with it's expensive high-end shops (think Tiffany's, Burberry, Ermenegildo Zegna, and Audi), interspersed with Levi Jeans, Esprit, Starbucks, Pizza Hut, KFC, Häagen-Dazs, and a modern cinema multicomplex. ✉ *Wangfujing, Dongcheng District.*

WORTH NOTING

Ditan Park (地坛公园 *Dìtán gōngyuán*). In this 16th-century green space, translated as "Temple of Earth Park," are the square altar where emperors once made sacrifices to the earth god and the Hall of Deities. This is a lovely place for a stroll, especially if you're already near the Drum Tower or Lama Temple. ✉ *Hepingli Xilu, just north of 2nd Ring Rd., Dongcheng District* ☏ *010/6421–4657* ✉ *Y2* ☉ *Daily 6 am–9 pm.*

Guijie (簋街 *Guǐjiè*). This nearly 2-km-long (1-mile-long) stretch, also known as Ghost Street, is lined with more than 100 restaurants, many open 24 hours a day and attracting the spill off from nightclubs. Although the restaurants here are generally just average, the lively atmosphere is enticing, with red lanterns strung across the sidewalks. There

MAO ZEDONG (1893–1976)

Some three decades after his passing, Mao Zedong continues to evoke radically different feelings. Was he the romantic poet-hero who helped the Chinese stand up against foreign aggression? Or was he a monster whose policies caused the deaths of tens of millions of people? Born into a relatively affluent farming family in Hunan, Mao became active in politics at a young age; he was one of the founding members of the Chinese Communist Party in 1921. When the People's Republic of China was established in 1949, Mao served as chairman. After a good start in improving the economy, he launched radical programs in the mid-1950s. The party's official assessment is that Mao was 70% correct and 30% incorrect. His critics reverse this ratio.

are a wide number of cuisines and restaurants that serve a diversity of dishes, though night owls tend to favor spicy dishes such as fiery Sichuan hotpot, crayfish in chili oil, and barbecued fish. ⊠ *Dongzhimennei Dajie, Dongcheng District.*

Mao Zedong Memorial Hall (毛主席纪念堂 *Máozhǔxí jìniàntáng*). Sentries here will assure that your communion with the Great Helmsman is brief. After waiting in a long and winding line, you'll be guided into a spacious lobby dominated by a marble Mao statue and then to the Hall of Reverence, where his embalmed body lies in state, wrapped in the red flag of the Communist Party of China inside a crystal coffin that's lowered each night into a subterranean freezer. In a bid to limit Mao's deification, a second-story museum was added in 1983; it's dedicated to the former Premier Zhou Enlai, former general Zhu De, and China's president before the Cultural Revolution, Liu Shaoqi (who was persecuted to death during the Cultural Revolution). The hall's builders willfully ignored Tiananmen Square's geomancy: the mausoleum faces north, boldly contradicting centuries of imperial ritual. ⊠ *Tiananmen Sq., Dongcheng District* ☎ *010/6513–2277* 🖅 *Free* ⏱ *Sept.–June, Tues.–Sun. 8 am–noon; July and Aug., Tues.–Sun. 7 am–11 am.*

Nan Luogu Xiang (南锣鼓巷*Nánluógǔxiàng*). The narrow Nan Luogu Xiang, or South Gong and Bell Alley, which dates back some 700 years, got a new lease on life when it was discovered by young entrepreneurs who raced in to open souvenir shops, boutiques, cafés, bars, and snack stalls in the aging but rustic structures that line the sidewalks. The narrow street is flanked by eight historic hutong to the east and west that are worth exploring, especially when the crowds in the main section get overwhelming. It's a great place to try some of the snacks popular with young Chinese, such as milk tea, chicken wings, and the famous custard-like yogurt at Wenyu Nailao. ⊠ *Nan Luogu Xiang, Dongcheng District.*

Nanxincang (南新仓 *Nánxîncâng*). China's oldest existing granary, dating back to the Yongle period (1403–24), is now Beijing's newest entertainment venue. It's home to three art galleries, a teahouse, and several bars and restaurants, including a branch of the famed Dadong Roast Duck. The structures at Nanxincang—just 10 years younger than those

Tiananmen Square

of the Forbidden City—were among the more than 300 granaries that existed in this area during imperial days. Have a glass of wine on the second floor of Yuefu, an audio and book shop, where you can admire the old interior, then have dinner at one of the excellent restaurants in the compound. ⊠ *Dongsi Shitiao, 1 block west of the 2nd Ring Rd., Dongcheng District.*

The Poly Art Museum (保利艺术博物馆 *Bǎolì yìshù bówùguǎn*). This very impressive museum, located in a gleaming new glass office tower called New Poly Plaza, was established in 1998 to promote traditional art and to protect Chinese art from being lost to foreign countries. The museum has focused on the overseas acquisition of ancient bronzes, sculpture, and painting. The museum is divided into two galleries, one for the display of early Chinese bronzes, and the other for Buddhist scriptures carved in stone. Also on display here are four bronze animal heads that were once located in the Old Summer Palace. ⊠ *New Poly Plaza, 1 Chaoyangmen Beidajie, located next to the Dongshisitiao subway stop on Line 2, Dongcheng District* ☎ *010/6500–8117* ☞ *Y20* ⊗ *Mon.–Sat. 9:30–4:30.*

| NEED A BREAK? | **Donghuamen Night Market** (东华门夜市 *Dōnghuāmén yèshì*). Crunchy deep-fried scorpions and other critters are sold at the northern end of Wangfujing's wide walking boulevard. Most street-market food is usually safe to eat as long as it's hot. The row of interesting outdoor evening stalls makes for an intriguing walk with great photo ops. ⊠ *Donganmen Dajie, on the northern side of Wangfujing, Dongcheng District.* |

XICHENG DISTRICT 西城区

Sightseeing
★★★☆☆

Dining
★★☆☆☆

Lodging
★☆☆☆☆

Shopping
★★☆☆☆

Nightlife
★★★☆☆

Xicheng District is home to a charming combination of some of the most distinctive things the city has to offer—cozy hutong, palatial courtyard houses, charming lakes, fine restaurants, and a buzzing nightlife scene—this is also the best area to fall in love with Beijing.

And the best way to do that is to take a walk or bicycle tour of the hutong here: there's no better way to scratch the surface of this sprawling city (before it disappears) than by exploring these courtyard houses as you wander in and out of historic sites in the area.

This is a great area for people-watching, especially along the shores of Houhai. As you wander, sample the local snacks sold from shop windows. Treats abound on Huguosi Jie (just west of Mei Lanfang's house) and on trendy Nan Luogu Xiang. In the evening, relax at a restaurant or bar with a view of the lake. The lakes at Shichahai are hopping day and night.

A GOOD WALK

Start just north of the Forbidden City at **Jingshan Park.** From here you can walk several blocks west to the south gate of **Beihai Park,** which is beautiful in August's lotus season. Exit at the north gate. After crossing Di'anmen Xidajie, you'll arrive at **Qianhai,** or "front lake."

Walk on the right, or east, side of the lake for about 10 minutes until you reach the famous Ming Dynasty **Silver Ingot Bridge.** Take a side trip to the **Bell Tower,** which is a short walk northeast of the bridge. (To get there, head down Yandai Xiejie, turn left at the end and you'll see the tower. Directly behind it is the Drum Tower.) Return to the Silver Ingot Bridge and follow the lake's northern shore until you arrive at **Soong Ching-ling's Former Residence.** Next, walk or take a short cab ride to **Prince Gong's Palace** behind the opposite side of the lake, to see how imperial relatives once lived. An alternative to those lavish interiors is the **Museum of Antique Currency,** where you can feast your eyes on rare Chinese coins.

Beihai Park

EXPLORING

TOP ATTRACTIONS

Beihai Park (北海 *Běihǎi gôngyuán*). A white stupa is perched on a small island just north of the south gate. Also at the south entrance is **Round City,** which contains a white-jade Buddha and an enormous jade bowl given to Kublai Khan. Nearby, the well-restored **Temple of Eternal Peace** houses a variety of Buddhas. Climb to the stupa from Yongan Temple. Once there, you can pay an extra Y1 to ascend the Buddha-bedecked **Shanyin Hall.**

The lake is Beijing's largest and most beautiful public waterway. On summer weekends the lake teems with paddleboats. The **Five Dragon Pavilion,** on Beihai's northwest shore, was built in 1602 by a Ming Dynasty emperor who liked to fish under the moon. ⊠ *Weijin Jie, Xicheng District* ☎ *010/6403–3225* ⊕ *www.beihaipark.com.cn* ⌷ *Y5; extra fees for some sites* ☉ *Apr., May, Sept., and Oct., daily 6 am–8:30 pm; Nov.–Mar., daily 6 am–8 pm; June–Aug., daily 6 am–10 pm.*

Capital Museum (首都博物馆 *Shǒdû bówùguǎn*). Moved to its architecturally striking new home west of Tiananmen Square in 2005, this is one of China's finest cultural museums. Artifacts are housed in the unique multistoried bronze cylinder that dominates the building's facade, while paintings, calligraphy, and photographs of historic Beijing fill the remaining exhibition halls. The museum gets extra points for clear English descriptions and modern, informative displays. Entry is free but foreign tourists must show their passports to get tickets. ⊠ *16 Fuxingmenwai Dajie, Xicheng District* ☎ *010/6337–0491* ⊕ *www. capitalmuseum.org.cn/en/* ⌷ *Free* ☉ *Tues.–Sun. 9–5.*

GETTING ORIENTED

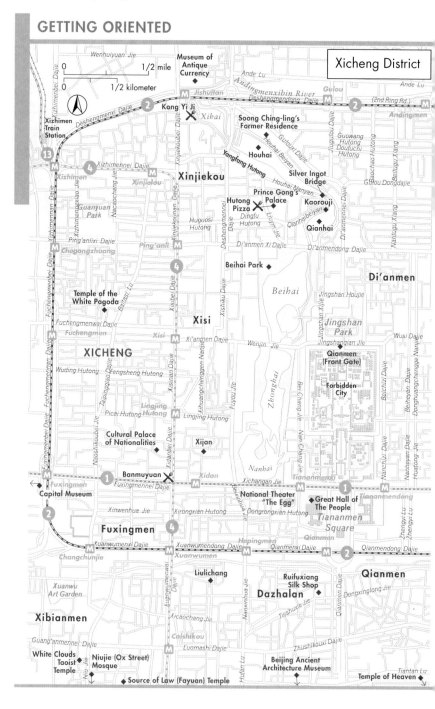

Xicheng District

Wenhuiyuan Jie
Museum of Antique Currency
Ande Lu
Ande Lu
Andingmenxibin River
Deshengmenxi Dajie
Gulou
(2nd Ring Rd.)
Andingmen
Jishuitan
Kong Yi Ji
Xizhimen Train Station
Deshengmenxi Dajie
Xibai
Soong Ching-ling's Former Residence
Houhai Beiyan
Xinjiekoubei Dajie
Guowang Hutong
Doufuchi Hutong
Guozhao Hutong
Beitingju Xiang
Gulou Dongdajie
Xizhimennei Dajie
Xizhimen
Yangfang Hutong
Houhai
Houhai Nanyan
Silver Ingot Bridge
Nahaju Xiang
Zhushikouxi Dajie
Xinjiekou
Nacaochang Jie
Guanyuan Park
Xinjiekou
Prince Gong's Palace
Hutong Pizza
Kaorouji
Qianhaibeiyan
Ping'anlixi Dajie
Chegongzhuang
Xinjiekounan Dajie
Deshengmennei Dajie
Huguosi Hutong
Dingfu Hutong
Liuyin Jie
Qianhai
Ping'anli
Di'anmen Xi Dajie
Di'anmendong Dajie
Di'anmen
Temple of the White Pagoda
Beihai Park
Beihai
Jingshan Houjie
Fuchengmennei Dajie
Xizhimen Dajie
Fuchengmenwai Dajie
Fuchengmen
Batasi Lu
Xisibei Dajie
Xishiku Dajie
Xisi
Jingshan Xijie
Jingshan Park
Wusi Dajie
Xisi
Xi'anmen Dajie
Wenjin Jie
Jingshanqian Jie
XICHENG
Fuchengmennei Dajie
Taipinggiao Dajie
Wuding Hutong
Fengsheng Hutong
Xisinan Dajie
Fuyou Jie
Zhonghai
Qianmen (Front Gate)
Beichizi Dajie
Beiheyan Dajie
Donghuangchengge Nanjie
Lingjing
Picai Hutong
Hutong
Lingjing Hutong
Xidanbei Dajie
Forbidden City
Nanchizi Dajie
Naohayan Dajie
Hutong Jie
Cultural Palace of Nationalities
Xijan
Xthuangchengmen Nanjie
Bei Chang Jie
Nan Chang Jie
Naoshikoubei Jie
Nanhai
Banmuyuan
Xidan
Xichang'an Jie
Tiananmenxi
Fuxingmen
Capital Museum
Fuxingmennei Dajie
National Theater "The Egg"
Great Hall of The People
Tiananmendong
Fuxingmen
Xinwenhua Jie
Xirongxian Hutong
Dongrongxian Hutong
Tiananmen Square
Zhengyi Lu
Zhengyi Lu
Xuanwumennei Dajie
Hepingmen
Qianmen
Changchunjie
Xuanwumen
Xuanwumendong Dajie
Qianmenxi Dajie
Qianmendong Dajie
Qianmen
Xuanwu Art Garden
Liulichang
Xicaochang Jie
Ruifuxiang Silk Shop
Qianmen Dajie
Dazhalan
Qianmen Dongxinglong Jie
Xibianmen
Xcatong Dajie
Nanxinhua Jie
Tieshuxie Jie
Guang'anmennei Dajie
Caishikou
White Clouds Taoist Temple
Niujie (Ox Street) Mosque
Niu Jie
Luomashi Dajie
Hutan Lu
Beijing Ancient Architecture Museum
Zhushikouxi Dajie
Tiantan Lu
Temple of Heaven
Source of Law (Fayuan) Temple

0 ———— 1/2 mile
0 ———— 1/2 kilometer

2

MAKING THE MOST OF YOUR TIME

Xicheng's must-see sites are few in number but all special. Walk around **Beihai Park** in the early afternoon. If you come to Beijing in the winter, **Qianhai** will be frozen and you can rent skates, runner-equipped bicycles to pedal across the ice, or the local favorite, a chair with runners welded to the bottom and a pair of metal sticks with which to propel yourself. Dinner along the shores of **Houhai** is a great option. Head toward the northern section for a more tranquil setting or join the crowds for a booming bar scene farther south. Plan to spend a few hours shopping at **Xidan** on your last day in Beijing; this is great place to pick up funky, cheap gifts.

QUICK BITES

Banmuyuan. For a simple meal in the Xidan area, try Banmuyuan, a Taiwanese-owned restaurant that serves chewy *zhajiang* noodles, beef dishes, and vegetarian pies. It's located directly behind the Bank of China headquarters (which was designed by I.M. Pei). ⊠ *45 Fuxingmen Neidajie, Xicheng District* ☎ *010/5851–8208* Ⓜ *Xidan.*

Cangsu Style Restaurant. Sleek Cangsu plates up beautiful creations along the shores of Houhai. It's located on the southwest corner of the lake, just two minutes north of Di'anmen Xidajie. Be sure to save room for a picture-perfect dessert. ⊠ *Xicheng District* ☎ *010/8328–6766.*

Hutong Pizza. Hutong Pizza is a great spot to take a break from Houhai and the hutong and enjoy a thin-crust square pie. It's located in a renovated courtyard house in a hutong just west of the Silver Ingot Bridge. ⊠ *9 Yindingqiao Hutong, Xicheng District* ☎ *010/8322–8916.*

Kong Yi Ji. The shores of Houhai and Qianhai are lined with great restaurants. Try Kong Yi Ji on the northwestern edge of Houhai. It's named after a story by famous writer Lu Xun and serves some of the dishes mentioned in the story. ⊠ *Houhai South Bank, 2A Deshengmennei Dajie, Xicheng District* ☎ *010/6618–4915.*

GETTING HERE

Houhai and Beihai Park are conveniently reached by taxi. Line 1 subway stops include Tiananmen West, Xidan, and Fuxingmen. Line 2 makes stops from Fuxingmen to the Drum Tower (Gulou), following Xicheng's perimeter.

NEIGHBORHOOD TOP 5

1. Sip coffee or an evening cocktail lakeside at **Houhai** or on one of the rooftop restaurants or bars overlooking the lake.

2. Explore Houhai's well-preserved hutong and historical sites by pedicab or bicycle.

3. Skate on **Houhai Lake** in winter, or, in the warmer months, take an evening boat tour of the lake. Dine onboard on barbecued lamb provided by Kaorouji.

Kaorouji. Kaorouji is an old lakeside restaurant specializing in Chinese-style barbecue. Romantics, take note: you'll be serenaded by your own personal *pipa* (four-stringed lute) musician. ⊠ *14 Qianhai Dongyan, just southeast of the Silver Ingot Bridge, Xicheng District* ☎ *010/6404–2554.*

4. Wander the hills and temples of historic Beihai Park. In the evening, eat the way the emperors did with an imperial banquet at **Fangshan Restaurant** (⇨ *Chapter 3)* in the park.

5. Shop for great gifts and snazzy clothes on the cheap at **Xidan**.

Drum Tower (鼓楼 *Gǔlóu*). Until the late 1920s, the 24 drums once housed in this tower were Beijing's timepiece. Sadly, all but one of these huge drums have been destroyed and the survivor is in serious need of renovation. Kublai Khan built the first drum tower on this site in 1272. You can climb to the top of the present tower, which dates from the Ming Dynasty. Old photos of hutong neighborhoods line the walls beyond the drum; there's also a scale model of a traditional courtyard house. The nearby **Bell Tower,** renovated after a fire in 1747, offers fabulous views of the hutong- from the top of a long, narrow staircase. The huge 63-ton bronze bell, supported by lacquered wood stanchions, is also worth seeing. ⊠ *North end of Dianmen Dajie, Xicheng District* ☎ *010/6404–1710* 🖃 *Drum Tower Y20, Bell Tower Y15* ⊙ *Daily 9–5* Ⓜ *Guloudajie.*

Niujie (Ox Street) Mosque (牛街清真寺 *Niújiē qīngzhēnsì*). Originally built during the Liao Dynasty in 996, Nuijie is Beijing's oldest and largest mosque. It sits at the center of the Muslim quarter and mimics a Chinese temple from the outside, with its hexagonal wooden structure. When the mosque was built, only traditional Chinese architecture was allowed in the capital. An exception was made for the Arabic calligraphy that decorates many of the mosque's walls and inner sanctums. The interior arches and posts are inscribed with Koranic verse, and a special moon tower helps with determining the lunar calendar. The Spirit Wall stands opposite the main entrance and prevents ghosts from entering the mosque. This wall is covered with carved mural works on the premise that ghosts can't turn sharp corners. Two dark tombs with Chinese and Arabic inscriptions are kept in one of the small courtyards. They belong to two Persian *imams* (the prayer leaders of a mosque) who came to preach at the mosque in the 13th and 14th centuries. Because Muslims must pray in the direction of Mecca, which is westward, the main prayer hall opens onto the east. At the rear of the complex is a minaret from which a muezzin calls the faithful to prayer. From this very tower, imams measure the beginning and end of Ramadan, Islam's month of fasting and prayer. Ramadan begins when the imam sights the new moon, which appears as a slight crescent.

The hall is open only to Muslims and can fit up to 1,000 worshippers. All visitors must wear long trousers or skirts and keep their shoulders covered. It's most convenient to get to the mosque by taxi. If you want to take the subway, it's about a 10-minute walk from Line 4's Caishikou station. ⊠ *18 Niu Jie, Xicheng District* ☎ *010/6353–2564* 🖃 *Y10* ⊙ *Daily 8–4.*

Qianhai and Houhai (前海,后海 *Qiánhǎi, Hòuhǎi*). Most people come to these lakes, along with Xihai to the northwest, to stroll and enjoy the shoreside bars and restaurants. In summer you can boat or fish. In winter, sections of the frozen lakes are fenced off for skating. This daytrip is easily combined with a visit to Beihai Park or the Bell and Drum towers. ⊠ *North of Beihai Lake, Xicheng District.*

Fodor's Choice
★
Temple of Heaven (天坛 *Tiāntán gōngyuán*). A prime example of Chinese religious architecture, this is where emperors once performed important rites. It was a site for imperial sacrifices, meant to please the gods so they would generate bumper harvests. Set in a huge, serene,

DID YOU KNOW?

The Temple of Heaven's overall layout symbolizes the relationship between Heaven and Earth. Earth is represented by a square and Heaven by a circle. The temple complex is surrounded by two cordons of walls; the taller outer wall is semicircular at the northern end (Heaven) and shorter and rectangular at the southern end (Earth). Both the Hall of Prayer for Good Harvests and the Circular Mound Altar are round structures on a square yard.

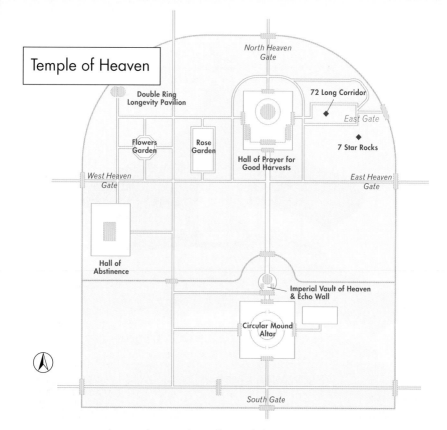

North Heaven Gate

Double Ring Longevity Pavilion

72 Long Corridor

East Gate

Flowers Garden

Rose Garden

7 Star Rocks

West Heaven Gate

Hall of Prayer for Good Harvests

East Heaven Gate

Hall of Abstinence

Imperial Vault of Heaven & Echo Wall

Circular Mound Altar

South Gate

mushroom-shape park southeast of the Forbidden City, the Temple of Heaven is surrounded by splendid examples of Ming Dynasty architecture, including curved cobalt blue roofs layered with yellow and green tiles. Construction began in the early 15th century under Yongle, whom many call the "architect of Beijing." Shaped like a semicircle on the northern rim to represent heaven and square on the south for the Earth, the grounds were once believed to be the meeting point of the two. The area is double the size of the Forbidden City and is still laid out to divine rule: buildings and paths are positioned to represent the right directions for heaven and Earth. This means, for example, that the northern part is higher than the south.

The temple's hallmark structure is a magnificent **blue-roofed wooden tower** built in 1420. It burned to the ground in 1889 and was immediately rebuilt using Ming architectural methods (and timber imported from Oregon). The building's design is based on the calendar: 4 center pillars represent the seasons, the next 12 pillars represent months, and 12 outer pillars signify the parts of a day. Together these 28 poles, which also correspond to the 28 constellations of heaven, support the structure without nails. A carved dragon swirling down from the ceiling represents the emperor.

Across the Danbi Bridge, you'll find the **Hall of Prayer for Good Harvests**. The middle section was once reserved for the Emperor of Heaven, who was the only one allowed to set foot on the eastern side, while aristocrats and high-ranking officials walked on the western strip. ■ TIP→ If you're coming by taxi, enter the park through the southern entrance (Tiantan Nanmen). This way you approach the beautiful Hall of Prayer for Good Harvests via the Danbi Bridge—the same route the emperor favored.

Directly east of this hall is a long, twisting platform, which once enclosed the animal-killing pavilion. The Long Corridor was traditionally hung with lanterns on the eve of sacrifices. Today it plays host to scores of Beijingers singing opera, playing cards and chess, and fan dancing.

Be sure to whisper into the echo wall encircling the **Imperial Vault of Heaven**. This structure allows anyone to eavesdrop. It takes a minute to get the hang of it, but with a friend on one side and you on the other it's possible to hold a conversation by speaking into the wall. Tilt your head in the direction you want your voice to travel for best results. Just inside the south gate is the **Round Altar**, a three-tiered, white-marble structure where the emperor worshipped the winter solstice; it's based around the divine number nine. Nine was regarded as a symbol of the power of the emperor, as it's the biggest single-digit odd number, and odd numbers are considered masculine and therefore more powerful.

The Hall of Abstinence, on the western edge of the grounds, is where the emperor would retreat three days before the ritual sacrifice. To understand the significance of the harvest sacrifice at the Temple of Heaven, it's important to keep in mind that the legitimacy of a Chinese emperor's rule depended on what is known as the *tian ming*, or the mandate of heaven, essentially the emperor's relationship with the gods.

A succession of bad harvests, for example, could be interpreted as the emperor losing the favor of heaven and could be used to justify a change in emperor or even in dynasty. When the emperor came to the Temple of Heaven to pray for good harvests and to pay homage to his ancestors, there may have been a good measure of self-interest to his fervor.

The sacrifices consisted mainly of animals and fruit placed on altars surrounded by candles. Many Chinese still offer sacrifices of fruit and incense on special occasions, such as births, deaths, and weddings.

■ TIP→ We recommend buying an all-inclusive ticket. If you only buy a ticket into the park, you'll need to pay an additional Y20 to get into each building.

Beijing's new subway Line 5 (purple line) makes getting to the Temple of Heaven easier than ever. Get off at the Tiantan Dongmen (Temple of Heaven East Gate) stop. The line also runs to the Lama Temple (Yonghegong), so combining the two sites in a day makes perfect sense.

Automatic audio guides (Y40) are available at stalls inside all four entrances. ✉ *Yongdingmen Dajie (South Gate), Xicheng District* ☎ *010/6702–8866* ⊕ *en.tiantanpark.com* ✑ *All-inclusive ticket Y35; entrance to park only Y15* ✆ *Daily 6 am–10 pm; ticket booth closes at 4:30.*

Shoppers enjoy a sunny day in the Xidan neighborhood.

Xidan (西单 *Xîdân*). This area teems with shopping malls and small stores selling clothing and accessories, and upwardly mobile Chinese consumers. There is also Tushu Dasha, aka Beijing Books Building, said to be the biggest bookstore in China, which has a small selection of English books in the basement. Ⓜ *Xidan.*

WORTH NOTING

Beijing Ancient Architecture Museum (北京古代建筑博物馆*Běijîng gǔdài jiànzhù bówùguǎn*). This little-known museum, located inside a Ming Dynasty temple, exhibits photos, objects, and elaborate models of ancient Chinese architecture from ancient huts and mud homes to Ming and Qing Dynasty palaces. The sand-table model of old Beijing is fascinating. ⊠ *21 Dongjing Lu, Xicheng District* ☎ *010/6317–2150* 💳 *Y15* ⏲ *Daily 9–4.*

Beijing Zoo (北京动物园 *Bìijîng dòngwù yuán*). Though visitors usually go straight to see the giant pandas, don't miss the other interesting animals, like tigers from the northeast, yaks from Tibet, enormous sea turtles from China's seas, and red pandas from Sichuan. The zoo started out as a garden belonging to one of the sons of Shunzhi, the first emperor of the Qing Dynasty. In 1750, the Qianlong emperor had it refurbished (along with other imperial properties, including the summer palaces) and turned it into a park in honor of his mother's 60th birthday. In 1901, the Empress Dowager gave it another extensive face-lift and used it to house a collection of animals given to her as a gift by a Chinese minister who had bought them during a trip to Germany. By the 1930s, most of the animals had died and were stuffed and put on display in a museum on the grounds. ⊠ *137*

Xizhimenwai Dajie, Xicheng District ☎ *010/6839–0274* ✉ *Apr.–Oct. Y15; Nov.–Mar. Y10 plus Y5 for panda site* ☉ *Apr.–Oct., daily 7:30–6; Nov.–Mar., daily 7:30–5.*

Cultural Palace of Nationalities (民族文化宫 *Mínzú wénhuà gōng*). Dedicated to the 56 official ethnic groups that make up China's modern population, this museum houses traditional clothing and artifacts from the country's remote border regions. Exhibits on topics like the "peaceful liberation of Tibet" are as interesting for the official government line as for what's left out. Entrance is free, but you'll need to show your passport to get in. ✉ *49 Fuxingmennei Dajie, next to the Minzu Hotel, Xicheng District* ☎ *010/6602–4433* ✉ *Free* ☉ *Daily 9–4.*

Great Hall of the People (人民大会堂 *Rénmín dàhuìtáng*). This solid edifice owes its Stalinist weight to the last years of the Sino-Soviet pact. Its gargantuan dimensions (205,712 square yards of floor space) exceed that of the Forbidden City. It was built by 14,000 laborers who worked around the clock for eight months. China's legislature meets in the aptly named Ten Thousand People Assembly Hall, beneath a panoply of 500 star lights revolving around a giant red star. Thirty-one reception rooms are distinguished by the arts and crafts of the provinces they represent. Have someone who speaks Chinese call a day ahead to confirm that it's open, as the hall often closes for political events and concerts. ✉ *West side of Tiananmen Sq., Xicheng District* ☎ *010/6309–6156* ✉ *Y30* ☉ *Dec.–Mar., daily 9–2; Apr.–June, daily 8:15–3; July and Aug., daily 7:30–4; Sept.–Nov., daily 8:30–3.*

Liulichang (琉璃厂 *Liúlíchǎng*). This quaint old street is best known for its antiques, books, and paintings. The street has been completely restored and a multitude of small shops, many privately owned, make it a fun place to explore, even if you're just window-shopping. Liulichang, often referred to as "Antiques Street," was built more than 500 years ago during the Ming Dynasty. It was the site of a large factory that made glazed tiles for the Imperial Palace. Gradually other smaller tradesmen began to cluster around and at the beginning of the Qing Dynasty, many booksellers moved here. The area became a meeting place for intellectuals and a prime shopping district for art objects, books, handicrafts, and antiques. In 1949, Liulichang still had more than 170 shops, but many were taken over by the state; the street was badly ransacked during the Cultural Revolution. Following large-scale renovation of the traditional architecture, the street reopened in 1984 under the policy that shops could only sell arts, crafts, and cultural objects. Today the street is a mixture of state-run and privately owned stores. ✉ *Liulichang, Xicheng District.*

Museum of Antique Currency (北京古代钱币博物馆 *Bǐijīng gǔdài qiánbì bówùguǎn*). This museum in a tiny courtyard house within the Deshengmen tower complex, showcases a small but impressive selection of rare Chinese coins. Explanations are in Chinese only. Also in the courtyard are coin and curio dealers. ✉ *Deshengmen Jianlou, Bei'erhuan Zhonglu, Xicheng District* ☎ *010/6602–4178* ✉ *Y10* ☉ *Tues.–Sun. 9–4.*

Liulichang (Antiques Street)

Prince Gong's Palace (恭王府 *Gōngwángfǔ*). This grand compound sits in a neighborhood once reserved for imperial relatives. Built in 1777 during the Qing Dynasty, it fell to Prince Gong—brother of Qing emperor Xianfeng and later an adviser to Empress Dowager Cixi—after the original inhabitant was executed for corruption. With nine courtyards joined by covered walkways, it was once one of Beijing's most lavish residences. The museum offers Beijing opera and tea to visitors who pay the higher ticket price. Some literary scholars believe this was the setting for *Dream of the Red Chamber,* one of China's best-known classical novels. ✉ *17 Qianhai Xijie, Xicheng District* ☎ *010/8328–8149* ⊕ *www.pgm.org.cn* ✐ *Y40–Y70* ⊙ *Mid-Mar.–mid.-Nov., daily 8–4; mid.-Nov.-mid.-Mar., daily 7:30–4:30.*

Qianmen (Front Gate) (前门大街 *Qiánmén dàjiē*). From its top looking south, you can see that the Qianmen is actually two gates: Sun-Facing Gate (Zhengyangmen) and Arrow Tower (Jian Lou), which was, until 1915, connected to Zhengyangmen by a defensive half-moon wall. The central gates of both structures opened only for the emperor's biannual ceremonial trips to the Temple of Heaven. The gate now defines the southern edge of Tiananmen Square. ✉ *Xuanwumen Jie, Xicheng District* ☎ *010/6522–9382* ✐ *Y10* ⊙ *8:30–4* Ⓜ *Qianmen.*

Ruifuxiang Silk Shop (瑞蚨祥绸布店 *Ruìfúxiáng chóubù diàn*). Established in 1893, this shop has thick bolts of silk, cotton, cashmere, and wool piled high, in more colors than you'll find in a box of crayons: chartreuse, candy-pink, chocolate-brown, fresh-cut-grass-green—you name it. Clerks deftly cut yards of cloth while tailors take measurements for colorful *qipaos* (traditional gowns). In this corner of Beijing, life seems to continue much as it did a century ago. ⊠ *5 Dazhalan Dajie, Xicheng District* ☎ *010/6303–5313.*

Soong Ching-ling's Former Residence (宋庆龄故居 *Sòng Qìnglíng gùjū*). Soong Ching-ling (1893–1981) was the youngest daughter of the wealthy, American-educated bible publisher, Charles Soong. At the age of 18, disregarding her family's strong opposition, she eloped to marry the much older Sun Yat-sen. When her husband founded the Republic of China in 1911, Soong Ching-ling became a significant political figure. In 1924 she headed the Women's Department of the Nationalist Party. Then in 1949 she became the vice president of the People's Republic of China. Throughout her career she campaigned tirelessly for the emancipation of women, and she helped lay the foundations for many of the rights that modern-day Chinese women enjoy today. This former palace was her residence and workplace and now houses a small museum, which documents her life and work. ⊠ *46 Houhai Beiyan, Xicheng District* ☎ *010/6404–4205* 💴 *Y20* ⊙ *Apr.–Oct., daily 9–6; Nov.–Mar., daily 9–4.*

Source of Law Temple (法源寺 *Fǎyuánsì*). This quiet temple is also a school for monks—the Chinese Buddhist Theoretical Institute houses and trains them here. Of course, the temple functions within the boundaries of current regime policy. You can observe both elderly practitioners chanting mantras in the main prayer halls, as well as robed students kicking soccer balls in a side courtyard. Before lunch the smells of a vegetarian stir-fry tease the nose. The dining hall has simple wooden tables set with cloth-wrapped bowls and chopsticks. Dating from the 7th century but last rebuilt in 1442, the temple holds a fine collection of Ming and Qing statues, including a sleeping Buddha and an unusual grouping of copper-cast Buddhas seated on a 1,000-petal lotus. ⊠ *7 Fayuan Si Qianjie, Xicheng District* ☎ *010/6353–4171* 💴 *Y5* ⊙ *Daily 8:30–4.*

Temple of the White Pagoda (白塔 *Báitǎ*). This 13th-century Tibetan stupa, the largest of its kind in China, dates from Kublai Khan's reign and owes its beauty to an unnamed Nepalese architect who built it to honor Shakyamuni Buddha. It stands bright and white against the Beijing skyline. Once hidden within the structure were Buddha statues, sacred texts, and other holy relics. Many of the statues are now on display in glass cases in the **Miaoying** temple, at the foot of the stupa. There's also a great English-language display on the temple's history and renovation. ⊠ *171 Fuchengmennei Dajie, Xicheng District* ☎ *010/6616–6099* 💴 *Y20* ⊙ *Tues.–Sun. 9–4.*

White Clouds Taoist Temple (白云观 *Báiyúnguàn*). This lively Taoist temple founded in the 8th century serves as a center for China's only indigenous religion. Monks wearing blue-cotton coats and black-satin hats roam the grounds in silence. Thirty of them now live at the monastery, which also houses the official All-China Taoist Association. Visitors bow and burn incense to their favorite deities, wander the back gardens in search of a master of *qigong* (a series of exercises that involve slow movements and meditative breathing techniques), and rub the bellies of the temple's three monkey statues for good fortune.

In the first courtyard, under the span of an arched bridge, hang two large brass bells. Ringing them with a well-tossed coin is said to bring wealth. In the main courtyards, the **Shrine Hall for Seven Perfect Beings** is lined with meditation cushions and low desks. Nearby is a museum of Taoist history (explanations in Chinese). In the western courtyard, the temple's

oldest structure is a shrine housing the **60-Year Protector.** Here the faithful locate the deity that corresponds to their birth year, bow to it, light incense, then scribble their names, or even a poem, on the wooden statue's red-cloth cloak as a reminder of their dedication. A trinket stall in the front courtyard sells pictures of each protector deity. Also in the west courtyard is a shrine to Taoist sage Wen Ceng, depicted in a 10-foot-tall bronze statue just outside the shrine's main entrance. Students flock here to rub Wen Ceng's belly for good luck on their college entrance exams. The area around the temple is packed with fortune-tellers. ⊠ *Lianhuachi Donglu, near Xibianmen Bridge, Xicheng District* ☎ *010/6344–3666* 🖃 *Y10* ⊗ *Daily 8:30–4.*

CHAOYANG DISTRICT 朝阳区

Sightseeing
★☆☆☆☆

Dining
★★★★☆

Lodging
★★★★☆

Shopping
★★★★☆

Nightlife
★★★★☆

Welcome to the new China. In fact, there's precious little of Beijing's ancient history found in Chaoyang District, where much of the old has been razed to make way for the blingy new. Impeccably dressed Chinese women shop the afternoons away at gleaming new malls, young tycoons and princelings park their Ferraris on the sidewalks, and everyone who's anyone congregates at the booming nightclubs filled with hip-hop music and VIP bottle service.

Sitting outside the Second Ring Road, which marks the boundary of the old walled imperial capital, Chaoyang represents the epitome of a rapidly modernizing China at its peak. Here's where you'll find the Central Business District, with the city's tallest towers and the architecturally impressive CCTV Building; Sanlitun, the longtime playground of expat residents, filled with swanky bars and restaurants that could just as well be in New York City or London; shopping centers filled with just about every major global brand, from Apple to Zegna; and almost all of Beijing's embassies, lending the area a distinctly international vibe.

For dining and nightlife, you can't beat Sanlitun, which was once upon a time a sleepy farming village. In the middle of it all is Sanlitun Beilu, wreathed in twinkling lights year-round. On one side is the luxurious open-air Village Sanlitun shopping center, on the other is a row of live music bars. There's also great shopping to be found around here.

EXPLORING

TOP ATTRACTIONS

798 Art District (798艺术区 *Qījiǔbâ yìshù qû*). The Art District, northeast of Beijing, is the site of several state-owned factories, including Factory 798, which originally produced electronics. Beginning in 2002, artists and cultural organizations began to move into the area, gradually developing the old buildings into galleries, art centers, artists' studios, design companies, restaurants, and bars. There are regularly scheduled art exhibits and events, some of the best can be found at the **Ullens Center for Contemporary Art** (⊕ *ucca.org.cn*). ✉ *Chaoyang District* ⊕ *www.798district.com/.*

Ancient Observatory (北京古观象台 *Bìijíng gǔguānxiàng tái*). This squat tower of primitive stargazing equipment peeks out next to the elevated highways of the Second Ring Road. It dates to the time of Genghis Khan, who believed that his fortunes could be read in the stars. Many of the bronze devices on display were gifts from Jesuit missionaries who arrived in Beijing and shortly thereafter ensconced themselves as the Ming court's resident stargazers. To China's imperial rulers, interpreting the heavens was key to holding onto power; a ruler knew when, say, an eclipse would occur, or he could predict the best time to plant crops. Celestial phenomena like eclipses and comets were believed to portend change; if left unheeded they might cost an emperor his legitimacy—or mandate of heaven. Records of celestial observations at or near this site go back more than 500 years, making this the longest documented astronomical viewing site in the world.

The main astronomical devices are arranged on the roof. Writhing bronze dragon sculptures adorn some of the astronomy pieces at Jianguo Tower, the main building that houses the observatory. Among the sculptures are an armillary sphere to pinpoint the position of heavenly bodies and a sextant to measure angular distances between stars, along with a celestial globe. Inside, the dusty exhibition rooms shelter ancient star maps with information dating back to the Tang Dynasty. A Ming Dynasty star map and ancient charts are also on display. Most of the ancient instruments were looted by the Allied Forces in 1900, only to be returned to China at the end of World War I. ✉ *2 Dongbiaobei Hutong, Jianguomenwai Dajie, Chaoyang District* ☎ *010/6524–2202* 💴 *Y10* 🕐 *Daily 9–4:30* Ⓜ *Jianguomen.*

BY THE LAKE

Bar Veloce. Secreted behind the walls of 1949–The Hidden City, Bar Veloce (originally from New York City) offers a fresh, minimalist ambience for enjoying a glass from the sommelier's carefully curated wine list, along with light bites such as chickpea bruschetta and delicate paninis. ✉ *Bldg. B, 1949–The Hidden City, Courtyard 4, Gongti Beilu, Chaoyang District* ☎ *010/6586–1006.*

Central Business District (CBD) (商业中心区 *Shāng yè zhōng xīn qū*). The fast-rising CBD encompasses the **China World Trade Center** (the recently completed third tower is the tallest building in Beijing) and a slew of new and impressive skyscrapers, some designed by internationally known architects. One example is the new CCTV Tower. The multimillion-dollar complex employs a continuous loop of horizontal and vertical sections, and its distinctive shape has earned it the moniker "big pants." Nearby is The Place, a shopping mall best known for its massive canopy-style LED screen that puts on impressive displays. ✉ *Chaoyang District.*

GETTING ORIENTED

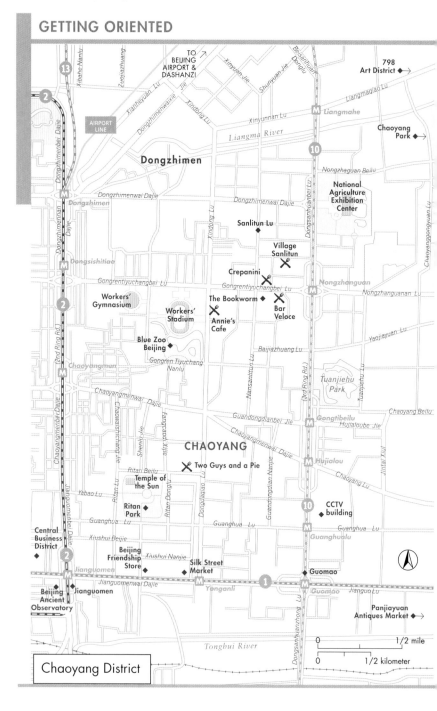

Chaoyang District

QUICK BITES

Annie's Café. Annie's Café serves up great pizza and Italian-American style specialties. ✉ *Chaoyang Park W. Gate, Chaoyang District* ☎ *010/6951–1931* ⊕ *en.annies.com.cn* ✉ *88 Jianguo Lu, west side of SOHO New Town.*

Crepanini. Crepes + Paninis = Crepanini, a great spot for sweet and savory snacks and it's open late. ✉ *Nali Patio, Sanlitun Lu, Chaoyang District.*

Two Guys And A Pie. This restaurant offers terrific savory pies. ✉ *Behind Sanlitun Houjie, west of the Sanlitun Police Station, Chaoyang District* ☎ *186/1105–3912.*

Village Sanlitun. If you're looking for Western food, the Village Sanlitun has many options, as does the surrounding area. ✉ *Sanlitun Lu, Chaoyang District.*

NEIGHBORHOOD TOP 5

1. Grab dinner in Sanlitun and check out one of the bars or nightclubs surrounding Workers' Stadium.

2. Check out what's really going on in Chinese art today in the **798 Art District.** After strolling through the galleries, browse the vast selection of art books at Timezone 8 and grab something to eat or a drink at its café.

3. Do some shopping at **Yashow Market,** where you can buy anything from knockoff jeans to a custom-tailored suit. Then take a half-hour walk north on **Sanlitun North Street** and pick a place to grab an espresso or some top-quality Western grub.

4. Enjoy a drink or meal, along with some great books, at **The Bookworm,** just off Sanlitun South Street. Readings and musical events take place throughout the week, usually in the evening.

5. Go for an early-morning stroll in **Chaoyang Park** and watch the traditional Chinese exercises.

GETTING HERE

The heart of Chaoyang District is accessible via Lines 1, 2, and 10 on the subway, but the district is huge and the sites are broadly distributed. Taking taxis between sites is usually the easiest way to get around. The 798 Art District is especially far away from central Beijing, and so a taxi is also the best bet (about Y30 from the center of town). Buses go everywhere, but they're slow.

MAKING THE MOST OF YOUR TIME

You can spend years lost in Chaoyang District and never get bored. There's plenty to do, but very few historical sights. Spend a morning shopping at **Silk Alley Market** or **Panjiayuan Antiques Market** (best on weekend mornings) and the afternoon cooling off at **Ritan Park** or **Chaoyang Park,** the latter a large and pleasant park with a lot of activities for kids. Next, head to one of the numerous bar streets for refreshments. If you like contemporary art, browse the galleries at **798 Art District.** There are a number of nice cafés here as well. **Vincent Café & Creperie** (☎ *010/8456–4823*) serves a variety of crepes and fondues. **Cafe Pause** has great coffee, a modest but good wine selection, and great atmosphere.

Ritan Park in the morning

Ritan Park (日坛公园 *Rìtán gōngyuán*). A cool oasis of water and trees just west of the Central Business District, Ritan Park (also known as "Temple of the Sun Park") is highly popular. Locals go to stretch their legs, but the embassy crowd is drawn in by the mojitos served at the Stone Boat. ⊠ *Ritan Lu, northeast of Jianguomen, Chaoyang District* ☎ *010/8561–4261* ✉ *Free* ⊘ *Daily 6 am–9 pm.*

Sanlitun (三里屯 *Sānlitún*). The famous Sanlitun Bar Street, several blocks east of the Workers' Stadium, is known for its nightlife offerings catering to foreigners, expats, and young Chinese. The hottest clubs are always changing, but Vics and Mix at the north gate of the Workers' Stadium are popular places, while the bars at the Opposite House hotel offer a swank reprieve. The Village Sanlitun, Beijing's hottest shopping complex, has changed the face of the formerly seedy area. The Japanese-designed open-air center includes a number of international shops as well as a movie theater and some of Beijing's best new restaurants and cafés, and has become *the* hangout for the city's in crowd, local and foreign alike. ⊠ *Chaoyang District.*

WORTH NOTING

Chaoyang Park (朝阳公园 *Cháoyáng gōngyuán*). The sprawling, modern Chaoyang Park lacks the imperial aura that marks other Beijing parks, but offers quite a bit in terms of recreation. About one-fourth of the park is water, and so boating of various kinds is available here, primarily pedal-powered paddleboats. There's a swimming pool with an artificial beach, tennis courts, beach volleyball grounds, a gymnasium, and a small amusement park. You can hire a slow-going electromobile for easy mobility around this sprawling park on your own, or hail a ride on a group trolley. There are many snack stands serving simple dishes, but if you're looking for something more substantive, walk around to the west gate of the park where you'll find a street lined with popular Western and Chinese eateries, or check out the Solana mall at the northwest corner of the park. ✉ *Nongzhanguan Rd. S, Chaoyang District* 🎫 *Y5* ⊙ *Mid-Mar.–mid-Nov., daily 6 am–9 pm; mid-Nov.–mid-Mar., daily 6 am–8 pm.*

Jianguomen (建国门 *Jiànguómén*). The embassy area has some good foreign restaurants, but is mostly quiet blocks of gated embassy compounds; in the center there's lovely Ritan Park with its winding paths, lotus-flower ponds, a climbing wall, and even a few upmarket restaurants. The area is close to the heart of Beijing's new Central Business District, aka CBD, home to some of the city's most impressive new architecture, including the new CCTV Tower, the Park Hyatt Hotel, and Tower III of the China World Trade Center, which at 81 stories is one of Beijing's tallest skyscrapers. ✉ *Chaoyang District.*

Workers' Stadium (工人体育场 *Gôngrén tǐyùchâng*). North of Ritan Park is the Workers' Stadium complex, where many of the biggest visiting acts perform. The famous Sanlitun Bar Street is several blocks east of Workers' Stadium and runs north–south; this is the area that's known for its nightlife catering to foreigners, expats, and young Chinese. ✉ *Gongti Rd., Chaoyang District* 🎫 *Varies according to event* ⊙ *Varies according to event* Ⓜ *Dongsishitiao.*

HAIDIAN DISTRICT 海淀区

Sightseeing
★★★☆☆

Dining
★☆☆☆☆

Lodging
★★☆☆☆

Shopping
★☆☆☆☆

Nightlife
★★☆☆☆

In the last decade or so, Haidian has become Beijing's educational and techno mecca. The major IT players are all located here (including offices of Microsoft, Siemens, NEC, and Sun). Here, in the Wudaokou and Zhongguancun neighborhoods, you'll find kids geeking out over the latest gadgets at electronics superstores, studying in one of the many cafés, or blowing off steam at some of the area's dance clubs.

The campuses of China's most elite educational institutions, Peking University and Tsinghua, are large by Chinese standards and provide a tranquil respite from the busy surrounding area, with wide lawns and Chinese gardens complete with scenic bridges and pagodas. A large number of foreign students attend Chinese universities, with South Koreans the most numerous, so restaurants and shops catering to their needs are easy to find, especially around Wudaokou station.

A GOOD TOUR

Haidian may be Beijing's technology and university district, but there's a lot of Old Beijing left here. Grab a taxi, or take the new Line 4, and head for the **Summer Palace.** Saunter around the lakes and ancient pavilions, and then head over to the East Gate. Nearby is the luxurious Aman Summer Palace resort, where you can enjoy a light meal or afternoon tea in the lobby lounge.

When you're done with sightseeing, hop in a cab and head to **Hailong Shopping Mall.** Go in and explore—the five-story shopping mall has every kind of computer or electronic device you could possibly want, often at deep discounts. ■TIP➔ Be careful when buying software, though, as most of it is pirated and illegal to bring back to the United States.

The Summer Palace

After you've shopped and you're ready to drop, head over to **Wudaokou Binguan** for a selection of wonderful "snacks" that usually add up to a great dinner, and don't miss the *zhapi*, or mugs of fresh-from-the-tap beer. Taxi it on home in the wee hours.

EXPLORING

TOP ATTRACTIONS

Beijing Botanical Garden (北京植物园*Běijīng zhíwù yuán*). Sitting at the feet of the Western Hills in Beijing's northwestern suburbs, the Beijing Botanical Garden, opened in 1955, hosts China's largest plant collection: 6,000 different plant species from all over northern China, including 2,000 types of trees and bushes, more than 1,600 species of tropical and subtropical plants, 1,900 kinds of fruit trees, and 500 flower species. With its state-of-the-art greenhouse and a variety of different gardens, this is a pleasant place to explore, especially in spring, when the peach trees burst with pretty blooms. An added feature is the wonderful Temple of the Reclining Buddha, which has an enormous statue that, it's said, took 7,000 slaves to build. ⊠ *Xiangshan Wofosi, Haidian District* ☎ *010/6259–1283* 🖾 *Outdoor garden Y5* ☉ *Daily 7–5 (outdoor garden).*

GETTING ORIENTED

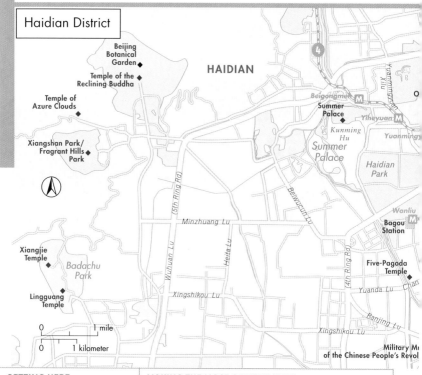

Haidian District

Beijing Botanical Garden

Temple of the Reclining Buddha

Temple of Azure Clouds

HAIDIAN

Xiangshan Park/ Fragrant Hills Park

Beigongmen

Summer Palace

Yiheyuan

Kunming Hu

Yuanmingy

Summer Palace

Haidian Park

Xiangjie Temple

Badachu Park

Wanliu

Bagou Station

Minzhuang Lu

Lingguang Temple

Xingshikou Lu

Five-Pagoda Temple

Yuanda Lu · Chan

0   1 mile

0   1 kilometer

Banjing Lu

Xingshikou Lu

Military M
of the Chinese People's Revol

GETTING HERE

Subway Line 13 stops at Wudaokou, the heart of Haidian. Line 4 runs far into the northwest of the city with stops at the Summer Palace and the Old Summer Palace, though Fragrant Hills Park and the Beijing Botanical Garden are farther out still and best reached by taxi. To save money, take Line 10 to Baguo station and catch a cab from there.

MAKING THE MOST OF YOUR TIME

Because the **Summer Palace** is so large, with its lovely lakes and ancient pavilions, it makes for an entire morning of great exploring. The **Old Summer Palace** is close by, so visiting the two sites together is ideal if you've got the energy.

Fragrant Hills Park makes for a charming outing, but keep in mind that it takes at least an hour and a half to get there from the city center. The **Botanical Garden**, with some 2,000 types of orchids, bonsai, and peach and pear blossoms, along with the **Temple of the Reclining Buddha**, is also fun, especially for green thumbs. Plan to spend most of a day if you go to either of these sites.

Hailong Shopping Mall. If you want to shop for electronics, spend an afternoon wandering the five floors of the Hailong Shopping Mall. ⊠ *1 Zhongguancun Dajie.*

Evenings in Wudaokou are a pleasure. After dinner, take advantage of the hopping beer gardens. A mug of Tsingtao is a great way to start a summer night off right.

2

NEIGHBORHOOD TOP 5

1. Spend a low-key day at the vast **Summer Palace** and **Old Summer Palace**. Don't miss getting out onto the water at either the Kunming Lake or the Fuhai Lake.

2. Eat and chat all evening at **Wudaokou Binguan** beer garden.

3. Browse the biggest selection of electronics and computer goods (both legitimate and pirated) this side of the Pacific at **Hailong Shopping Mall**.

4. Listen to China's biggest bell toll at the **Big Bell Temple**. Here you'll find bells, both large and small, from the Ming, Song, and Yuan dynasties.

5. Get out of town with a day trip to **Fragrant Hills Park** or **Beijing Botanical Garden**.

QUICK BITES

There are plenty of restaurants on campus and around Zhongguancun, but the coolest places to eat in Haidian are in Wudaokou.

Bridge Café. The Bridge Café, also on Chengfu Lu one block west of the subway station, serves up great sandwiches, salads, and desserts popular with the student crowd. ⊠ *Haidian District* ☎ *010/8286–7026.*

Isshin. Another hopping eatery is Isshin, a Japanese restaurant popular with students from the surrounding campuses. ⊠ *35 Chengfu Lu, Haidian District* ☎ *010/8261–0136.*

Tan Tan Da Lu. Try excellent and innovative Korean barbecue at Tan Tan Da Lu. ⊠ *35 Chengfu Lu, Haidian District* ☎ *010/6256–0471* Ⓜ *Wudaokou.*

Big Bell Temple (大钟寺 *Dàzhōngsì*). This 18th-century temple shields China's biggest bell and more than 400 smaller bells and gongs from the Ming, Song, and Yuan dynasties. The Buddhist temple—originally used for rain prayers—has been restored after major damage inflicted during the Cultural Revolution. Before it opened as a museum in 1985, the buildings were used as Beijing No. 2 Food Factory. The bells here range from a giant 23 feet high to hand-size chimes, many of them corroded to a pale green by time.

The giant, two-story bell, inscribed with the texts of more than 100 Buddhist scriptures (230,000 Chinese characters), is also said to be China's loudest. Believed to have been cast during Emperor Yongle's reign, the sound of this 46-ton relic can carry more than 15 km (10 miles) when struck forcibly. The bell rings 108 times on special occasions like Spring Festival, one strike for each of the 108 personal worries defined in Buddhism. People used to throw coins into a hole in the top of the bell for luck. The money was swept up by the monks and used to buy food. Enough money was collected in a month to buy provisions that would last for a year. ▓TIP→ You can ride the subway to the temple: transfer from Dongzhimen on Line 2 to the aboveground Line 13 and go one stop north to Dazhong Si station. ⊠ *1A Beisanhuanxi Lu, Haidian District* ☎ *010/8213–2630* ☞ *Y20* ☉ *Tues.–Sun. 9–4:30* Ⓜ *Dazhong Si.*

Fodor'sChoice
★
Old Summer Palace (圆明园 *Yuánmíngyuán*). About the size of New York's Central Park, this ruin was once a grand collection of palaces—the emperor's summer retreat from the 15th century to 1860, when it was looted and blown up by British and French soldiers. More than 90% of the original structures were Chinese-style wooden buildings, but only the European-style stone architecture (designed after Versailles by Jesuits and added during the Qing Dynasty) survived the fires. Many of the priceless relics that were looted are still on display in European museums, and China's efforts to recover them have been mostly unsuccessful. Beijing has chosen to preserve the vast ruin as a "monument to China's national humiliation," though the patriotic slogans that were once scrawled on the rubble have now been cleaned off.

The palace is made up of three idyllic parks: Yuanmingyuan (Garden of Perfection and Light) in the west, Wanchunyuan (Garden of 10,000 Springs) in the south, and Changchunyuan (Garden of Everlasting Spring) where the ruins are like a surreal graveyard to European architecture. Here you'll find ornately carved columns, squat lion statues, and crumbling stone blocks that lie like fallen dominoes. An engraved concrete wall maze, known as Huanghuazhen (Yellow Flower), twists and turns around a European-style pavilion. Recently restored and located just to the left of the west gate of Changchunyuan, it was once the site of lantern parties during mid-autumn festivals. Palace maids would race each other to the pavilion carrying lotus lanterns. The park costs an extra Y15 to enter, but it's well worth it. The park and ruins take on a ghostly beauty if you come after a fresh snowfall. There's also skating on the lake when it's frozen over. ▓TIP→ It's a long trek to the European ruins from the main gate. Electric carts buzz around the park; hop on one heading to Changchunyuan if you feel tired. Tickets are Y5.

The ruins of the Old Summer Palace

If you want to save money, take subway Line 13 to Wudaokou and then catch a cab to Yuanmingyuan. The recently opened Line 4 stops at the Old Summer Palace. ⊠ *28 Qinghua Xilu, northeast of the Summer Palace, Haidian District* ☎ *010/6262–8501* 🖃 *Park Y10; extra Y15 fee for sites* ⊘ *Park, daily 7–7; exhibits, daily 8:30–5.*

Fodor'sChoice
★
Summer Palace (颐和园 *Yíhéyuán*). Emperor Qianlong commissioned this giant royal retreat for his mother's 60th birthday in 1750. Anglo–French forces plundered, then burned, many of the palaces in 1860, and funds were diverted from China's naval budget for the renovations. Empress Dowager Cixi retired here in 1889. Nine years later it was here that she imprisoned her nephew, Emperor Guangxu, after his reform movement failed. In 1903, she moved the seat of government from the Forbidden City to the Summer Palace, from where she controlled China until her death in 1908.

Nowadays the place is undoubtedly romantic. Pagodas and temples perch on hillsides; rowboats dip under arched stone bridges; and willow branches brush the water. The greenery provides a welcome relief from the loud, bustling city. It also teaches a fabulous history lesson. You can see firsthand the results of corruption: the opulence here was bought with siphoned money as China crumbled, while suffering repeated humiliations at the hands of colonialist powers. The entire gardens were for Empress Dowager's exclusive use. UNESCO placed the Summer Palace on its World Heritage list in 1998.

The **Hall of Benevolent Longevity** is where Cixi held court and received foreign dignitaries. It's said that the first electric lights in China shone here. Just behind the hall and next to the lake is the **Hall of Jade Ripples,**

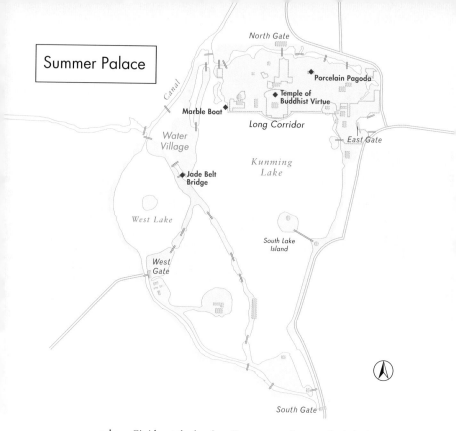

where Cixi kept the hapless Guangxu under guard while she ran China in his name. Strung with pagodas and temples, including the impressive Tower of the Fragrance of Buddha, Glazed Tile Pagoda, and the Hall that Dispels Clouds, **Longevity Hill** is the place where you can escape the hordes of visitors—take your time exploring the lovely northern side of the hill.

Most of this 700-acre park is underwater. **Kunming Lake** makes up around three-fourths of the complex, and is largely man-made. The excavated dirt was used to build Longevity Hill. This giant body of water extends southward for 3 km (2 miles); it's ringed by tree-lined dikes, arched stone bridges, and numerous gazebos. In winter, you can skate on the ice. The less-traveled southern shore near Humpbacked Bridge is an ideal picnic spot.

At the west end of the lake you'll find the **Marble Boat,** which doesn't actually float and was built by Dowager Empress Cixi with money meant for the navy. The **Long Corridor** is a wooden walkway that skirts the northern shoreline of Kunming Lake for about half a mile until it reaches the marble boat. The ceiling and wooden rafters of the Long Corridor are richly painted with thousands of scenes from legends and nature—be on the lookout for Sun Wukong (the Monkey King). Cixi's home, in the Hall of Joyful Longevity, is near the beginning of the Long

2

Corridor. The residence is furnished and decorated as Cixi left it. Her private theater, called the **Grand Theater Building,** just east of the hall, was constructed for her 60th birthday and cost 700,000 taels of silver.

Subway Line 4 stops at the Summer Palace. Get off at Beigongmen and take exit C for the easiest access to the north gate of the park. Otherwise, you'll have to take a taxi. It's best to come early in the morning to get a head start before the busloads of visitors arrive. You'll need the better part of a day to explore the grounds. Automatic audio guides can be rented for Y40 at stalls near the ticket booth. ⊠ *Yiheyuan Lu and Kunminghu Lu, 12 km (7½ miles) northwest of downtown Beijing, Haidian District* ☎ *010/6288–1144* ⊕ *www.summerpalace-china.com* ✉ *Y60 summer all-inclusive, Y50 winter* ☉ *Apr.–Oct., daily 8:30–5; Nov.–Mar., daily 9–4* Ⓜ *Beigongmen.*

Xiangshan Park (香山公园 *Xiāngshān gōngyuán*). This hillside park, also known as Fragrant Hills Park, is northwest of Beijing and was once an imperial retreat. From the eastern gate you can hike to the summit on a trail dotted with small temples. If you're short on time, ride a cable car to the top. Note that the park becomes extremely crowded on pleasant fall weekends, when Beijingers turn out en masse to view the changing colors of the autumn leaves. ⊠ *Haidian District* ☎ *010/6259–1155* ✉ *Y10, one-way cable car Y60* ☉ *Daily 6–6.*

WORTH NOTING

Five-Pagoda Temple (五塔寺 *Wǔ tǎ sì*). Hidden among trees just behind the zoo and set amid carved stones, the temple's five pagodas reveal obvious Indian influences. It was built during the Yongle years of the Ming Dynasty (1403–24), in honor of an Indian Buddhist who came to China and presented a temple blueprint to the emperor. Elaborate carvings of curvaceous figures, floral patterns, birds, and hundreds of Buddhas decorate the pagodas. Also on the grounds is the **Beijing Art Museum of Stone Carvings,** with its collection of some 1,000 stelae and stone figures. ⊠ *24 Wuta Si, Baishiqiao Lu, Haidian District* ☎ *010/6217–3543* ✉ *Y20* ☉ *Tues.–Sun. 9–4.*

FAMILY **Military Museum of the Chinese People's Revolutions** (中国人民革命军事博物馆 *Zhōngguó rénmín gémìng jūnshì bówùguǎn*). Stuffed with everything from AK-47s to captured tanks to missile launchers, this is a must-see for military buffs. Five thousand years of Chinese military history are on display, and kids especially love every minute of it. This museum is easily accessible by taking a 10-minute subway ride west from Tiananmen Square. Admission is free; just show your passport for a ticket. ⊠ *9 Fuxing Rd., Haidian District* ☎ *010/6686–6244* ⊕ *eng.jb.mil.cn* ✉ *Free* ☉ *Daily 8:30–5.*

Temple of Azure Clouds (碧云寺 *Bìyún sì*). Once the home of a Yuan Dynasty official, the site was converted into a Buddhist temple in 1366 and enlarged during the 16th and 17th centuries by imperial eunuchs who hoped to be buried here. The temple's five main courtyards ascend a slope in **Fragrant Hills Park.** Although severely damaged during the Cultural Revolution, the complex has been beautifully restored.

The main attraction is the Indian-influenced **Vajra Throne Pagoda.** Lining its walls and five pagodas are gracefully carved stone-relief

Buddhas and bodhisattvas. The pagoda once housed the remains of Nationalist China's founding father, Dr. Sun Yat-sen, who lay in state here between March and May 1925, while his mausoleum was being constructed in Nanjing. A hall in one of the temple's western courtyards houses about 500 life-size wood and gilt arhats (Buddhists who have reached enlightenment)—each displayed in a glass case. ⊠ *Xiangshan Park, Haidian District* ☏ *010/6259–1155* 🎟 *Park Y10, temple Y10* 🕙 *Daily 8–4:30.*

Temple of Longevity (万寿寺 *Wànshòu sì*). A Ming empress built this temple to honor her son in 1578. Qing emperor Qianlong later restored it as a birthday present to his mother. From then until the fall of the Qing, it served as a rest stop for imperial processions traveling by boat to the Summer Palace and Western Hills. The site also served as a Japanese military command center during occupation. Today the temple is managed by the Beijing Art Museum and houses a small but exquisite collection of Buddha images. The statues in the main halls include dusty Ming-period Buddhas and one of Shakyamuni sitting on a 1,000-petal, 1,000-Buddha bronze throne. ⊠ *Suzhou Jie, Xisanhuan Lu, on the north side of Zizhu Bridge, Haidian District* ☏ *010/6845–6995* 🎟 *Y20* 🕙 *Tues.–Sun. 9–4.*

Temple of the Reclining Buddha (卧佛寺 *Wòfó sì*). Although the temple was damaged during the Cultural Revolution and poorly renovated afterward, the Sleeping Buddha remains. Built in 627–629, during the Tang Dynasty, the temple was named after the reclining Buddha that was brought in during the Yuan Dynasty (1271–1368). An English-language description explains that the casting of the beautiful bronze, in 1321, enslaved 7,000 people. The temple is inside the **Beijing Botanical Garden**; stroll north from the entrance through the neatly manicured grounds. ⊠ *Xiangshan Lu, 2 km (1 mile) northeast of Xiangshan Park, Haidian District* ☏ *010/6259–1283* 🎟 *Temple Y5, gardens Y10* 🕙 *Daily 8:30–4:30.*

WHERE TO EAT

Updated by
Sky Canaves

Since imperial times, China's capital has drawn citizens from all corners of this vast nation, and along with them have come the myriad cuisines of far-flung regions. China's economic boom has only accelerated the culinary diversity of Beijing, with just about every kind of food well represented in the capital. You can enjoy a nationwide tour of China's many regional tastes without ever leaving the city. Highlights include unusual specialties from Yunnan, earthy Hakka cooking from southern China, Tibetan yak and *tsampa* (barley flour), kebabs and flatbreads from Xinjiang, numbingly spicy Sichuan cuisine, and chewy noodles from Shaanxi.

The capital also offers an array of international cuisines, including Italian, French, German, Thai, Japanese, and Korean among others.

You can spend as little as $5 per person for a decent meal or $100 and up on a lavish banquet. The variety of venues is also part of the fun, ranging from five-star hotel dining rooms to holes-in-the-wall to refurbished courtyard houses. Reservations are always a good idea so book as far ahead as you can, and reconfirm as soon as you arrive.

Beijingers tend to eat dinner around 6 pm, though most restaurants continue to serve food until 10 pm or later, and restaurants that stay open until the wee morning hours aren't hard to find. Tipping can be tricky. Though it isn't required, some of the larger, fancier restaurants will add a 15% service charge to the bill, as do hotel restaurants. Be aware before you go out that small and medium venues only take cash payments; more-established restaurants usually accept credit cards.

Great local beers and some international brands are available everywhere in Beijing, and many Chinese restaurants now have extensive wine menus.

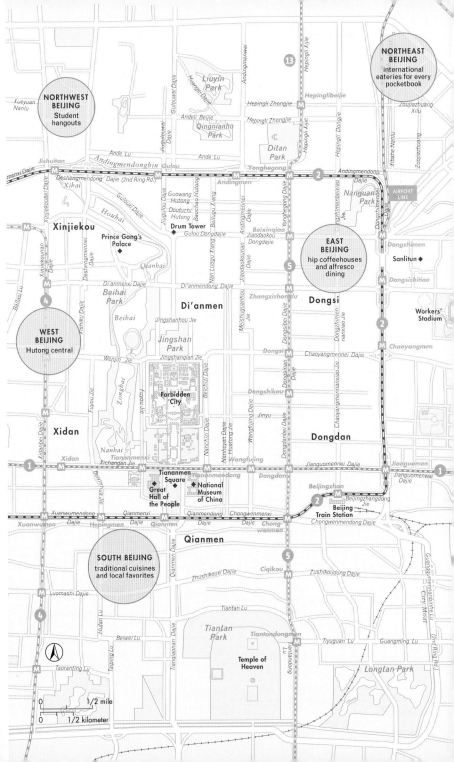

BEST BETS FOR BEIJING DINING

With thousands of restaurants to choose from, how will you decide where to eat? Fodor's writers and editors have selected their favorite restaurants by price, cuisine, and experience in the Best Bets lists here. In the first column, Fodor's Choice properties represent the "best of the best" in every price category. You can also search by neighborhood for excellent eats—just peruse our reviews on the following pages.

Fodor's Choice ★

Aria, p. 114
Capital M, p. 93
Din Tai Fung, p. 116
Huang Ting, p. 98
Li Qun Roast Duck Restaurant, p. 105
Made in China, p. 107
Maison Boulud, p. 107
Mei Fu, p. 111
Peking Duck, Private Kitchen, p. 121
The Source, p. 109
Temple Restaurant Beijing, p. 110
Transit, p. 123
Yotsuba, p. 123

Best By Price

$

Baoyuan Dumpling, p. 114
Bellagio, p. 115
Crescent Moon, p. 93
In and Out, p. 117
Ju'er Renjia, p. 105

Lei Garden, p. 105
Madam Zhu's Kitchen, p. 118
Paomo Guan, p. 107
Peking Duck, Private Kitchen, p. 121
Qin Tangfu, p. 108
Still Thoughts, p. 109
Xiheyaju, p. 123
Yue Bin, p. 110
Yuxiang Renjia, p. 123

$$

Alameda, p. 113
Din Tai Fung, p. 116
Ssam, p. 122

$$$

Bei, p. 114
Huang Ting, p. 98
Mosto, p. 120

$$$$

Aria, p. 114
Capital M, p. 93
Fangshan, p. 110
Maison Boulud, p. 107

Temple Restaurant Beijing, p. 110

Best By Experience

BUSINESS DINING

Aria, p. 114
Barolo, p. 114
Maison Boulud, p. 107

GREAT VIEW

Assaggi, p. 114
Capital M, p. 93

HUTONG EATERIES

Café Sambal, p. 93
Dali Courtyard, p. 97
Dezhe Xiaoguan, p. 97
Guo Yao Xiao Ju, p. 98
Huang Ting, p. 98
Li Qun Roast Duck Restaurant, p. 105
Mei Fu, p. 111
Saffron, p. 109
The Source, p. 109
Susu, p. 110
Yue Bin, p. 110

Best By Cuisine

GUIZHOU

Jia No. 21, p. 117

HUNAN

Karaiya Spice House, p. 118

BEIJING

Duck de Chine, p. 116
Shaguo Ju, p. 112

SHANGHAINESE AND JIANGZHE

Kong Yi Ji, p. 111

SICHUAN

The Source, p. 109
Transit, p. 123

TAIWANESE

Bellagio, p. 115
Din Tai Fung, p. 116
Shin Yeh, p. 122

YUNNAN

Dali Courtyard, p. 97

NORTHERN CHINESE

Baoyuan Dumpling, p. 114
Ding Ding Xiang, p. 124
Jinyang Fanzhuang, p. 111
Old Beijing Noodle King, p. 107
Paomo Guan, p. 107
Qin Tangfu, p. 108

RESTAURANT REVIEWS

Listed alphabetically within neighborhoods

Use the coordinate (✛ A1) at the end of each listing to locate a site on the corresponding map.

DONGCHENG DISTRICT 东城区

Dongcheng runs from the eastern flank of the Forbidden City to the Second Ring Road. There are plenty of good restaurants here, along with an impressive wealth of historical sights. Try one of Beijing's growing number of traditional courtyard eateries, where you can dine alfresco in the warmer months. Or walk down Nan Luogu Xiang, an old alleyway, where you pick from more than a dozen Western and Chinese restaurants, coffeehouses, snack vendors, and bars.

$ ╳ **Café de la Poste** (云游驿 *Yúnyóu yì*). In almost every French village, FRENCH town, or city there's a Café de la Poste, where people go for a cup of coffee, a beer, or a simple family meal. This haunt lives up to its name: It's a steak-lover's paradise, with such favorites as finely sliced marinated beefsteak served with lemon-herb vinaigrette and steak tartare. If the next table orders banana flambé, we promise the warm scent of its rum will soon have you smitten enough to order it yourself. $ *Average main: Y100* ✉ *58 Yonghegong Dajie, Dongcheng District* ☎ *010/6402–7047* ⊕ *www.cafedelaposte.net* ▭ *No credit cards* Ⓜ *Yonghegong* ✛ *E2.*

$ ╳ **Café Sambal.** Tucked away in a cozy traditional courtyard house, MALAYSIAN this mainstay of Beijing's international dining scene offers some of the city's best Southeast Asian flavors. This spot lives up to the promise of its name, which refers to the chili sauce used in many of the dishes served. Best bets include fiery beef rendang, butter prawns, and the four-sided beans in cashew nut sauce. A recent renovation has enhanced the spaciousness of the formerly snug surroundings, while retaining the signature antique furnishings and chilled-out vibe that have long made this a great place to relax over a Malaysian meal. $ *Average main: Y100* ✉ *43 Doufuchi Hutong, Jiugulou Dajie, Dongcheng District* ☎ *10/6400–4875* ⊕ *www.cafesambal.com* ✛ *D2.*

$$$$ ╳ **Capital M.** This is one of the few restaurants in the capital with both ECLECTIC stunning views and food worthy of the divine setting in front of Tianan-
Fodor'sChoice men Square. Australian-influenced classics with a Mediterranean twist
★ are the order of the day here, served amid a vibrantly modern, muraled interior. Try the crispy suckling pig or roasted leg of lamb, and save room for the famed pavlova dessert: a heavenly cloud of meringue and whipped cream sprinkled with fresh fruit. On weekends, hearty brunches and afternoon high tea are served. $ *Average main: Y268* ✉ *2 Qianmen Pedestrian St., Dongcheng District* ☎ *010/6702–2727* ⊕ *www.m-restaurantgroup.com* ✍ *Reservations essential* ✛ *D5.*

$ ╳ **Crescent Moon** (弯弯的月亮 *Wānwānde yuèliàng*). Unlike many of the ASIAN bigger Xinjiang restaurants in town, there's no song and dance performance at this Uygur family-run spot, and none needed, as the solid cooking stands on its own merits. The heaping platters of grilled lamb skewers, *da pan ji* (chicken, potato, and green pepper stew), homemade yogurt,

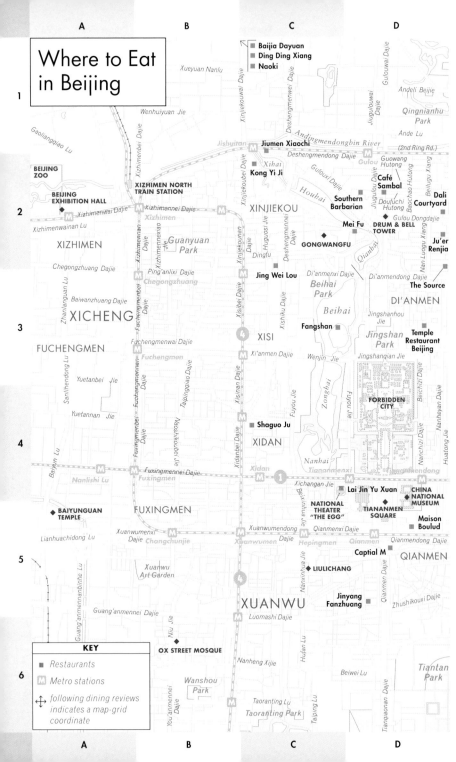

Where to Eat in Beijing

KEY
- ■ Restaurants
- Ⓜ Metro stations
- ✛ following dining reviews indicates a map-grid coordinate

■ Baijia Dayuan
■ Ding Ding Xiang
■ Naoki

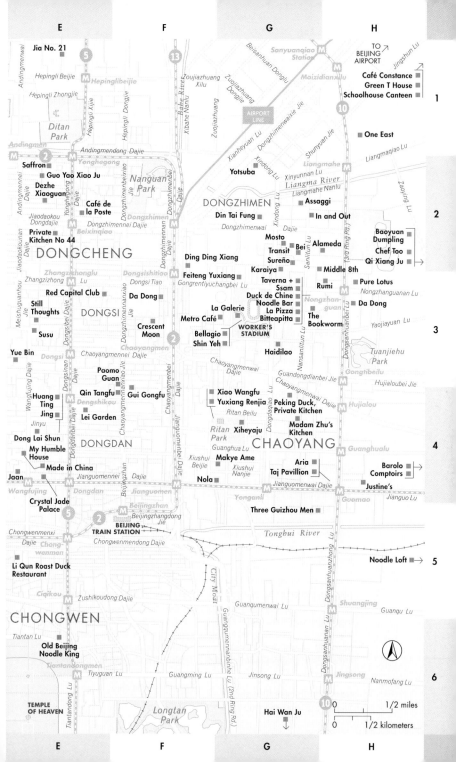

CHINESE CUISINE

We use the following terms in our restaurant reviews.

Beijing: As the seat of government for several dynasties, Beijing has produced cuisine that melds the culinary traditions of many cultures. Specialties include Peking duck, *ma doufu* (mashed fermented soybeans), zhajiang noodles, flash-boiled tripe, and a wide variety of snack foods.

Cantonese: A diverse cuisine that roasts and fries, braises and steams. Spices are used in moderation. Dishes include steamed fish, sweet-and-sour pork, roasted goose, and dim sum.

Chinese: Catchall term used for restaurants that serve cuisine from multiple regions of China.

Chiu chow: Known for its vegetarian and seafood dishes, which are mostly poached, steamed, or braised. Specialties include *popiah* (non-fried spring rolls) and fish-ball noodle soup.

Guizhou: The two most important cooking condiments that are used to prepare Guizhou's fiery hot cuisine are *zao lajiao* (pounded dried peppers brined in salt) and fermented tomatoes. The latter are used to make sour fish soup, the region's hallmark dish.

Hunan: Flavors are spicy, with chili peppers, ginger, garlic, and dried salted black beans and preserved vegetables. Signature dishes are Mao's braised pork, steamed fish head with coarse chopped salted chilies, and cured pork with smoked bean curd.

Northern Chinese (Dongbei): Staples are lamb and mutton, preserved vegetables, noodles, steamed breads, pancakes, stuffed buns, and dumplings.

Shanghainese and Jiangzhe: Cuisine characterized by rich, slightly sweet flavors produced by braising and stewing, and the use of rice wine in cooking. Signature dishes are steamed hairy crabs and "drunken chicken."

Sichuan (central province): Famed for bold flavors and spiciness from chilies and numbing Sichuan peppercorns. Dishes include kung pao chicken, mapo bean curd, "dandan" spicy noodles, twice-cooked pork, and tea-smoked duck.

Taiwanese: Diverse cuisine centers on seafood. Specialties include "three cups chicken" with a sauce made of soya, rice wine, and sugar; oyster omelets; cuttlefish soup; and dried tofu.

Tan Family Cuisine: Tan family cuisine originated in the home of Tan Zongjun (1846–88), a native of Guangdong, who secured a high position in the Qing inner court in Beijing. He added other regional influences into his cooking, which resulted in this new cuisine.

Tibetan: Cuisine reliant on foodstuffs grown at high altitudes including barley flour, yak meat, milk, butter, and cheese.

Yunnan (southern province): This region's cuisine is noted for its use of vegetables, fresh herbs, and mushrooms in its spicy preparations. Dishes include rice noodle soup with chicken, pork, and fish; steamed chicken with ginseng and herbs; and cured Yunnan ham.

and freshly baked flatbreads are all terrific, as are the light and dark Xinjiang beers available here. The traditional green-and-white Islamic decor, Uygur CDs playing on the stereo, and clouds of hookah smoke lend an authentic Central Asian vibe to the dining experience. $ *Average main: Y60* ⊠ *16 Dongsi Liutiao, Dongcheng District* ☎ *010/6400–5281* ▭ *No credit cards* ✚ *F3.*

$ ✕ **Crystal Jade Palace** (翡翠皇宫酒家
CANTONESE *Fěicuì huánggōng jiǔjiā*). Don't let the dark granite floors and crystal chandeliers intimidate you—the food at this Cantonese favorite is familiar, and the service is sincere. Weekdays see wheeler-dealers closing deals over abalone and sea cucumber, while the weekends bustle with families from Singapore and Hong Kong lingering over dim sum and many pots of excellent teas. Plenty of pricey seafood dishes are on the menu, but you can opt for the less expensive stir-fry dishes and dim sum. $ *Average main: Y100* ⊠ *Oriental Plaza, 1 Dongchang'an Jie, BB82, Dongcheng District* ☎ *010/8515–0238* ⊕ *www.crystaljade.com* ✚ *E4.*

$$ ✕ **Dali Courtyard** (大理 *Dàlǐ*). Yunnan's tranquility and bohemian spirit
YUNNAN are captured in this enchanting traditional courtyard house, just a short walk from the Drum and Bell towers. On breezy summer nights the best seats are in the central courtyard with its overflowing greenery; these are popular so reservations are essential. The restaurant offers only set menus for the table, starting at Y128 per person. Offerings change on a daily basis depending on what's fresh, but are sure to include a fair measure of heat as well as meat. $ *Average main: Y128* ⊠ *67 Xiaojingchang Hutong, Gulou Dongdajie, Dongcheng District* ☎ *010/8404–1430* ▭ *No credit cards* ✚ *D2.*

$ ✕ **Dezhe Xiaoguan** (得着小馆 *Dézhé xiǎo guǎn*). This simple, rustic,
SICHUAN and adorable hutong restaurant is appropriately named *Dezhe* or "you got it"—a local phrase which means the best of something. Dezhe serves up a memorable poached chicken dish drenched in aromatic young and green Sichuan peppercorns, which permeate the entire dish. Other standard Sichuan fare includes kung pao chicken, classic twice-cooked pork, and mapo bean curd. $ *Average main: Y50* ⊠ *1 Beijixiang Hutong, Jiaodaokou Nandajie, Dongcheng District* ☎ *010/6407–8615* ✚ *E2.*

$ ✕ **Dong Lai Shun** (东来顺饭 *Dōngláishùn*). Founded in 1903, this clas-
CHINESE sic Beijing Hui (Chinese Muslim) restaurant now has branches all over the city. Their specialty is a mutton dish famous for three attributes: paper-thin slices, high-quality meat, and an excellent dipping sauce. The hotpot dishes are amazingly flavorful: the best part is near the end, when the broth reaches a tongue-tingling climax. If you like, drop some cilantro into the bowl. *Zhima shaobing* (small, baked sesame

ON THE MENU

Peking duck is the capital's best-known dish, but there's much more to the city's cuisine than just the famous fowl. Beijing-style eateries offer many little-known but excellent specialties, such as *dalian huoshao* (meat- and vegetable-filled dumplings) and *zhajiangmian* (thick noodles with meat sauce). If you're adventurous, sample a bowl of intestines brewed in an aromatic broth mixed with bean curd, baked bread, and chopped cilantro.

3

Kebabs are a favorite street food all over China.

bread) is the perfect accompaniment. $ *Average main: Y80* ✉ *198 Wangfujing Dajie, Dongcheng District* ☎ *010/6513–9661* Ⓜ *Wangfujing* ⊕ *E4.*

$$ ✕ **Guo Yao Xiao Ju** (国肴小居 *Guó yáo xiǎo jū*). Tucked inside a small

CHINESE hutong, the food served in this award-winning restaurant, which dates back to the Qing Dynasty, is phenomenal. The owner's brother-in-law is a veteran of the Beijing Hotel and the fourth generation trained in Tan cooking. Chef Guo has also prepared state banquets for U.S. presidents Nixon and Clinton, and for Chinese leaders such as Deng Xiaoping. Go for the Tan cuisine set menu for a thorough experience of China's haute cuisine. An à la carte menu is also available, featuring enticing specialties such as homemade wine-flavored sausages, delightful duck and chive rolls, king-size breaded shrimp, and comforting spaetzle in rich tomatoey soup. $ *Average main: Y150* ✉ *58 Jiaodaokou Bei Santiao, Andingmennei, Dongcheng District* ☎ *010/6403–1940* ⊕ *E2.*

$$$ ✕ **Huang Ting** (凰庭 *Huángtíng*). Beijing's traditional courtyard houses,

CANTONESE facing extinction as entire neighborhoods are demolished to make way

Fodor's Choice for high-rises, provide an exquisite setting here. The walls are con-

★ structed from original hutong bricks taken from centuries-old courtyard houses that have been destroyed. This is arguably one of Beijing's best Cantonese restaurants, serving southern favorites such as braised shark fin with crabmeat and seared abalone with seafood, as well as a classic Peking duck. The dim sum is delicate and refined, and the deep-fried taro spring rolls and steamed pork buns are not to be missed. $ *Average main: Y200* ✉ *The Peninsula, 8 Jinyu Hutong, Wangfujing, Dongcheng District* ☎ *010/6512–8899* Ⓜ *Dongdan* ⊕ *E4.*

Continued on page 105

Edmonton Public Library Express Check STR 2

Customer ID: **********5356

Title: The rough guide to first-time Asia
ID: 31221093503527
Due: 10/9/2014,23:59

Title: The rough guide to Shanghai
ID: 31221110762437
Due: 10/9/2014,23:59

Title: Fodor's Beijing
ID: 31221110222754
Due: 10/9/2014,23:59

Total items: 3
9/18/2014 5:16 PM

www.epl.ca

A CULINARY TOUR OF CHINA

For centuries the collective culinary fragrances of China have drifted far beyond its borders and tantalized the entire world. Now with China's arms open to the world, a vast variety of Chinese flavors—from the North, South, East, and West—are more accessible than ever.

Four corners of the Middle Kingdom

In dynasties gone by, a visitor to China might have to undertake a journey of a thousand li just to feel the burn of an authentic Sichuanese hotpot, and another to savor the crispy skin and juicy flesh of a genuine Beijing roast duck. Luckily for us, the vast majority of regional Chinese cuisines have made successful internal migrations. As a result, Sichuanese cuisine can be found in Guangzhou, Cantonese dim sum in Urumuqi, and the cumin-spiced lamb-on-a-stick, for which the Uigher people of Xinjiang are famous, is now grilled all over China.

Before you begin your journey, remember, a true scholar of Middle Kingdom cuisine should first eliminate the very term "Chinese food" from their vocabulary. It hardly encompasses the variety of provincial cuisines and regional dishes that China has to offer, from succulent Shanghainese dumplings to fiery Sichuanese hotpots.

To guide you on your gastronomic journey, we've divided the country's gourmet map along the points of the compass—North, South, East, and West. Bon voyage and bon appétit!

Following the revolution, it was hard to find authentic Chinese cuisine.

NORTH

THE BASICS

Cuisine from China's Northeast is called dongbei cai, and it's more wheat than rice based. Vegetables like kale, cabbage, and potatoes are combined with robust, thick soy sauces, garlic (often raw), and scallions.

Even though many Han Chinese from southern climates find mutton too gamey, up north it's a regular staple. In many northern cities, you can't walk more than a block without coming across a small sidewalk grill with yang rou chua'r, or lamb-on-a-stick.

NOT TO BE MISSED

The most famous of all the northern dishes is Peking duck, and if you've ever had it well prepared, you'll know why Beijingers are proud of the dish named for their city.

The fowl is cleaned, stuffed with burning millet stalks and other aromatic combustibles, and then slow-cooked in an oven heated by a fire made of fragrant wood. Properly cooked, Peking duck should have crispy skin, juicy meat, and none of the grease. Peking duck is served with pancakes, scallions,

Peking duck sliced table-side.

and a delicious soy-based sauce with just a hint of sweetness.

LEGEND HAS IT

Looking for the best roast duck in Beijing? You won't find it in a luxury hotel. But if you happen to find yourself wandering through the Qianmendong hutong just south of Tiananmen Square, you may stumble upon a little courtyard home with a sign in English reading LI QUN ROAST DUCK. This small and unassuming restaurant is widely considered as having the best Peking roast duck in the capital. Rumor has it that the late leader Deng Xiaoping used to send his driver out to bring him back Li Qun's amazing ducks.

THE CAPITAL CITY'S NAMESAKE DISH

A perfectly prepared duck

Scallions

Soy based hoisin sauce

Pancakes

SOUTH

(left) Preparing for the feast. (top right) Dim sum as art. (bottom right) Place your order.

THE BASICS

The dish most associated with Southern Chinese cuisine is dim sum, which is found in great variety and abundance in Guangdong province, as well as Hong Kong and Macau. Bite-size dim sum is usually eaten early in the day. Any good dim sum place should have dozens of varieties. Some of the most popular dishes are *har gao*, a shrimp dumpling with a rice-flour skin, *siu maai*, a pork dumpling with a wrapping made of wheat flour, and *chaa-habao*, a steamed or baked bun filled with sweetened pork and onions. Adventurous eaters should order the chicken claws. Trust us, they taste better than they look.

> The Cantonese saying *"fei qin zou shou"* roughly translates to "if it flies, swims or runs, it's food."

For our money, the best southern food comes from Chaozhou (Chiuchow), a coastal city only a few hours' drive north of its larger neighbors. Unlike dim sum, Chaozuo cuisine is extremely light and understated. Deep-fried bean curd is also a remarkably fresh Chaozuo dish.

NOT TO BE MISSED

One Chaozuo dish that appeals equally to the eye and the palate is the plain-sounding mashed vegetable with minced chicken soup. The dish is served in a large bowl, and resembles a green-and-white yin-yang. As befitting a dish resembling a Buddhist symbol, a vegetarian version substituting rice gruel for chicken broth is usually offered.

SOUTHWEST AND FAR WEST

Southwest

THE BASICS

When a person from the Southwest asks you if you like spicy food, consider your answer well. Natives of Sichuan and Hunan take the use of chilies, wild pepper, and garlic to blistering new heights. These two areas have been competing for the "spiciest province in China" title for centuries. The penchant for fiery food is likely due to the weather—hot and humid in the summer and harshly cold in the winter. But no matter what the temperature, if you're eating Sichuan or Hunan dishes, be prepared to sweat.

Southwest China shares some culinary traits with both Southeast Asia and India. This is likely due to the influences of travelers from both regions in centuries past. Traditional Chinese medicine also makes itself felt in the regional cuisine. Theory has it that sweating expels toxins and equalizes body temperature.

As Chairman Mao's province, Hunan has a number of dishes with revolutionary names. The most popular are red-cooked Hunan fish *(hongshao wuchangyu)* and red-cooked pork *(hongshao rou)*, which was said to have been a personal favorite of the Great Helmsman.

Sichuan pepper creates a tingly numbness.

NOT TO BE MISSED

One dish you won't want to miss out on in Sichuan is *mala zigi,* or "peppery and hot chicken." It's one part chicken meat and three parts fried chilies and a Sichuanese wild pepper called *huajiao* that's so spicy it effectively numbs the tongue. At first it feels like eating Tiger Balm, but the hot-cool-numb sensation produced by crunching on the pepper is oddly addictive.

KUNG PAO CHICKEN

One of the most famous Chinese dishes, Kung Pao chicken (or gongbao jiding), enjoys a legend of its own.

Though shrouded in myth, its origin exemplifies the improvisational skills found in any good Chinese chef. The story of Kung Pao chicken has to do with a certain Qing Dynasty era (1644–1911) provincial governor named Ding Baozhen, who arrived home unexpectedly one day with a group of friends in tow. His cook, caught in between shopping trips, had only the chicken breast and a few vegetables he was planning to cook for his own dinner. The crafty chef diced the chicken into tiny bits and fried it up with everything he could find in the cupboard—some peanuts, sugar, onion, garlic, bits of ginger, and a few handfuls of dried red peppers—and hoped for the best.

(top left) Tibetan dumplings. (center left) Uyghur-style pilaf. (bottom left) Monk stirring tsampa barley. (right) Juggling hot noodles in the Xinjiang province.

Far West

THE BASICS

Religion is the primary shaper of culinary tradition in China's Far West. Being a primarily Muslim province, chefs in Xinjiang don't use pork products of any kind. Instead, meals are likely to be heavy on spiced lamb. Baked flat breads coated in sesame seeds are a specialty. Whole lamb roasted on a spit, fine spicy tomato salads, and lightly spiced mutton and vegetable soups are also favorites.

NOT TO BE MISSED

In Tibet, climate is the major factor dictating cuisine. High and dry, the Tibetan plateau is hardly suited for rice cultivation. Whereas a Han meal might include rice, Tibetan cuisine tends to include tsampa, a ground barley usually cooked into a porridge. Another staple that's definitely an acquired taste is yak butter tea. Dumplings, known as *momo,* are wholesome and filling. Of course, if you want to go all out, order the yak penis with caterpillar fungus.

EAST

(top left) Cold tofu with pork and thousand-year-old eggs. (top right) Meaty dumplings. (bottom right) Letting off the steam of Shanghai: soup dumplings. (bottom left) Steamed Shanghai hairy crabs.

THE BASICS

The rice, seafood, and fresh vegetable-based cooking of the southern coastal provinces of Zhejiang and Jiangsu are known collectively as huiyang cai. As the area's biggest city, Shanghai has become a major center of the culinary arts. Some popular dishes in Shanghai are stir-fried freshwater eels and finely ground white pepper, and red-stewed fish—a boiled carp in sweet and sour sauce. Another Shanghai favorite are xiaolong bao, or little steamer dumplings. Similar to Cantonese dim sum, xiaolong bao tend to be more moist. The perfect steamed dumpling is meant to explode in your mouth in a juicy burst of meat.

NOT TO BE MISSED

Drunken anything! Shanghai chefs are known for their love of cooking with wine. Dishes like drunken chicken, drunken pigeon, and drunken crab are all delectable meals cooked with prodigious amounts of Shaoxing wine. People with an aversion to alcohol should definitely avoid these. Another meal not to be missed is hairy freshwater crabs, which only come into season in October. One enthusiast of the dish was 15th-century poet and essayist Li Yu, who wrote of the dish in near-erotic terms. "Meat as white as jade, golden roe . . . to use seasoning to improve its taste is like holding up a torch to brighten the sunshine."

$$$
FRENCH
✕ **Jaan** (家安 *Jiāān*). If you're looking for Old World elegance, this is the place. You'll be transported back to the 1920s, complete with wood-plank floors, an antique piano, and graceful arched doorways. The French-influenced dishes have yet to disappoint, and crossover classics such as caramelized foie gras terrine with Sichuan peppercorns are a pleasant discovery. The wine list is staggeringly long and befits a place that's been around since 1917. $ *Average main: Y200* ⊠ *Raffles Beijing Hotel, 33 E. Chang'an Ave., Wangfujing, Dongcheng District* ☎ *010/6526–3388* ✦ *E4.*

$$$$
INTERNATIONAL
✕ **Jing** (京). East–West fusion cuisine is served in an ultramodern setting replete with polished red wooden floors, gauzy curtain dividers, and theatrical open kitchens. For dinner, a concise à la carte menu is available but the main draw is the lavish international buffet, with more than a dozen stations serving up lobster, foie gras, prime rib, and delectable desserts. There's also an excellent selection of international wines. $ *Average main: Y398* ⊠ *The Peninsula, 8 Jinyu Hutong, Wangfujing, Dongcheng District* ☎ *010/6510–6714* Ⓜ *Dongdan* ✦ *E4.*

$
CHINESE
✕ **Ju'er Renjia** (菊儿人家 *Júer rénjiā*). This modest little eatery really offers only one option: a set meal of tasty *lurou fan*, or rice with an aromatic ground pork topping complemented with flavorful boiled egg, mixed pickled vegetables, and a delicious clear soup, for less than $4. A vegetarian stew and rice set is also available. The home-brewed teas are excellent, especially the red date, longan, and ginger selections. Not to be missed is the homemade chilled milk custard called *shuang pi nai*, or double-skin milk. $ *Average main: Y26* ⊠ *63 Xiao Ju'er Hutong, Dongcheng District* ☎ *010/6400–8117* 🖿 *No credit cards* ✦ *D2.*

$
CHINESE
✕ **Lai Jin Yu Xuan** (来今雨轩). A gem tucked inside Zhongshan Park on the west side of the Forbidden City, Lai Jin is known for its Red Mansion banquet, based on dishes from Cao Xueqin's classic 18th-century novel, *The Dream of the Red Chamber*. The two-level restaurant sits beside a small pond amid willow and peach trees. The two daily dishes are *qie xiang* (eggplant with nuts) and *jisi haozigan* (shredded chicken with crown-daisy chrysanthemum). After your meal, take a lazy stroll across the park to the nearby teahouse with the same name, where you can enjoy a cup of tea in the courtyard surrounded by ancient cypress and scholar trees. $ *Average main: Y60* ⊠ *Inside Zhongshan Park, on the west side of the Forbidden City, Dongcheng District* ☎ *010/6605– 6676* 🖿 *No credit cards* ✦ *C4.*

$
CANTONESE
✕ **Lei Garden** (利苑 *Lìyuàn*). Bright and bustling on any day of the week, Lei Garden really packs them in on Sunday afternoons for dim sum amid glamorous surroundings. The panfried turnip cake is juicy and topped with generous amounts of grated veggies, and the shrimp dumplings are bursting with sweet plump shrimp and crunchy bamboo shoots. A platter of roast pork, with bite-size pieces laced with buttery fat and capped with crisp, crunchy skin, hits the spot. Private dining rooms offer sanctuary from the crowd. $ *Average main: Y100* ⊠ *Jinbao Tower, 89 Jinbao Jie, Dongcheng District* ☎ *010/8522–1212* ⊕ *www.leigarden.hk* ✦ *E4.*

$$
BEIJING
Fodor'sChoice
★
✕ **Li Qun Roast Duck Restaurant** (利群烤鸭店 *Lìqún kǎoyādiàn*). Juicy, whole ducks roasting over fragrant pear wood greet you upon entering this simple courtyard restaurant in a ramshackle hutong neighborhood. This family-run affair, far from the crowds and commercialism

Fast Food: Beijing's Best Street Snacks

Part of the fun of exploring Beijing's lively hutong is the chance to munch on the city's traditional snacks, served up by itinerant food sellers. Sweet-potato sellers turn their pedicabs into restaurants on wheels. An oil drum, balanced between the two rear wheels, becomes a makeshift baking unit, with small cakes of coal at the bottom roasting sweet potatoes strung around the top. In fall and winter, sugarcoated delicacies are a popular treat. Crab apples, water chestnuts, grapes, and yams are placed on skewers, about half a dozen to a stick; the fruit is then bathed in syrup that hardens into a shiny candy coating, providing a sugar rush for those all-day walks.

Wangfujing Snack Street and nearby Donghuamen Night Market are fun for browsing and sampling. The two markets have an extensive lineup of cooked-food stalls, many selling food items designed to shock. Sure, it's extremely touristy, and you'll be elbow-to-elbow with wide-eyed travelers fresh off the tour buses, but they're also incredibly fun. Cheerful vendors call out to potential customers, their wares glowing under red lanterns. Kebabs are popular, and it seems as though anything under the sun can be skewered and fried. There are the outlandish skewers of scorpion, silkworm cocoons, and even starfish, all fried to a crisp and covered with spices. There are also the more palatable (and more authentic) lamb kebabs flavored with cumin and chili flakes.

Worried about hygiene? The turnover at vendor carts and street-side stands is rapid, so it's unusual that anything has been sitting around long. It's easy to tell if the food is fresh, because it will be furiously hot when served. If you have any doubts, ask the vendor to cook yours to order, rather than accepting the ready-made food on display.

On the banks of Houhai, near the historical residence of Soong Ching-ling, is the entrance to Xiaoyou Hutong. Down this narrow alley you'll find Jiumen Xiaochi, a traditional courtyard house occupied by a collection of old Beijing eateries forced to relocate due to urban redevelopment. Some of these small eateries have been producing the same specialty dishes for decades. Look out for *lu dagun*, a pastry made of alternate layers of glutinous rice and red bean paste; *dalian huoshao*, northern-style pork pot stickers; and *zha guanchang*, deep-fried slices of mung bean starch dipped in a raw garlic sauce.

Some modern snacks are ubiquitous, such as the *jianbing*, a thin flour crepe topped with an egg and a crispy fried cracker. Briny fermented bean paste and hot chili sauce are spread thick and a sprinkling of cilantro and spring onion is added before it's rolled into a tidy package for munching on the go. Also on the streets: *baozi*, fluffy steamed buns filled with all manner of meat and vegetables, and *xianbing*, wheat flour pockets typically stuffed with chives and eggs.

of Quanjude, remains a popular choice for the city's signature dish. The spot is a bit tricky to find: It's about a five-minute walk east from Qianmen Donglu, and you may have to stop to ask for directions until you start seeing duck graffiti and arrows pointing the way. Sure, the restrooms and dining room are a bit shabby, but it's hosted everyone from Al Gore to Anthony Bourdain. ⑤ *Average main: Y140* ✉ *11 Beixiangfeng Hutong, Zhengyi Lu, Dongcheng District* ☎ *010/6705–5578* ⚲ *Reservations essential* ▬ *No credit cards* Ⓜ *Chongwenmen* ✛ *E5.*

$$$
NORTHERN
CHINESE
Fodor's Choice
★
✘ **Made In China** (长安壹号 *Cháng'ān yīhào*). Discover one of Beijing's most exciting dining rooms at the Grand Hyatt: A glossy, deep cavern dotted with glassed-in kitchens where you can watch the chefs work their magic. From Peking duck to noodles to vegetable dishes, all are meticulously prepared before your eyes. The Peking duck is the standout dish, and some say it's the best to be found in this duck-crazed city. ⑤ *Average main: Y200* ✉ *Grand Hyatt, 1 Dong Chang Anjie, Dongcheng District* ☎ *010/8518–1234* ⚲ *Reservations essential* ✛ *E4.*

$$$$
FRENCH
Fodor's Choice
★
✘ **Maison Boulud** (布鲁宫法餐厅 *Bùlǔgōng fǎ cāntīng*). Internationally acclaimed chef Daniel Boulud's first foray in China is this much-lauded restaurant in the historic Legation Quarter. Arrive early for your reservation to sip an aperitif in the parlor and admire the chic colonial decor. Entering the understated dining room, you'll find yourself in the company of the city's movers and shakers. Peruse the concise à la carte menu for all the usual suspects—foie gras, duck confit, a beef duo of short ribs and tenderloin—or splurge on a seasonal tasting menu for Y888. The brunch here is justifiably legendary. ⑤ *Average main: Y298* ✉ *23 Qian Men Dongdajie, Dongcheng District* ☎ *010/6559–9200* ✛ *D5.*

$$$
ASIAN
✘ **My Humble House** (寒舍 *Hánshè*). From its decor to the dinnerware, there's nothing humble about this fusion restaurant. The dramatic main dining area is designed around a pool covered with rose petals; gingko leaves scatter the hallway. Many find this to be one of the few restaurants that successfully creates fusion dishes, tapping Western ingredients while retaining a distinct Chinese flavor, such as in the panfried foie gras with Chinese mushrooms and abalone jam, or the unforgettable wok-fried beef tenderloin with black pepper. For dessert, try the almond tofu, a silken pudding made from ground apricot kernels. ⑤ *Average main: Y180* ✉ *W307 Oriental Plaza, 1 Dong Changanjie, Dongcheng District* ☎ *010/8518–8811* Ⓜ *Wangfujing* ✛ *E4.*

$
NORTHERN
CHINESE
✘ **Old Beijing Noodle King** (老北京炸酱面大王 *Lǎo Běijīng zhájiàngmiàn dàwáng*). This small chain of noodle houses serves hand-pulled noodles and traditional local dishes in a lively old-time atmosphere, with waiters shouting across the room to announce customers arriving. Try the classic *zhajiang* noodle served in a ground-meat sauce with accompaniments of celery, bean sprouts, green beans, soybeans, slivers of cucumber, and red radish. ⑤ *Average main: Y30* ✉ *56 Dong Xinglongjie, Dongcheng District* ☎ *010/6701–9393* ▬ *No credit cards* ✛ *E6.*

$
NORTHERN
CHINESE
✘ **Paomo Guan** (泡馍馆 *Pào mó guǎn*). The colorful murals decorating the front porch of this adorable spot will immediately catch your eye. Paomo Guan focuses on *paomo*—a Shaanxi trademark dish. Guests break a large piece of hardened flat bread into little pieces and then put them in a bowl. After adding condiments, the waiter takes your bowl

Street snacks at Wangfujing, Beijing's premier shopping spot

to the kitchen where broth—simmered with spices, including star anise, cloves, cardamom, cinnamon sticks, and bay leaves—is poured over the bread bits. It's Chinese comfort food at its best. ⑤ *Average main: Y20* ⊠ *53 Chaoyangmennei Nanxiaojie, Dongcheng District* ☎ *010/6525–4639* ▭ *No credit cards* ✛ *F3.*

$ ✕ **Private Kitchen No. 44** (44号私家厨房). This place is worth the risk
CHINESE of getting lost in the maze of alleyways in which it's located. Call ahead to order the signature dish called *suantang yu*, meaning fish in a sour tomato broth. Fermented tomatoes brought from western China are essential to achieve the bright tangency of this dish. The service is notoriously slow but sincere. You may find your patience increases with a cup of house-made rice wine. ⑤ *Average main: Y40* ⊠ *44 Xiguan Hutong, Dongcheng District* ☎ *010/6400–1280* ▭ *No credit cards* ✛ *E2.*

$ ✕ **Qin Tangfu** (秦唐府 *Qíntáng fǔ*). Pull up a tiny stool to a low table for
NORTHERN stick-to-your-ribs goodness at this rustic haven for Shaanxi fare. Hearty
CHINESE wheat-based specialties include *roujia mo* (bread stuffed with meat, aka "Chinese hamburger"), chewy hand-pulled noodles, and flavorful dumplings, all served up next to the traditional stove that produces baked goods. Lending a bit of charm are framed paper cuts (a form of Chinese folk art in which red paper is cut into animal, flower, or human shapes), traditional handicrafts, and large woven baskets (where you can store your purse or bags while you eat). ⑤ *Average main: Y40* ⊠ *69 Chaoyangmennei Nanxiaojie, Dongcheng District* ☎ *010/6559–8135* ▭ *No credit cards* ✛ *F4.*

$$$ ✕ **Red Capital Club** (新红资俱乐部 *Xīnhóngzī jùlèbù*). Occupying a
CHINESE restored courtyard home, replete with a Cold War–era bomb shelter down below, the Red Capital Club oozes nostalgia for the early days of

revolutionary China. Kitschy Cultural Revolution memorabilia and books dating from the Great Leap Forward era adorn every nook of the small bar, while the theme of the dining room is more imperial. The fancifully written menu serves old favorites of Communist leaders, though flavors are somewhat toned down for the foreign palate. $ *Average main: Y180* ⊠ *66 Dongsi Jiutiao, Dongcheng District* ☎ *010/6402–7150* ⌲ *Reservations essential* ⊘ *No lunch* ✚ *E3.*

$
SPANISH

✕**Saffron** (藏红花 *Cánghónghuā*). An early pioneer in the uber-chic Wudaoying Hutong, Saffron is still going strong with refined Mediterranean food served in a romantic courtyard house. Tapas, paella, sangria, and desserts (displayed in a glass case), served with warmth, provide the makings for a fine evening. $ *Average main: Y100* ⊠ *64 Wudaoying Hutong, Dongcheng District* ☎ *010/8404–4909* ✚ *E2.*

$$$
SICHUAN
Fodor's Choice
★

✕**The Source** (都江源 *Dōujiāngyuán*). Amid a loftlike courtyard setting, this restaurant serves a set menu of Sichuan specialties that changes every two weeks. The menu includes several appetizers, both hot and mild dishes, and a few surprise concoctions from the chef. On request, the kitchen will tone down the spiciness. The location was once the backyard of a Qing Dynasty general regarded by the Qing court as "The Great Wall of China" for his military exploits. The grounds have been painstakingly restored; an upper level overlooks a small garden filled with pomegranate and date trees. Dining in the central yard is serene and acoustically protected from the hustle and bustle from outside the walls. $ *Average main: Y188* ⊠ *14 Banchang Hutong, Kuanjie, Dongcheng District* ☎ *010/6400–3736* ⌲ *Reservations essential* ✚ *D2.*

$
YUNNAN

✕**Southern Barbarian** (南蛮子 *Nánmánzi*). After taking Shanghai by storm, this trendy Yunnan eatery has invaded the capital with delicious southwestern fare served in a gallery-like space in the up-and-coming Baochao Hutong. The home-style menu includes many regional favorites: Think mint salad, fried goat cheese, and mixed mushrooms in a banana leaf. A creative cocktail list and a large selection of imported beers keep this place hopping with hipsters late into the evening. It's a good spot in which to unwind after braving the youthful throngs of Nan Luogu Xiang. $ *Average main: Y80* ⊠ *107 Baochao Hutong, Gulou Dongdajie, Dongcheng District* ☎ *010/8408–3372* ✚ *D2.*

$
VEGETARIAN

✕**Still Thoughts** (静思素食坊 *Jìngsī sùshí fāng*). Soft Buddhist chants hum in this clean, cheerful restaurant. Even though there's no meat on the menu, carnivores may still be happy here as much of the food is

A BOOKWORM'S FOOD TOUR

Throughout China's history, there has been a love affair between the literati and food. So grab a copy of these books and try the following plates:

Qiexiang: a simple eggplant dish depicted in the classic *Dream of the Red Chamber*, a novel about scholar-gentry life in the 1700s.

Huixiang dou: a bean boiled with star anise, made famous through Lu Xun's short story "Kong Yi Ji," which takes place in a traditional wine house.

Lu Yu zhucha: beef cooked in tea leaves, inspired by Lu Yu, the author of the *Book of Tea*.

3

prepared to look and taste like meat. Try the crispy Peking "duck," or a "fish" (made of tofu skin) that even has scales carved into it. *Zaisu jinshen*, another favorite, has a filling that looks and tastes like pork. It's wrapped in tofu skin, deep-fried, and coated with a light sauce. $ *Average main: Y50* ⊠ *18A Dafosi Dongjie, Dongcheng District* ☎ *010/6405–2433* ▭ *No credit cards* ✛ *E3*.

$
VIETNAMESE

✕ **Susu** (苏苏会 *Sūsū huì*). Tucked away down a dim alley north of the National Art Museum, this hip hutong eatery has quickly gained a following for Beijing's best Vietnamese food. Choose from an array of light and fresh summer rolls and salads to start, and be sure to order the succulent barbecued La Vong Fish, served on a bed of vermicelli with herbs, peanuts, crispy rice crackers, and shrimp, which goes well with beer from local Slow Boat Brewery. The lovingly restored courtyard house offers a gorgeous patio and rooftop seating for pleasant weather, but the beautifully furnished and perfectly lighted interiors aren't too shabby either. $ *Average main: Y80* ⊠ *10 Qianlang Hutong Xixiang, Dongcheng District* ☎ *010/8400–2699* ✛ *E3*.

$$$$
MODERN
EUROPEAN
Fodor's Choice
★

✕ **Temple Restaurant Beijing.** Worship at the altar of Epicureanism and surround yourself with serenity at the city's best new restaurant, nestled in the heart of Old Beijing. TRB (as it's also known) serves high-end European cuisine in a spacious, minimalist dining room within a fabulously restored Ming Dynasty Buddhist temple complex. The four-course tasting menu offers a selection of dishes such as hamachi carpaccio and broiled pigeon for Y398, or go all out with the Y980 eight-course degustation. The wine list is excellent, with a deep focus on Champagne, Bordeaux, and Burgundy. $ *Average main: Y250* ⊠ *23 Songzhusi, Shatan Beijie, Dongcheng District* ☎ *010/8400–2232* ⊕ *www.temple-restaurant.com* ⌂ *Reservations essential* ✛ *D3*.

$
CHINESE

✕ **Yue Bin** (悦宾饭馆 *Yuèbīn fànguǎn*). Holding the historic distinction of being the first private restaurant to open in Beijing after the Cultural Revolution era, Yue Bin's home-style cooking still attracts neighborhood residents, as well as hungry visitors from the nearby National Museum of Art. The no-frills dining room is just big enough for half a dozen spotless tables, where you'll see families chowing down on local favorites such as *suanni zhouzi*, garlic-marinated braised pork shoulder; *guota doufuhe*, tofu pockets stuffed with minced pork; and *wusitong*, a spring roll filled with duck and vegetables. $ *Average main: Y50* ⊠ *43 Cuihua Hutong, Dongcheng District* ☎ *010/6524–5322* ▭ *No credit cards* ✛ *E3*.

XICHENG DISTRICT 西城区

Xicheng extends north and west of the Forbidden City, and includes Beihai Park and *Houhai*. Dive into the hutong here and try one of the excellent local restaurants, such as Jiumen Xiaochi, which serves Old Beijing favorites, or Kong Yi Ji, for its *huixiang dou*, boiled bean with star anise, and *Dongpo rou*, or red braised pork belly.

$$$$
CHINESE

✕ **Fangshan** (仿膳 *Fǎngshàn*). You can dine in imperial style at this extravagant courtyard villa on the shore of Beihai. Established in 1925 by three palace chefs, Fangshan serves elaborate dishes once prepared for the imperial family, based on recipes gathered across China. The place is best known for its filled pastries and steamed breads—traditional snack foods developed to satisfy Empress Dowager Cixi's sweet tooth. Banquet-style set meals are also available starting at Y228 per person. Be sure to make reservations two or three days in advance. ⑤ *Average main: Y228* ⊠ *Beihai Park, northwest of the Forbidden City, Xicheng District* ☎ *010/6401–1879* ⊕ *www.fangshanfanzhuang.com. cn* ⌖ *Reservations essential* Ⓜ *Tiananmen West* ✛ *C3.*

$ ✕ **Jing Wei Lou** (京味楼 *Jngwèilóu*). Always crowded with locals, this
CHINESE "House of Beijing Flavors" focuses on traditional local fare. Dishes include *ma doufu* (mashed fermented soybeans), *zha guanchang* (fried mung-bean chips), and a variety of mutton dishes. The two-story building has red pillars; the entrance is guarded by a statue of a man traditionally dressed and holding a birdcage—check out his Manchu queue (the hair braid men were forced to wear during the Qing Dynasty). A semi-open kitchen around the inner dining room gives the restaurant the flavor of an Old Beijing courtyard house. ⑤ *Average main: Y78* ⊠ *181 A Di'anmen Xidajie, Xicheng District* ☎ *010/6617–6514* ▭ *No credit cards* ✛ *C2.*

$ ✕ **Jinyang Fanzhuang** (晋阳饭庄 *Jìnyáng fànzhuāng*). Reliable, standard
NORTHERN Shanxi fare is the order of the day here, alongside famous crispy duck
CHINESE and cat-ear-shape pasta stir-fried with meat and vegetables. End your meal with a "sweet happiness" pastry. Jinyang Fangzhuang is attached to the ancient courtyard home of Ji Xiaolan, a Qing Dynasty scholar, the chief compiler of the *Complete Library of the Four Branches of Literature.* You can visit the old residence without admission fee and see Ji Xiaolan's study, where he wrote his famous essays. The crabapple trees and wisteria planted during his lifetime still bloom in the courtyard. ⑤ *Average main: Y70* ⊠ *241 Zhushikou Xidajie, Xicheng District* ☎ *010/6303–1669* ▭ *No credit cards* ✛ *D5.*

$ ✕ **Kong Yi Ji** (孔乙己 *Kŏngyĭjĭ*). Named for the down-and-out protago-
SHANGHAINESE nist of a short story by Lu Xun (one of China's most famous writers), the first thing you'll see upon entering this restaurant is a bust of the author. The old-fashioned menu, which is bound with thread in a traditional fashion, features dishes from Lu's hometown of Shaoxing, near Shanghai. Also served is a wide selection of the region's famed *huangjiu*, sweet rice wine; it comes in heated silver pots and you can sip it from a special ceramic cup. The peaceful lakeside location is a perfect launching point for an after-dinner stroll. ⑤ *Average main: Y80* ⊠ *South shore of Shichahai, Deshengmenneidajie, Xicheng District* ☎ *010/6618–4915* ✛ *C2.*

$$$$ ✕ **Mei Fu** (梅府家 *Méi fŭ*). In a plush courtyard on Houhai's south bank,
CHINESE Mei Fu oozes intimate elegance. The interior is filled with antique furni-
Fodor's Choice ture and velvet curtains punctuated by pebbled hallways and waterfalls.
★ Black-and-white photos of Mei Lanfang, China's famous opera star, who performed female roles, hang on the walls. Diners choose from set menus, starting at Y500 per person, which feature typical Jiangsu and Zhejiang cuisine, such as stir-fried shrimp, tender leafy greens, and dates filled with glutinous rice. A Y244 (per person) lunch is also available. ⑤ *Average main: Y500* ⊠ *24 Daxiangfeng Hutong, south bank of Houhai Lake, Xicheng District* ☎ *010/6612–6845* ⊕ *chinameilanfang. oinsite.cn* ⌖ *Reservations essential* ✛ *D2.*

Legendary Eats in the Xiaoyou Hutong

A dozen well-known restaurants, some dating back more than a century and threatened by the urban renewal of the old Qianmen business district, have found refuge in a large traditional courtyard house in **Xiaoyou Hutong.** Some of Beijing's oldest and most famous eateries have regrouped here under one roof. Our favorites are:

Baodu Feng. This vendor specializes in tripe. The excellent accompanying dipping sauce is a long-guarded family secret. You'll see upon entering that this stall has the longest line.

Chatang Li. On offer here is *miancha,* a flour paste with either sweet or salty toppings. Miancha was created by an imperial chef who ground millet, poured boiling water into it, mixed it into a paste, and added brown sugar and syrup. The imperial family loved it, and it soon became a breakfast staple.

Niangao Qian. This stall makes sticky rice layered with red-bean paste. It's the most popular sticky rice snack made by the Hui, or Chinese Muslims.

Yangtou Ma. Known for thin-sliced meat from boiled lamb's head, this shop was once located on Ox Street, in the old Muslim quarter.

Doufunao Bai. These folks sell soft bean curd, recognized for its delicate texture. It's best topped with braised lamb and mushrooms.

En Yuan Ju. Sample the *chaogeda,* which are small, stir-fried noodles with vegetables and meat.

Yue Sheng Zhai. Line up for excellent *jiang niurou* (braised beef), *shao yangrou* (braised lamb), and *zasui tang* (mutton soup).

Xiaochang Chen. The main ingredient of this vendor's dish is intestines, complemented with pork, bean curd, and *huoshao* (unleavened baked bread). The contents are simmered slowly in an aromatic broth.

Dalian Huoshao. This stall serves pot stickers in the shape of old-fashioned satchels that the Chinese once wore. These pot stickers were the creation of the Yao family of Shunyi, who set up their small restaurant in the old Dong'an Market in 1876.

The Jiumen Xiaochi. The Jiumen Xiaochi (Nine Gates Snacks). The archway by the lake in front of Xiaoyou Hutong refers to the former nine gates in the inner city of the Forbidden City. The private dining rooms in the courtyard are named after these gates. ✉ *1 Xiaoyou Hutong, Xicheng District* ☎ *010/6402–5858* ▭ *No credit cards.*

$

BEIJING

✕ **Shaguo Ju** (沙锅居 *Shāguō jū*). Established in 1741, Shaguo Ju serves a simple Manchu favorite—*bairou,* or white-meat pork, which first became popular 300 years ago. The first menu pages list all the dishes cooked in the *shaguo* (the Chinese term for a casserole pot). The classic shaguo bairou consists of strips of pork neatly lined up, concealing bok choy and glass noodles below. Shaguo Ju emerged as a result of ceremonies held by imperial officials and wealthy Manchus in the Qing Dynasty, which included sacrificial offerings of whole pigs. The meat offerings were later given away to the nightwatch guards, who shared

Dishing up hotpot

the "gifts" with friends and relatives. Such gatherings gradually turned into a small business, and white meat became very popular. $ *Average main: Y60* ✉ *60 Xisi Nandajie, Xicheng District* ☎ *010/6602–1126* ▭ *No credit cards* Ⓜ *Xidan* ✢ *C4.*

CHAOYANG DISTRICT 朝阳区

Vast Chaoyang District extends east from Dongcheng, encompassing Beijing's Jianguomen diplomatic neighborhood, the Sanlitun bar area, the Central Business District, and several outdoor markets and upscale shopping malls. The large foreign population living and working here has attracted a bevy of international restaurants, making this a fine place to sample dishes from around the world. If you're in Sanlitun, try Korean food at Ssam. Near Guomao, visit the excellent Peking Duck, Private Kitchen for its namesake dish, or indulge in divine Italian at Aria.

$$ ✕ **Alameda.** Specializing in Brazilian fare, Alameda serves simple but BRAZILIAN delicious dishes in a funky outdoor mall tucked behind the hubbub of Sanlitun's bar street. The weekday lunch specials, at Y78–Y98, are one of the best deals in town. Their menu is light yet satisfying, with plenty of Latin influences. Crowds seek out the *feijoada*—Brazil's national dish—a hearty black-bean stew with pork and rice, served only on Saturday. The glass walls and ceiling make it a bright, pleasant place to dine but magnify the din of the crowded room. $ *Average main: Y120* ✉ *Nali Mall, Sanlitun Lu, Chaoyang District* ☎ *010/6417–8084* ✢ *H2.*

$$$$
INTERNATIONAL
Fodor's Choice
★

✕ **Aria** (阿郦雅 *Āliyǎ*). Enjoy deluxe hotel dining amid murals and paintings of cheerful Italian Renaissance characters at Aria. Choose from three settings: the posh dining and bar area on the first floor, intimate private rooms upstairs, or alfresco on a terrace, protected by the din of downtown by neatly manicured bushes and roses. A perfectly decadent meal would include foie gras and seafood bisque, followed by one of the excellent steaks, with the playful deconstructed cheesecake for dessert. The best deal at this elegant restaurant is the three-course weekday business lunch for just Y198. ⑤ *Average main: Y300 ⊠ China World Hotel, 1 Jianguomenwai Dajie, Chaoyang District* ☎ *010/6505–2266* Ⓜ *Guomao* ⊹ *H4.*

$
ITALIAN

✕ **Assaggi** (尝试 *Chángshì*). Your mood brightens the minute you walk up the sunny spiral staircase to the rooftop patio, which includes glassed-in and open-air sections and overlooks the wide, tree-lined streets of the surrounding embassy district. It's a fine setting in which to enjoy a few glasses of wine accompanied by Parma ham or one of the pastas on offer. Check out the reasonable prix-fixe business lunches for around Y100. ⑤ *Average main: Y100 ⊠ 1 Sanlitun Bei Xiaojie, Chaoyang District* ☎ *010/8454–4508* ⊹ *G2.*

$
NORTHERN
CHINESE

✕ **Baoyuan Dumpling** (宝源饺子屋 *Bǎo yuán jiǎozi wū*). There's so much more to dumplings than standard pork and veggie fillings at this cheerfully homey joint. The photo-filled menu here offers dozens of creative filling options, many wrapped in bright skins of purple, green, and orange, thanks to the addition of vegetable juice to the dough. The options are mind-boggling, but feel free to mix and match: the minimum order for any kind of dumpling is 100 grams, or about six dumplings. If you can manage not to completely stuff yourself on dumplings, there's a separate menu with a solid selection of classic Chinese dishes—you'll see the popular *ma doufu* on many tables. ⑤ *Average main: Y40 ⊠ North of 6 Maizidian Jie, Chaoyang District* ☎ *010/6586–4967* ▭ *No credit cards* ⊹ *H2.*

$$$$
ITALIAN

✕ **Barolo** (巴罗洛 *Bāluóluò*). Beautifully executed Italian food in plush surroundings makes this luxury hotel eatery as appropriate for a power lunch as for a romantic dinner. A love of wine clearly is the inspiration, from the bold burgundies of the decor to the impressive list of Italian vintages to the use of the restaurant's namesake in dishes such as tagliolini with sea urchin, suckling pig, and *wagyu* beef cheek. A three-course lunch set is available Monday through Saturday for Y178. ⑤ *Average main: Y300 ⊠ Ritz Carlton Hotel, 83A Jianguo Lu, China Central Place, Chaoyang District* ☎ *010/5908–8888* ⊹ *H4.*

$$$
ASIAN

✕ **Bei** (北 *Běi*). This sleek little joint has attitude to spare. Perch at the sassy sushi bar or book a wood-paneled private room to enjoy the cuisines of northern Asia. Regional dishes from Japan, Korea, and northern China are transformed by creative presentation and haute techniques, so dishes like miso pork belly and smoked wagyu are fit for an emperor. The sashimi is flown in directly from Tokyo, and the competent staff will help you navigate their comprehensive list of sakes and wines. ⑤ *Average main: Y160 ⊠ The Opposite House, Bldg. 1, 11 Sanlitun Lu, Chaoyang District* ☎ *010/6410–2538* ☺ *Dinner only* ⊹ *G2.*

$ **Bellagio** (鹿港小镇 *Lùgǎng xiǎo zhèn*). This popular chain of bright,
TAIWANESE trendy-but-comfortable restaurants dishes up Taiwanese favorites to a
largely young and upwardly mobile clientele. A delicious choice is their
"three-cup chicken" (*sanbeiji*), served in a fragrantly sizzling pot with
ginger, garlic, and basil. You can finish your meal with a Taiwan-style
mountain of crushed ice topped with condensed milk and beans, man-
goes, strawberries, or peanuts. This branch is open until 4 am, making
it a favorite with Beijing's clubbing set. The smartly dressed all-female
staff—clad in black and white—have identical short haircuts. $ *Aver-
age main: Y60* ✉ *6 Gongti Xilu, Chaoyang District* ☎ *010/6551–3533*
🖎 *Reservations essential* ✢ *G3.*

$ **Biteapitta** (吧嗒饼 *Batà bǐng*). Located upstairs in a dive behind
MIDDLE EASTERN Sanlitun's bar street, this bright and spacious kosher falafel joint is a
breath of fresh air. Biteapitta has been filling Beijing tummies for over a
decade with quick and tasty Mediterranean fare such as baba ghanoush,
roasted chicken, and pita sandwiches brimming with yogurt, tahini,
cucumbers, and tomatoes. The cheerful room encourages diners to linger over a lemonade or mint tea. $ *Average main: Y60* ✉ *Tongli Studio,
Sanlitun Houjie, 2nd floor, Chaoyang District* ☎ *010/6467–2961* ✢ *G3.*

$ **The Bookworm** (书虫 *Shūchóng*). We love this Beijing spot when we're
CAFÉ craving a double-dose of intellectual stimulation and decent café food.
Thousands of English-language books fill the shelves and may be bor-
rowed for a fee or read inside. New books and magazines are also for
sale. This is a popular venue for guest speakers, poetry readings, film
screenings, and live-music performances. The French chef offers a three-
course set lunch and dinner. For a nibble, rather than a full meal, sandwiches, salads, and a cheese platter are also available. $ *Average main:
Y80* ✉ *Bldg. 4, Nan Sanlitunlu, Chaoyang District* ☎ *010/6586–9507*
⊕ *www.beijingbookworm.com* ▭ *No credit cards* ✢ *G3.*

$ **Café Constance.** Teutonic timbers frame the facade of this two-story res-
GERMAN taurant and bakery offering specialties from southern Germany. Down-
stairs, find excellent breads, pastries, prepared sandwiches, and a fantastic
Sacher torte, for take away or eating in at one of the café's tables. For
more filling fare, head upstairs, where a hearty menu of sausages, schnit-
zels, and dumplings awaits, along with a selection of imported beers.
$ *Average main: Y90* ✉ *No. 27 Lucky St., Zaoying Lu, Chaoyang Dis-
trict* ☎ *010/5867–0201* ⊕ *www.germanbakery.com.cn* ✢ *H1.*

$$ **Chef Too** (美西西餐厅 *Měixī xīcāntīng*). Beijing's best American
DINER grub can be found at this restaurant, housed in a sunny, cozy, and
family-friendly cottage near Chaoyang Park. During the day, massive
diner-style breakfasts, huge burgers, and bottomless cups of coffee offer
simple and satisfying comfort to homesick Americans. At night, the
ambience is slightly more refined, with perfectly cooked steaks serving
as the main draw, and a wine list focused on the U.S. West Coast. Save
room for a scoop (or two) of the homemade ice cream. $ *Average main:
Y140* ✉ *Chaoyang Gongyuan Xilu, opposite the West Gate of Chaoy-
ang Park, Chaoyang District* ☎ *010/6591–8676* ✢ *H2.*

$ **Comptoirs de France Bakery** (法派 *Fǎpài*). This small chain of contem-
FRENCH porary French-managed patisseries is the go-to place in Beijing for fine
cakes and pies, and makes an especially decadent chocolate tart. A variety

of other goodies are on offer: airy macaroons, flaky croissants, savory croquettes and quiches, as well as hot beverages. Beside the standard coffee options of Americano, cappuccino, and latte, Comptoirs has a choice of unusual hot chocolate flavors. In the Sichuan pepper–infused chocolate drink, peppercorns float in the brew, giving it a pleasantly spicy aroma. ⑤ *Average main: Y50* ✉ *China Central Place, Bldg. 15, N 102, 89 Jianguo Rd.(just northeast of Xiandai Soho), Chaoyang District* ☎ *010/6530–5480* ⊕ *www. comptoirsdefrance.com* 🚭 *No credit cards* ✛ *H4.*

$ | ✕ **Da Dong Roast Duck** (北京大董烤鸭店 *Běijīng Dàdǒng kǎoyā diàn*).
NORTHERN | You can't go wrong with the namesake dish at this world-famous spot,
CHINESE | where it's served with panache. Crispy, caramel skin over lean but juicy meat is the signature here, and comes with crisp sesame pockets in addition to the more usual thin pancakes. Newer branches of the eatery (such as this one) provide an atmosphere far better suited to the quality of the food than the original restaurant farther east. Upon entering, pause for a look into the glassed-in kitchen as chefs maneuver their hooks to pull glistening ducks from the oven, then peruse the enormous, photo-laden menu of innovative dishes to choose the rest of your meal. Don't miss the braised eggplant. ⑤ *Average main: Y100* ✉ *1–2 Nanxincang Guoji Dasha, 22 Dongsishitiao, Chaoyang District* ☎ *010/5169–0328* ⊕ *www. dadongdadong.com* 🍴 *Reservations essential* ✛ *H3.*

$$ | ✕ **Din Tai Fung** (鼎泰丰 *Dǐngtàifēng*). Taipei's best known restaurant is
TAIWANESE | this high-quality chainlet, now with several branches in Beijing, special-
Fodor's Choice | izing in *xiaolong bao*—steamed dumplings with piping hot soup inside.
★ | Din Tai Fung offers several variations on the standard pork xiaolong bao, such as crab, chicken, or shrimp, and a luxurious pork and black truffle soup dumpling. At the risk of getting completely stuffed on carbs, the dandan noodles, fried rice, and sweet dessert dumplings are also worth a try. ⑤ *Average main: Y120* ✉ *24 Xinyuan Xili Zhongjie, Chaoyang District* ☎ *010/6462–4502* ✛ *G2.*

$$ | ✕ **Duck de Chine** (全鸭季 *Quányājì*). This duck eatery is located in a large
BEIJING | courtyard complex that also houses an art gallery, a wine bar, a café, and a noodle shop. The restaurant is set up in a traditional-style building with a skylight across the roof ridge, bathing the room in natural light, while the dark bricks, wooden floors, and red lanterns give the venue a rustic feel. In addition to the classic roast Peking duck, the menu offers French-inspired renditions of duck, as well as an extensive wine list. The amazingly rich duck soup is fortified with tonic herbs such as wolfberries and huaishan. A second outlet has recently opened at Jinbao Jie. ⑤ *Average main: Y130* ✉ *1949 The Hidden City, Courtyard 4, Gongti Beilu, behind Pacific Century Place, Chaoyang District* ☎ *010/6501–8881* ✛ *G3.*

$
SICHUAN
✗**Feiteng Yuxiang** (沸腾鱼乡 *Fèiténgyúxiāng*). Be warned: Sichuan spices can be addictive. This restaurant's signature dish is *shuizhuyu*, sliced fish cooked in broth brimming with scarlet chili peppers and piquant peppercorns. The fish is impossibly delicate, melting in your mouth like butter, while the chilies and peppercorns tingle the lips. It's an overwhelming experience that heat-seekers will want to repeat over and over. Red-faced diners test the limits of their spice tolerance over dandan noodles and *koushuiji*, or mouthwatering chicken. The service is unfriendly but efficient. **$** *Average main: Y70* ✉ *1 Gongti Beilu, Chaoyang District* ☎ *010/6417–4988* ✛ *G3.*

$
CHINESE
✗**Haidilao** (海底捞 *Hǎidǐlāo huǒguō*). There's often a wait for a table at this upscale hotpot haven, but don't despair, because there's plenty to do in the meantime. Enjoy a complimentary manicure or shoe shine while you munch on crunchy snacks to whet your appetite for the main draw: bubbling pots of broth (spices optional), a variety of fresh ingredients for dipping, and a DIY sauce bar with loads of choices. Order the Kungfu Noodles, and you'll get a show as a young waiter hand-pulls the noodles table-side. More than a dozen locations can be found around town. **$** *Average main: Y90* ✉ *2A Baijiazhuang Lu, Chaoyang District* ☎ *010/6595–2982* ✛ *G3.*

$
NORTHERN
CHINESE
✗**Hai Wan Ju** (海碗居 *Hǎiwǎnjū*). Haiwan means "a bowl as deep as the sea," fitting for this eatery that specializes in crockery filled with hand-pulled noodles. The interior is simple, with traditional wooden tables and benches. A *xiao er* (a "young brother" in a white mandarin-collar shirt and black pants) greets you with a shout, which is then echoed in a thundering chorus by the rest of the staff. The clanking dishes and constant greetings re-create the busy atmosphere of an old teahouse. There are two types of noodles here: *guoshui*, noodles that have been rinsed and cooled; and *guotiao*, meaning "straight out of the pot," ideal for winter days. Vegetables, including diced celery, radish, green beans, bean sprouts, cucumber, and scallions, are placed on individual small dishes. Nothing tastes as good as a hand-pulled noodle: it's doughy and chewy, a texture that can only be achieved by strong hands repeatedly stretching the dough. **$** *Average main: Y50* ✉ *36 Songyu Nanlu, Chaoyang District* ☎ *010/8731–3518* ✛ *G6.*

$
YUNNAN
✗**In and Out** (一坐一忘 *Yīzuò yīwàng*). In a loftlike setting, the atmosphere here is as light and fresh as the Yunnan cuisine on offer. Sink into a sofa by the big windows that look out onto a tree-lined street and enjoy some of the delightful treats: a soul-warming bowl of steamed chicken in broth, crispy potato pancakes, or eggs scrambled with fragrant jasmine flowers. **$** *Average main: Y60* ✉ *1 Sanlitun Beixiaojie, Chaoyang District* ☎ *010/8454–0086* ✛ *G2.*

$
GUIZHOU
✗**Jia No. 21** (甲21号 *Jiǎ èrshíyī hào*). This trendy spot, started by a Taiwanese pop singer, stands out from its drab neighborhood thanks to its contemporary decor and large, sloping windows, with avant-garde paintings and sculptures against bare walls. The dishes served here are a collection of the best of Guizhou and Yunnan with a Thai twist. Try the sour fish-head soup with lemongrass for a sophisticated flavor. **$** *Average main: Y80* ✉ *21 Beitucheng Donglu, Chaoyang District* ☎ *010/6489–5066* ⌑ *Reservations essential* ▭ No credit cards ✛ *E1.*

$$$
FRENCH

✕**Justine's** (杰斯汀 *Jiésītīng*). Classic French cuisine and wine, including foie gras, escargot, and Château Haut-Brion, are served with the utmost attention at Beijing's oldest French restaurant. Justine's is well known for its delicious desserts. ⑤ *Average main: Y200 ⊠ Jianguo Hotel, 5 Jianguomenwai Dajie, Chaoyang District* ☎ *010/6500–2233* ✣ *H4.*

$
HUNAN

✕**Karaiya Spice House** (辣屋 *Làwū*). The tangy smell of chili wafts through the air as you step into this stylish, two-story Hunan eatery, known for its spicy and delectable dishes. Sweet-and-sour pork ribs, butterflied Mandarin fish with chopped chilies, and shredded duck served in a copper pot are among the favorites. ⑤ *Average main: Y90 ⊠ Sanlitun Village S, 19 Sanlitun Rd., S10–30, Chaoyang District* ☎ *010/6415–3535* ✣ *G2.*

$
CANTONESE

✕**La Galerie** (中国艺苑 *Zhōngguó yìyuàn*). Choose between two outdoor dining areas: one a wooden platform facing bustling Guanghua Road; the other well hidden in the back, overlooking the greenery of Ritan Park. Inspired Cantonese food and dim sum fill the menu. *Changfen* (steamed rice noodles) are rolled and cut into small pieces then stir-fried with crunchy shrimp, strips of lotus root, and baby bok choy, accompanied by sweet soybean, peanut, and sesame pastes. *Xiajiao* (steamed shrimp dumplings) envelop juicy shrimp and water chestnuts. ⑤ *Average main: Y90 ⊠ South gate of Ritan Park, Guanghua Lu, Chaoyang District* ☎ *010/8562–8698* Ⓜ *Jianguomen* ✣ *G3.*

$
PIZZA

✕**La Pizza** (辣匹萨 *Là bǐsà*). An Italian pizzaiolo can often be seen working the massive brick oven at this glass-enclosed corner pizza joint in Sanlitun, which serves some of the best pies in town. The classic Margherita is top-notch, with a thin crust, bubbled and charred at the edges, topped with creamy buffalo mozzarella and a perfectly tangy tomato sauce. Or you can say "when in Beijing" and try the Peking duck pizza, one of many available options. A good selection of antipasti, salads, and pastas round out the straightforward menu. ⑤ *Average main: Y80 ⊠ 3.3 Mall, 33 Sanlitun Lu, Chaoyang District* ☎ *010/5136–5582* ✣ *G3.*

$
CHINESE

✕**Madam Zhu's Kitchen** (汉舍 *Hànshè*). This sprawling basement dining venue is brightly lighted and decked out with sofas, heaps of green plants, and fun celebrity photos that line the walls. While the doors are whitewashed with an antique look and the European cabinets display blue-and-white china, there's nothing ye olde country inn about this industrial-chic space. The menu features classic regional dishes with new twists—mouthwatering *xun changyu* (a cold smoked fish appetizer), scallion chicken, and poached egg white filled with crabmeat are among their best dishes. ⑤ *Average main: Y90 ⊠ Vantone Center, 6A Chaoyangmenwai Dajie, B1/F, Bldg. D, Chaoyang District* ☎ *010/5907–1625* ✣ *G4.*

$
TIBETAN

✕**Makye Ame** (玛吉阿米 *Mǎjíāmǐ*). Prayer flags lead you to the secondfloor entrance of this Tibetan restaurant, where a pile of mani stones and a large prayer wheel greet you. Long Tibetan Buddhist trumpets, lanterns, and handicrafts decorate the walls, and the kitchen serves a range of hearty dishes that run well beyond the staples of yak-butter tea and *tsampa* (roasted barley flour). Try the vegetable *pakoda* (a deepfried dough pocket filled with vegetables), curry potatoes, or roasted lamb spareribs. Heavy wooden tables with brass corners, soft lighting,

and Tibetan textiles make this an especially soothing choice. $ *Average main: Y70* ✉ *11 Xiushui Nanjie, 2nd floor, Chaoyang District* ☎ *010/6506–9616* Ⓜ *Jianguomen* ⊕ *G4.*

$ ✕ **Metro Café** (美特柔 *Měitèróu*). A good assortment of fresh Italian
ITALIAN   pastas, soups, bruschettas, and meat dishes round out the menu at this long-standing eatery. Although service is inconsistent, the food is usually very good, and the outdoor tables are wonderful (if you can get one) on spring and summer evenings. $ *Average main: Y100* ✉ *6 Gongti Xilu, Chaoyang District* ☎ *010/6552–7828* ☾ *Closed Mon.* ⊕ *G3*

$ ✕ **Middle 8th** (中8楼 *Zhōngbālóu*). Perched at the very top of Village
YUNNAN   Sanlitun South, this modern Yunnan restaurant is a great place to wrap up a day of exploring the city. Deep earthy tones, soaring ceilings, and traditional handicrafts provide a relaxing setting in which to peruse the long photo-filled menu book. Dishes served on sizzling platters or in heated copper pots are especially tasty, and mushroom dishes are a Yunnan specialty. Wash it down with a pot of the region's famed Pu'Er tea or a refreshing vanilla mint cooler. $ *Average main: Y80* ✉ *Village Sanlitun S, Sanlitun Lu, 4th floor, Chaoyang District* ☎ *010/6415–8858* ⊕ *G3.*

$$$ ✕ **Mosto.** This Latino-inspired restaurant is located in the Nali Patio
INTERNATIONAL   complex, just off Sanlitun's bar street, with an interior that combines traditional and industrial elements. The open kitchen turns out innovative interpretations of South American classics, such as braised oxtail and black bean napoleon, grilled tuna steak with *mojo* (a spicy sauce), and chocolate soufflé with Sichuan pepper ice cream. A solid wine list and good cocktails keep the cosmopolitan crowd in high spirits. $ *Average main: Y180* ✉ *Nali Patio, 81 Sanlitun Beilu, 3rd floor, Chaoyang District* ☎ *010/5208–6030* ⊕ *www.mostobj.com* ⊕ *G2.*

$ ✕ **Nola.** This is the only place in the capital to get genuine New Orleans
AMERICAN   grits, jambalaya, and other Creole fare. Don't miss the pork tenderloin served with plums wrapped in bacon. For dessert, try the warm apple cobbler with a scoop of homemade nutmeg-flavored ice cream. Park yourself on the lovely rooftop terrace for romantic alfresco dining overlooking the surrounding green. $ *Average main: Y100* ✉ *11A Xiushui St. S, Chaoyang District* ☎ *010/8563–6215* ⊕ *G4.*

$ ✕ **Noodle Bar** (面吧 *Miàn bā*). With a dozen seats surrounding the open
CANTONESE   kitchen, this petite dining room lives large when it comes to flavor. The brief menu lists little more than beef brisket, tendon, and tripe, which are stewed to chewy perfection and complemented with noodles handpulled right before your eyes. For those seeking a moment of respite in Beijing's busy Sanlitun District, this is the place for a light lunch and a quick noodle-making show. The service is efficient and friendly. $ *Average main: Y70* ✉ *1949 The Hidden City, Gongti Beilu, behind Pacific Century Place, Chaoyang District* ☎ *010/6501–1949* ⊕ *G3.*

$ ✕ **Noodle Loft** (面酷 *Miànkù*). Watch the dough masters work in a
NORTHERN   flurry while you slurp your noodles at this bright and bustling res-
CHINESE   taurant. Sit at the bar to watch chefs snipping, shaving, and pulling dough into noodles amid clouds of steam. The black-and-white color scheme plays backdrop to a trendy crowd. Do as they do and order yummy fried "cat ears," which are actually small nips of dough, boiled

and then topped with meat, scrambled eggs, and shredded cabbage. ⑤ *Average main: Y50* ⊠ *33 Guangshun Beidajie, Chaoyang District* ☎ *010/8472–4700* ✛ *H5.*

$$$
AMERICAN

✕ **One East** (东方路一号 *Dōngfāng lù yīhào*). Contemporary American-style fine dining brings business travelers to the Hilton's flagship restaurant. With an emphasis on seasonal ingredients, the kitchen serves dishes that are fresh and light, such as sea bass with a sweet garlic puree. Or try one of Beijing's fanciest burgers, made with wagyu beef and served with foie gras and a choice of toppings. You'll find one of this town's best wine lists here, sampled by a crowd that's a mix of longtime residents and hotel guests drifting down from their rooms. ⑤ *Average main: Y200* ⊠ *Beijing Hilton Hotel, 1 Dongfang Lu, 2nd floor, Chaoyang District* ☎ *010/5865–5030* ✛ *H1.*

$
NORTHERN
CHINESE
Fodor'sChoice
★

✕ **Peking Duck, Private Kitchen** (私房烤鸭 *Guǒguǒ sīfáng kǎoyā*). Delicious duck in comfortable surroundings, what more could one ask for? Doing away with the formal, banquet-style scene that accompanies most places serving roast duck, diners here lounge on comfortable sofas in a moderately sized, warmly lighted dining room where the signature dish is made to perfection. The set menus, all including succulent Peking duck, are a terrific value and include other northern-style dishes such as kung pao shrimp and green beans in sesame sauce. Despite the name, this restaurant is very much open to the public, and it's quite popular so it's best to book ahead. ⑤ *Average main: Y80* ⊠ *Vantone Center, 6A Chaowai Dajie, FS2015, Chaoyang District* ☎ *010/5907–1920* ✛ *G4.*

$$
VEGETARIAN

✕ **Pure Lotus** (净心莲 *Jingxīnliányu*). You'd never guess, but this glamorous vegetarian haven is owned and operated by Buddhist monks. The warm jewel tones and traditional artwork will calm and restore frazzled nerves, and dishes served on mother-of-pearl amid dry ice will delight the senses. The exhaustive menu amply transcends the typical tofu and salad offerings by including mock meat dishes such as Sichuan-style fish or Beijing-style duck. (It's all made from wheat gluten and soy protein.) Alcohol isn't served, but a wide range of rare teas and fruit drinks are available. ⑤ *Average main: Y140* ⊠ *Metropark Lido Hotel, 6 Jiangtai Lu, Chaoyang District* ☎ *010/6437–6288* ✛ *H3.*

$
SICHUAN

✕ **Qi Xiang Ju** (其香居 *Qíxiāngjū*). Named after a famous teahouse in Sichuan, the beautiful stone-carved entrance of this restaurant gives way to a plush maze of modern dining areas and private rooms. The menu's main focus is hot-and-spicy fare, including Rabbit Crossing the River, boiled fish fillet in fiery broth, and delicious duck tongue paired with lotus roots. ⑤ *Average main: Y80* ⊠ *Chaoyang Gongyuan Xilu, inside No. 8 Gongguan, Chaoyang District* ☎ *010/6508–8855* ✛ *H2.*

$
MIDDLE EASTERN

✕ **Rumi** (入迷 *Rùmí*). Soaring ceilings in a split-level room and enormous mirrors decorated with Arabic script create a casually exotic atmosphere at this all-white Persian favorite. Portions are family-size, and a mixed appetizer of three choices from the menu is more than enough for a summertime supper. Try the chicken braised in a tangy pomegranate sauce or a platter of generously sized kebabs of meat and seafood. For dessert, take your rosewater and pistachio ice cream to the patio to enjoy the breeze. The Baha'i owner doesn't offer alcohol, but you're welcome to bring your own. ⑤ *Average main: Y100* ⊠ *1–1A*

Gongti Beilu, Chaoyang District ☎ *010/8454–3838* ⊕ *www.rumigrill. com* ▭ *No credit cards* ✢ *H3*.

$
TAIWANESE
✕ **Shin Yeh** (欣叶 *Xīnyè*). The focus here is on Taiwanese flavors and freshness. *Caipudan* is a scrumptious turnip omelet and *fotiaoqiang* ("Buddha jumping over the wall") is a delicate soup with medicinal herbs and seafood. Last but definitely not least, try the *mashu*, a glutinous rice cake rolled in ground peanuts. Service is friendly and very attentive. ⑤ *Average main: Y100* ⊠ *Xin Zhongguancun Shopping Center, 19 Zhongguancun Dajie, 4th floor, Chaoyang District* ☎ *010/8248–6288* ✢ *G3*.

$$
KOREAN
✕ **Ssam.** Beijing has no shortage of solid Korean food, but few that tweak the traditions of the cuisine. At Ssam, chef-owner Andrew Ahn's innovative creations include Korean beef carpaccio with truffle, pear, and quail egg; glass noodles with stir-fried vegetables and sesame foam; and a multi-part dessert of dried persimmon, lemon yogurt cake, and cinnamon jelly cubes. It's all served in a slightly industrial, minimalist space that complements the experimental qualities of the food, with helpful and friendly service. ⑤ *Average main: Y120* ⊠ *Sanlitun SOHO, Gongti Beilu, Tower 2, B1–238, Chaoyang District* ☎ *010/5395–9475* ✢ *G3*.

$$$$
MEDITERRANEAN
✕ **Sureño.** This chic, modern escape from the bustle of Beijing is housed in the city's coolest hotel, which makes it a great spot for people-watching over fine tapas and a glass of wine. But don't ignore the more substantial fare. An open, wood-fired oven takes center stage here, turning out exquisite thin-crust pizzas and grilled meats, including wagyu steaks, tuna, and tender baby chicken. The Florentine steak (for two or more people) is a hefty showstopper. ⑤ *Average main: Y300* ⊠ *Opposite House, 11 Sanlitun Lu, Chaoyang District* ☎ *010/6417–6688* ⊕ *www. surenorestaurant.com* ⌖ *Reservations essential* ✢ *G2*.

$
INDIAN
✕ **Taj Pavilion** (泰姬楼 *Tàijī lóu*). Beijing's best Indian restaurant, Taj Pavilion has been serving up all the classics since 1998, including chicken tikka masala, *palak panir* (creamy spinach with cheese), and *rogan josh* (tender lamb in curry sauce). Consistently good service and an informal atmosphere make this a well-loved neighborhood haunt. Newer branches have opened in Lido and Shunyi. ⑤ *Average main: Y75* ⊠ *China Overseas Plaza North Tower, No 8 Guanghua Dong Li, Jianguomenwai Ave., 2nd floor, F2-03, Chaoyang District* ☎ *010/6505– 5866* ⊕ *www.thetajpavilion.com* Ⓜ *Guomao* ✢ *H4*.

$$$
MEDITERRANEAN
✕ **Taverna+** (塔瓦娜+ *Tǎwǎnà*). Rustic dishes are a perfect contrast to the industrial-chic interior of this former factory. The young, well-heeled crowd fuels up on tapas and wine before heading out into the nightclubs of Sanlitun. Perch yourself on the luxe leather seats against exposed brick walls and sip on a selection from the modern wine list. Or dig in for a heftier meal of paella or prime rib. ⑤ *Average main: Y180* ⊠ *Courtyard 4, Gongti Beilu, Chaoyang District* ☎ *010/6501–8882* ✢ *G3*.

$
CHINESE
✕ **Three Guizhou Men** (三个贵州人 *Sāngèguìzhōurén*). The popularity of this cuisine prompted three Guizhou artist friends to set up shop in Beijing. There are many dishes here to recommend, but among the best are "beef on fire" (pieces of beef placed on a bed of chives over burning charcoal) accompanied by ground chilies; pork ribs; spicy lamb with

mint leaves; and *ma doufu,* a rice-flour cake in spicy sauce. ⑤ *Average main: Y70* ⊠ *Jianwai SOHO, Bldg. 7, 39 Dong Sanhuanzhonglu, Chaoyang District* ☎ *010/5869–0598* Ⓜ *Guomao* ✛ *G5.*

$ ✕ **Transit** (渡金湖 *Dùjīnhú*). This is one of Beijing's hottest restaurants,
SICHUAN   and we're not just talking about the chilies at this glam Sichuan estab-
Fodor'sChoice   lishment. Located in the upscale Sanlitun Village North, Transit holds
★   its own amid the surrounding luxury retailers, with designer interiors as sleek as a chic boutique. The region's fiery classics are stunningly prepared, with cold chicken in chili oil and dandan noodles garnering some of the ravest reviews. ⑤ *Average main: Y100* ⊠ *Sanlitun Village North, N4–36, Chaoyang District* ☎ *010/6417–9090* 🖉 *Reservations essential* ⊗ *No lunch* ✛ *G2.*

$ ✕ **Xiao Wangfu** (小王府 *Xiǎowángfǔ*). Beijing residents—locals and
CHINESE   expats—enjoy Xiao Wangfu's home-style cooking. Thanks to rampant reconstruction, it's moved from location to location as neighborhoods have been torn down. But fans can now happily find the newest site inside Ritan Park, located in a small, two-story building, with a rooftop area overlooking the park's greenery. The Peking duck is good, and the *laziji* (deep-fried chicken smothered in dried red chilies) is just spicy enough. The second-floor dining area overlooks the main floor, with plenty of natural sunlight pouring through the surrounding windows. ⑤ *Average main: Y80* ⊠ *Ritan Park North Gate, Chaoyang District* ☎ *010/8561–5985* Ⓜ *Jianguomen* ✛ *F4.*

$ ✕ **Xiheyaju** (义和雅居 *Yìhéyǎjū*). Nestled in Ritan Park, in one of Bei-
CHINESE   jing's embassy neighborhoods, Xiheyaju is a favorite of diplomats and journalists, many of whom live and work nearby. The outdoor court-yard is perfect on a sunny spring day. Not many places can do as well as Xiheyaju in four regional cuisines: Sichuan, Shandong, Cantonese, and Huaiyang. The tasty *ganbian sijidou* (stir-fried green beans), *mapo doufu* (spicy bean curd), and *gongbao jiding* (chicken with peanuts) are all great choices. ⑤ *Average main: Y100* ⊠ *Northeast corner of Ritan Park, Chaoyang District* ☎ *010/8561–7643* ✛ *G4.*

$$$ ✕ **Yotsuba** (四叶 *Sìyè*). This tiny, unassuming restaurant is arguably the
JAPANESE   best Japanese restaurant in town. It consists of a sushi counter—manned
Fodor'sChoice   by a Japanese master working continuously and silently—and two small
★   tatami-style dining areas, evoking an old-time Tokyo restaurant. The seafood is flown in from Tokyo's Tsukiji fish market. Reservations are a must for this dinner-only Chaoyang gem. A second location has opened nearby at Sanlitun Beixiaojie. ⑤ *Average main: Y200* ⊠ *2 Xinyuan Xili Zhongjie, Bldg. 2, Chaoyang District* ☎ *010/6464–2365* 🖉 *Reservations essential* ⊗ *No lunch* ✛ *G2.*

$ ✕ **Yuxiang Renjia** (渝乡人家 *Yúxiāngrénjiā*). Of the many Sichuan res-
SICHUAN   taurants in Beijing, the Yuxiang Renjia chain is the top choice for many Sichuan natives living in the capital. Huge earthen vats filled with pick-led vegetables, hanging bunches of dried peppers and garlic, and simply dressed servers evoke the Sichuan countryside. The restaurant does an excellent job of preparing provincial classics such as *gongbao jiding* (diced chicken stir-fried with peanuts and dried peppers) and *ganbian sijidou* (green beans stir-fried with olive leaves and minced pork). Thirty different Sichuan snacks are served for lunch on weekends, all at very

reasonable prices. There are now more than a dozen locations around the city. ⑤ *Average main: Y50* ⊠ *Lianhe Dasha, 101 Chaowai Dajie, 5th floor, Chaoyang District* ☎ *010/6588–3841* ⊕ *www.yuxiangrenjia. com* Ⓜ *Chaoyangmen* ✛ *F4.*

HAIDIAN DISTRICT 海淀区

Whether you're visiting the Summer Palace, Beijing's university area, or the electronics mecca of Zhongguancun, you certainly won't go hungry. And if you're hankering for the familiar, wander around the university campuses and pick one of the many Western-style restaurants or cafés catering to the local and international student population.

$$$$
CHINESE
✕ **Baijia Dayuan** (白家大宅门 *Báijiā dà zháimén*). Staff dressed in rich-hued, Qing Dynasty attire welcome you at this grand courtyard house. Bowing slightly, they'll say *"Nin jixiang"* ("May you have good fortune"). The mansion's spectacular setting was once the garden of Prince Li, son of the first Qing emperor. Cao Xueqin, the author of the Chinese classic *Dream of the Red Chamber*, is said to have lived here as a boy. Featured delicacies include bird's-nest soup, braised sea cucumber, abalone, and authentic imperial snacks. On weekends, diners are treated to short, live performances of Beijing opera. ⑤ *Average main: Y250* ⊠ *15 Suzhou St., Haidian District* ☎ *010/6265–4186* ⚏ *Reservations essential* ✛ *C1.*

$$
NORTHERN
CHINESE
✕ **Ding Ding Xiang** (鼎鼎香 *Dǐngdǐngxiāng*). Hotpot restaurants are plentiful in northern China, but few do it better than Ding Ding Xiang, a self-proclaimed "hotpot paradise." A variety of meats, seafood, and vegetables can be cooked in a wide selection of broths (the wild mushroom broth is a must for mycophiles), and the pot can be divided to accommodate several kinds. Should you be visiting Beijing in the bitter winter months, look forward to paper-thin lamb slices dipped in a bubbling pot of broth. Despite the surly service and gaudy decor, this place is perennially crowded. ⑤ *Average main: Y120* ⊠ *Bldg. 7, Guoxing Jiayuan, Shouti Nanlu, Haidian District* ☎ *010/8835–7775* ▭ *No credit cards* ⑤ *Average main: Y120* ⊠ *40 Dongzhong Jie, Dongzhimenwai, Dongcheng District* ☎ *010/6417–9289* ✛ *C1.*

$$$
JAPANESE
FUSION
✕ **Naoki** (直树怀石料理餐厅 *Zhíshùhuáishí liàolǐcāntīng*). Modern Beijing doesn't lack for fancy restaurants, but few are able to approach the level of refinement found at this Japanese haven, set in the ultra-luxe, restored imperial grounds of the Aman Resort at the Summer Palace. The multicourse set menu introduces diners to chef Naoki Okumura's selection of small dishes that marries French cooking techniques to Japanese traditions, such as seared foie gras served on steamed egg custard. If the weather is fine, sit outside by the reflecting pool for a transcendent experience. ⑤ *Average main: Y180* ⊠ *Aman at Summer Palace, 1 Gongmenqian Jie, Summer Palace, Haidian District* ☎ *010/5987–9999* ⚏ *Reservations essential* ✛ *C1.*

4

WHERE TO STAY

Updated
by Adrian
Sandiford

The first real wave of tourists to visit China in the 1980s had no need for guidebooks—foreigners were only allowed to stay in ugly, state-run, Stalinist-style blocks. But thankfully times have changed. Now Beijing has it all: a glorious glut of the world's best hotel brands; cheap and breezy places to make your base; intimate boutique beauties; and historical courtyard conversions. Whatever you're looking for, you'll find it in China's thriving capital.

The main hub of hotels is around Wangfujing (Beijing's famous shopping strip) and along Chang'an/Jianguomen, one of the city's main thoroughfares that connect the Central Business District (CBD) to Tiananmen Square. This is where you'll find the city's most recognizable and reputable hotels, all of which offer luxurious rooms, international-standard facilities, and attentive service. Don't despair if you're on a budget: there are plenty of decent dwellings next to the tourist trail at a fraction of the cost.

Busy execs should choose wisely in order to avoid getting snarled up in Beijing's horrific traffic, which most likely means staying a little farther west near Financial Street (the clue's in the name) or in the other commercial hub of Guomao (the CBD) in the east. Those in search of nightlife will want to be by Sanlitun, home to the capital's best bars and restaurants. And visitors after a taste of Old Beijing may want to try Gulou, where you'll find the city's fast-disappearing alleyways—or *hutong*—the ancient network of lanes increasingly under threat in the rush to modernity.

If you're after a one-of-a-kind Beijing experience, check out the city's courtyard hotels. These distinctive lodgings are converted from Beijing's historical *siheyuan*—traditional homes built as residential quadrangles among the hutong.

BEST BETS FOR BEIJING LODGING

Fodor's offers a selective listing of quality lodging experiences in every price range, from the city's best budget beds to its most sophisticated luxury hotels. Here we've compiled our top recommendations by price and experience. The very best properties—in other words, those that provide a particularly remarkable experience in their price range—are designated in the listings with the Fodor's Choice logo.

4

PLANNING

MONEY-SAVING TIPS

Beijing's busiest seasons are spring and fall, with summer following closely behind. Special rates can be had during the low season, so make sure to ask about deals involving weekends or longer stays. If you are staying more than one night, you can often get some free perks—ask about free laundry service or free airport transfers. Children 16 and under can normally share a room with their parents at no extra charge—although there may be a modest fee for adding an extra bed. Ask about this when making your reservation.

HOTEL RATINGS

The local rating system doesn't correspond to those of any other country. What is called a five-star hotel here might only warrant three or four elsewhere. This is especially true of the state-run hotels, which often seem to be rated higher than they deserve.

TIPPING

Tipping isn't the norm in China—a remnant from the country's Communist past. This may perhaps partly explain why service, in general, isn't as smooth or smiling as you would normally expect, even in the more established hotels.

LANGUAGE

English isn't widely spoken in Beijing, so it's best to print out the address (in Chinese) and telephone number of your hotel before departure. This will save you a lot of trouble upon arrival—taxi drivers, in particular, will be thankful for your forethought. If you're absolutely set on staying somewhere with English-speaking staff, look to the international chains, but call ahead, if you can, to check up on their language proficiency.

RESTAURANT REVIEWS

Listed alphabetically within neighborhoods.

Use the coordinate (✛ A1) at the end of each listing to locate a site on the corresponding map.

DONGCHENG DISTRICT 东城区

Dongcheng District covers the eastern half of Beijing's inner core, stretching from the Forbidden City in the center out to the Second Ring Road, which marks the boundary of the old city walls. This area incorporates some of the city's most important historic sites. The hotels off Dongchang'an Jie and Wangfujing Dajie are within walking distance of Tiananmen Square.

$$
HOTEL
Fodor's Choice
★

 ☷ **3+1 Bedrooms.** Modern, minimalist design—pure white interiors, free-standing bathtubs, individual courtyards—meets old Beijing at this intimate four-bedroom boutique hidden away within the quaint alleyways (*hutong*) near the historic Drum and Bell towers. **Pros:** spacious rooms; free in-room Wi-Fi and minibar; private terraces. **Cons:** no health club; no restaurants; some staff struggle with English. $ *Rooms from:*

Y1360 ✉ 17 Zhangwang Hutong, Jiu Guloudajie, Drum Tower, Dongcheng District ☎ *010/6404–7030* ⊕ *www.3plus1bedrooms. com* ✍ *3 rooms, 1 suite* ⫶◎⫶ *Breakfast* Ⓜ *Gulou Dajie* ✦ *C2.*

$$$
HOTEL

▢ **Beijing Hotel** (北京饭店 *Běijīng fàndiàn*). History-steeped, flush with an old-fashioned splendor, and close to the Forbidden City and Tiananmen Square, this hotel has been welcoming grandees and high rollers ever since it opened in 1900 (Nixon stayed here on his historic visit). **Pros:** short walk from the Forbidden City; close to shopping; a sense of history. **Cons:** mediocre restaurants; a lack of local nightlife; hard to get taxis. ⑤ *Rooms from: Y1500 ✉ 33 Dongchang'an Jie, off Wangfujing Dajie, Dongcheng District* ☎ *010/6513–7766* ⊕ *www.chinabeijinghotel.com.cn* ✍ *733 rooms, 51 suites* ⫶◎⫶ *No meals* Ⓜ *Wangfujing* ✦ *D5.*

$$
HOTEL

▢ **Beijing International** (北京国际饭店 *Běijīng Guójì fàndiàn*). Located on Beijing's main east–west central axis and close to Beijing's train station, this white monolith—spectacularly curved like Miami's Fontaineableau hotel—symbolised the rebirth of China's tourism industry in 1987. **Pros:** close to key transport links; near popular sites; good health facilities. **Cons:** expensive restaurants; can lack character; outdated in places. ⑤ *Rooms from: Y1400 ✉ 9 Jianguomennei Dajie, off Wangfujing Dajie, Dongcheng District* ☎ *010/6512–6688* ⊕ *www.bih.com.cn* ✍ *909 rooms, 60 suites* ⫶◎⫶ *No meals* Ⓜ *Dongdan* ✦ *F5.*

$$$$
HOTEL

▢ **Beijing Marriott Hotel City Wall** (北京万豪酒店 *Běijīng Wànháo jiǔdiàn*). At the edge of a restored section of the city wall—there are great views from the lobby coffee shop—this hotel is in a good location, relatively near key tourist sites, and is a reliable choice for those wanting clean, spacious rooms and excellent service. **Pros:** close to tourist sites; near the old city wall; spacious rooms. **Cons:** some rooms have odd shapes; lacks intimacy; extra charge for in-room Internet. ⑤ *Rooms from: Y1900 ✉ 7 Jianguomen Nanlu, Dongcheng District* ☎ *010/5811–8888* ⊕ *www.marriott.com* ✍ *649 rooms, 30 suites* ⫶◎⫶ *No meals* Ⓜ *Jianguomen* ✦ *F5.*

$
HOTEL

▢ **Beijing Sihe Courtyard Hotel** (北京四合宾馆 *Běijīng Sìhé bīnguǎn*). Small, quiet, and cute, this lovely courtyard hotel—tucked away inside one of the city's quaint hutongs and featuring a centuries-old date tree, red lanterns, and other such traditional Chinese decorations—was once the home of Mei Lanfang, the legendary male Peking opera star known for playing female roles. **Pros:** lots of privacy; homey atmosphere; authentic experience. **Cons:** not all rooms have courtyard views; no restaurant; bad plumbing. ⑤ *Rooms from: Y759 ✉ 5 Dengcao Hutong, Dongcheng District* ☎ *010/5169–3555* ⊕ *www.sihehotel.com* ✍ *12 rooms, 6 suites* ⫶◎⫶ *Breakfast* Ⓜ *Dongsi (Exit C)* ✦ *E4.*

$$
HOTEL

▢ **Crowne Plaza Beijing Wangfujing** (北京国际艺苑皇冠假日酒店 *Běijīng Guójì yìyuàn huángguàn jiàrì jiǔdiàn*). The best thing about this hotel is its location on Wangfujing, thereby putting you in the center of

LOCALE CONCERNS

As traffic conditions worsen, more travelers are choosing hotels closer to their interests. That said, Beijing's new subway lines are providing good alternatives to reaching distant places without getting stuck in traffic.

4

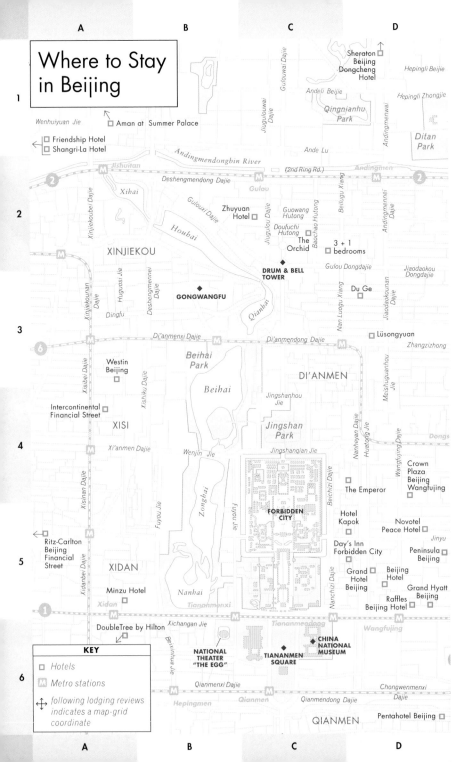

Where to Stay in Beijing

A · **B** · **C** · **D**

Wenhuiyuan Jie

☐ Aman at Summer Palace

☐ Friendship Hotel
☐ Shangri-La Hotel

Gulouwai Dajie

Sheraton Beijing Dongcheng Hotel ☐

Hepingli Beijie

Andeli Beijie

Hepingli Zhongjie

Qingnianhu Park

Andingmenwai

Ditan Park

Jishuitan Ⓜ

Andingmendongbin River

(2nd Ring Rd.)

Ande Lu

Andingmen

Ⓜ

②

Deshengmendong Dajie

Gulou Ⓜ

②

Xinjiekoubei Dajie

Xihai

Gulouxi Dajie

Houhai

Jugulouwai Dajie

Jiugulou Dajie

Zhuyuan Hotel ☐

Guowang Hutong

Beilugu Xiang

Baochao Hutong

Andingmennei Dajie

XINJIEKOU

Doufuchi Hutong

The Orchid

3 + 1 bedrooms ☐

Ⓜ

Gulou Dongdajie

Jiaodaokou Dongdajie

Xinjiekounan Dajie

Huguosi Jie

Deshengmennei Dajie

DRUM & BELL TOWER ◆

Nan Luogu Xiang

Du Ge ☐

Jiaodaokounan Dajie

GONGWANGFU ◆

Dingfu

Qianhai

Ⓜ

Ⓜ

Di'anmenxi Dajie

Ⓜ

Di'anmendong Dajie

Ⓜ

Lüsongyuan ☐

⑥

Xisibei Dajie

Westin Beijing ☐

Xishiku Dajie

Beihai Park

Beihai

DI'ANMEN

Jingshanhou Jie

Meishuguanhou Jie

Zhangzizhong

Intercontinental Financial Street ☐

XISI

Xi'anmen Dajie

Ⓜ

Wenjin Jie

Jingshan Park

Nanheyan Dajie

Huatdng Jie

Wangfujing Dajie

Dongs

Jingshanqian Jie

Crown Plaza Beijing Wangtujing ☐

Xisinan Dajie

Zonghai

Fuyou Jie

Fuyou Jie

FORBIDDEN CITY

Beichizi Dajie

The Emperor ☐

Ritz-Carlton Beijing Financial Street
☐←

Hotel Kapok ☐

Novotel Peace Hotel ☐

Jinyu

Day's Inn Forbidden City ☐

Peninsula Beijing ☐

Ⓜ

XIDAN

Nanhai

Nanchizi Dajie

Grand Hotel Beijing ☐

Beijing Hotel ☐

Grand Hyatt Beijing ☐

Minzu Hotel ☐

Tiananmenxi

Raffles Beijing Hotel ☐

①

Xidan Ⓜ

Ⓜ

Tiananmenxi

Ⓜ

Tiananmeadong

Wangfujing

DoubleTree by Hilton ☐
↙

Xichangan Jie

Beixinhua Jie

NATIONAL THEATER "THE EGG"

TIANANMEN SQUARE ◆

CHINA NATIONAL MUSEUM ◆

KEY

☐ Hotels

Ⓜ Metro stations

⟺ following lodging reviews indicates a map-grid coordinate

Ⓜ

Qianmenxi Dajie

Ⓜ

Chongwenmenxi Dajie

Hepingmen

Qianmen

Qianmendong Dajie

QIANMEN

Pentahotel Beijing ☐

A · **B** · **C** · **D**

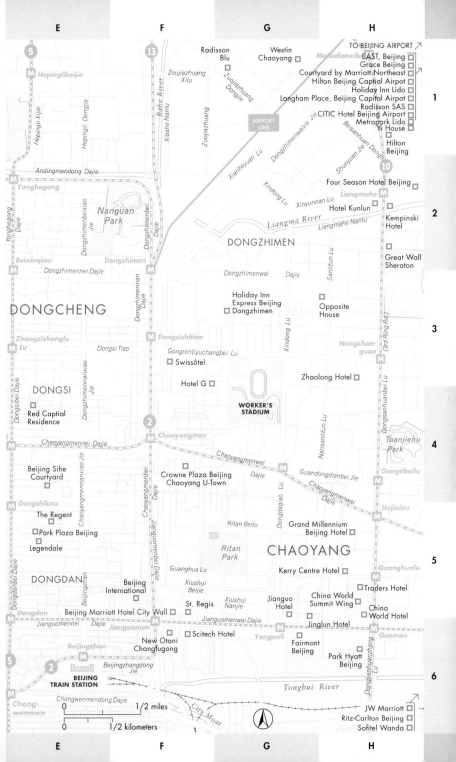

E   **F**   **G**   **H**

⑤ Hepinglibeijie

Zoujiazhuang Xilu

Radisson Blu

Westin Chaoyang

TO BEIJING AIRPORT ↗

Maizidianxilu

EAST, Beijing □
Grace Beijing □
Courtyard by Marriott Northeast □
Hilton Beijing Capital Airpot □
Holiday Inn Lido □
Langham Place, Beijing Capital Airpot □
Radisson SAS □
CITIC Hotel Beijing Airport □
Metropark Lido □
Yi House □

Hilton Beijing □

1

AIRPORT LINE

Hepingli Xijie

Zuojiazhuang Dongjie

Dongzhimenwaixie Jie

Bensanhuan Dongjie

Shunyuan Jie Dongjie

Zuojiazhuang Dongjie

Bahe River

Xibahe Nanlu

Andingmendong Dajie

Yonghegong

Yonghegong Dajie

Dongzhimenbeixiao Jie

Dongzhimenbei

Nanguan Park

Xianheyuan Lu

Xindong Lu

Xinyunnan Lu

Four Season Hotel Beijing □

Liangmahe

⑩

2

Hotel Kunlun □

Liangma River

Liangmahe Nanlu

Kempinski Hotel

Beixinqiao

Dongzhimen

Dongzhimennei Dajie

Dongzhimennan Dajie

Dongzhimen

DONGZHIMEN

Dongzhimenwai Dajie

Sanlitun Lu

Great Wall Sheraton

DONGCHENG

Holiday Inn Express Beijing □ Dongzhimen

Opposite House □

Xindong Lu

Nongzhan-guan

3

Zhangzizhonglu Lu

Dongsishitiao

Dongsi Tiao

Gongrentiyuchangbei Lu
□ Swissôtel

Hotel G □

Zhaolong Hotel □

Dongsanhuanbei Lu

(3rd Ring Rd.)

DONGSI

Dongzhimennanxiao Jie

WORKER'S STADIUM

Tuanjiehu Park

4

Dongsibei Dajie

Red Captial Residence

Chaoyangmennei Dajie

② Chaoyangmen

Chaoyangmenwai

Dajie

Nansanlitun Lu

Guandongdianbei Jie

Chaoyangmenwai Dajie

Gongtibeilu

Hujialou

Beijing Sihe Courtyard

Chaoyangmennanxiao Jie

Crowne Plaza Beijing Chaoyang U-Town

Dongdaqiao Lu

Dangshikou

The Regent

□ Park Plaza Beijing

Legendale

Ritan Beilu

Ritan Park

Grand Millennium Beijing Hotel □

CHAOYANG

5

Guanghua Lu

Kerry Centre Hotel □

Guanghualu

DONGDAN

Beijingzhan

Jianguomenbei Dajie

Beijing International

Xiushui Beijie

Xiushui Nanjie

Jianguo Hotel

China World Summit Wing

□ Traders Hotel

Dongdanbei Dajie

St. Regis □

□

China World Hotel

Dongdan

Beijing Marriott Hotel City Wall □

Jianguomennei Dajie

Jianguomen

Jianguomenwai Dajie

Jinglun Hotel

Yonganli

Guomao

Jianguomennei Dajie

New Otani Changfugong

Scitech Hotel □

Beijingzhan

Fairmont Beijing

Park Hyatt Beijing

Dongsanhuanzhong

6

⑤

②

BEIJING TRAIN STATION

Beijingzhangdong Jie

Tonghui River

Chongwenmendong Dajie

Chong-wenmen

0 ————— 1/2 miles

0 ————— 1/2 kilometers

City Moat

JW Marriott □
Ritz-Carlton Beijing □
Sofitel Wanda □

E   **F**   **G**   **H**

Beijing's most famous shopping street, a spectacle unto itself, with China's largest Apple store at one end and a bustling food market—scorpions-on-a-stick, anyone?—at the other. **Pros:** near the main sights; close to shopping; reputable brand. **Cons:** chain-hotel feel; service can be hit and miss; boring design. $ *Rooms from: Y1400* ⌖ *48 Wangfujing Dajie, Dongcheng District* ☎ *010/5911–9999* ⊕ *www.crownplaza.com/beijingchn* ⇗ *360 rooms, 27 suites* ⦿ *Breakfast* Ⓜ *Wangfujing* ✛ *D4.*

> **WORD OF MOUTH**
>
> "After we got into the cab, I gave the driver the phone number for the hotel, which he seemed to appreciate since he promptly pulled over and called the hotel for directions."
>
> —Wiselindag

$
HOTEL ⬚ **Day's Inn Forbidden City Beijing** (北京香江戴斯酒店 *Běijīng Xiāngjiāng dàisī jiǔdiàn*). Functional more than fancy, the Day's Inn offers a lot of pluses: it's inexpensive, clean, comfortable, and located within striking distance of the Imperial Wall Ruins Park, Wangfujing, the Forbidden City, and Tiananmen Square. **Pros:** fantastic price for the location; close to tourist sites; free Internet. **Cons:** restaurant is average at best; bad basement rooms; onset of mold in some shower rooms. $ *Rooms from: Y500* ⌖ *99 Nanheyan Dajie, Dongcheng District* ☎ *010/6512–7788* ⊕ *www.daysinn.cn* ⇗ *164 rooms* ⦿ *No meals* Ⓜ *Tiananmen East* ✛ *D5.*

$$$
HOTEL
Fodor's Choice
★ ⬚ **Du Ge** (杜革 *Dù gé*). One step beyond the striking Moon Gate doorway of this 18th-century hutong home—once owned by the Minister of the Imperial Household to Emperor Xianfeng (1860)—and you're gorgeously transported, thanks to swaying bamboos, flickering lanterns, blazing red walls, and a chic and sleek lobby, to a nobleman's courtyard house. **Pros:** gorgeous decor; great location; free soft drinks at the bar all day; outstanding breakfast. **Cons:** small rooms; patchy Internet; no in-room phones. $ *Rooms from: Y1500* ⌖ *26 Qian Yuan En Si Hutong, Dongcheng District* ☎ *010/6406–0686* ⊕ *www.dugecourtyard.com* ⇗ *6 rooms* ⦿ *No meals* Ⓜ *Gulou Dajie* ✛ *D3.*

$$$
HOTEL ⬚ **The Emperor** (皇家驿栈 *Huángjiā yìzhàn*). Though fronted by a boring brick facade, this hotel features a "cutting-edge" interior created by a team of international designers: guest rooms, replete with tube pillows, built-in sofas, angled desks, and color schemes bold enough to rely on bright yellows, rich reds, or sleek grays, and perhaps best be described as minimalist sci-fi chic (look for the wall-mounted flat-screen TVs and Wi-Fi)—whether or not you'll spend most of your time at the rooftop terrace and bar (with great Forbidden City views) remains to be seen. **Pros:** best rooftop terrace in the city; unbeatable views of the Forbidden City; unique, modern room design. **Cons:** no elevator; limited gym facilities; far from the subway. $ *Rooms from: Y1800* ⌖ *33 Qihelou Jie, Dongcheng District* ☎ *010/6526–5566* ⊕ *www.theemperor.com.cn* ⇗ *46 rooms, 9 suites* ⦿ *No meals* Ⓜ *Dengshikou* ✛ *D4.*

$$
HOTEL ⬚ **Grand Hotel Beijing** (北京贵宾楼饭店 *Běijīng Guìbīnlóu fàndiàn*). This high-end option on the north side of Chang'an Avenue blends ancient traditions with modern comforts—the classic Chinese gateway at the hotel's entrance is a particularly nice touch—and true convenience (it's close to Tiananmen Square and the Forbidden City, and some

rooms have views of the latter), along with some grandly decorated suites. **Pros:** good location; classic decor; great rooftop views. **Cons:** disappointing dining; confusing layout; little atmosphere. $ *Rooms from:* Y1200 ⊠ *35 Dongchang'an Jie, Dongcheng District* ☎ *010/6513–7788* ⊕ *www.grandhotelbeijing.com* ⌁ *214 rooms, 50 suites* ⏐⊙⏐*No meals* Ⓜ *Wangfujing* ✛ *D5.*

$$$$
HOTEL
Fodor's Choice
★

Grand Hyatt Beijing (北京东方君悦酒店 *Běijīng Dōngfāngjūnyuè jiǔdiàn*). The wow factor at the Grand Hyatt Beijing—located close to Tiananmen Square and the Forbidden City—comes via its huge glass facade and even more extraordinary Olympic-size swimming pool: surrounded by lush vegetation, waterfalls, and statues, it has a "virtual sky" ceiling that imitates different weather patterns. **Pros:** great dining; plenty of shopping; very impressive pool and gym. **Cons:** dull rooms; overpriced bar; Internet is extra. $ *Rooms from: Y2500* ⊠ *1 Dongchang'an Jie, corner of Wangfujing, Dongcheng District* ☎ *010/8518–1234* ⊕ *www.beijing.grand.hyatt.com* ⌁ *825 rooms, 155 suites* ⏐⊙⏐*No meals* Ⓜ *Wangfujing* ✛ *D5.*

$
HOTEL
FAMILY
Fodor's Choice
★

Holiday Inn Express Beijing Dongzhimen (北京东直门智选假日酒 *Běijīng dōngzhīmén zhìxuǎn jiàrì jiǔdiàn*). Cheap and cheerful does it at this budget hotel close to Sanlitun (Beijing's lively nightlife center)—yes, it lacks the facilities you'd expect in pricier establishments (such as a pool and gym), and the guest rooms are somewhat small, but everything here is super spick-and-span, from the gleaming lobby to the surprisingly comfortable beds, while touches such as six shiny Apple Macs next to the front desk (free for use), plus a games area complete with Xbox, Wii, and foosball table add a little something extra; book yourself here for great value from a Holiday Inn that goes beyond brand expectations. **Pros:** cheap yet extremely modern and clean; tour operator next door; close to some great nightlife. **Cons:** breakfast can be crowded (and no lunch or dinner options); small rooms; subway is a long walk away. $ *Rooms from: Y558* ⊠ *1 Chunxiu Rd., Dongcheng District* ☎ *010/6416–9999* ⊕ *www.holidayinnexpress.com* ⌁ *350 rooms* ⏐⊙⏐*Breakfast* Ⓜ *Dongzhimen* ✛ *G3.*

$
HOTEL

Hotel Kapok (木棉花酒店 *Mùmiánhuā jiǔdiàn*). Designed by Studio Pei Zhu (who also worked on the Olympics), this minimalist-style offering helped kick-start the boutique hotel movement in Beijing. **Pros:** comfortable rooms; near top sites; friendly staff. **Cons:** no pool; not everyone will like the glass-walled bathrooms; refurbishment needed. $ *Rooms from: Y800* ⊠ *16 Donghuamen, Dongcheng District* ☎ *010/6525–9988* ⊕ *www.kapokhotelbeijing.com* ⌁ *89 rooms* ⏐⊙⏐*Breakfast* Ⓜ *Tiananmen East* ✛ *D5.*

$$$$
HOTEL
Fodor's Choice
★

Legendale (励骏酒店 *Lìjùn jiǔdiàn*). Those fond of a classic European ambience will be drawn to the Old World spectacle that is the Legendale, a gigantic "château" from the outside, while inside a breathtaking gilded staircase winds upward to the towering atrium—a veritable "theater" with gilt balconies and a domelike atrium—with plenty of sparkling chandeliers and an antique Parisian fireplace at the center of it all. **Pros:** plenty of pampering; in a great neighborhood; luxurious rooms. **Cons:** high prices; vast size can make it feel empty; the faux European style will put off those in search of a more traditional Chinese

Red Capital Residence

Hotel G Beijing

Aman at Summer Palace

experience. ⑤ *Rooms from: Y2100* ⊠ *90–92 Jinbao St., Dongcheng District* ☎ *010/8511–3388* ⊕ *www.legendalehotel.com* ⬎ *390 rooms, 81 suites* ⦿| *Breakfast* Ⓜ *Dengshikou* ✛ *E5.*

$ LüSongyuan (侣松园宾馆 *Lǚsōngyuán bīnguǎn*). The traditional
HOTEL wooden entrance to this delightful courtyard hotel, on the site of an old
Fodor's Choice Mandarin's residence, is guarded by two *menshi* (stone lions)—this is a
★ classic old-Beijing experience, turned over to tourism, with no attempts
at modern updates or fancy design, but, rather, just a good choice for
cheap, traditional living. **Pros:** convenient location; near restaurants;
unfussy courtyard conversion. **Cons:** a lack of luxury; can be hard to
find; carpets are in need of a cleaning. ⑤ *Rooms from: Y850* ⊠ *22 Banchang Hutong, Kuanjie, Dongcheng District* ☎ *010/6401–1116* ⬎ *55 rooms* ⦿| *No meals* Ⓜ *Zhangzizhonglu* ✛ *D3.*

$ Novotel Peace Hotel (和平宾馆 *Hépíng bīnguǎn*). This tower of shim-
HOTEL mering glass has rooms with floor-to-ceiling windows that afford decent
FAMILY views, but, other than that, there's nothing spectacular here: service is
fairly basic and the ambience is decidedly low-key; the big plus is the
surrounding area, with plenty of shops and restaurants nearby (as well
as Wangfujing and Tiananmen Square), making it a solid base at a good
price for the location. **Pros:** convenient location; near plenty of restaurants; close to the sites. **Cons:** mixed room quality; not much ambience;
lackluster service. ⑤ *Rooms from: Y850* ⊠ *3 Jinyu Hutong, Wangfujing Dajie, Dongcheng District* ☎ *010/6512–8833* ⊕ *www.accorhotels-asia.com* ⬎ *402 rooms, 25 suites* ⦿| *No meals* Ⓜ *Wangfujing* ✛ *D5.*

$ The Orchid (兰花 *Lán Huā*). A smash hit in recent years, and a firm
HOTEL favorite among cool, independent travelers after somewhere trendy,
Fodor's Choice and yet down-to-earth, the Orchid may be located in the middle of
★ the action but is actually hidden away in an old network of hutong
alleyways, rewarding guests after their search with its beautiful internal courtyard and rooftop terraces (with great views), it's simple yet
cozy and modern rooms; and hugely knowledgeable staff. **Pros:** great
location; cool interiors; some rooms with gardens. **Cons:** reservations
a must; can be hard to locate. ⑤ *Rooms from: Y735* ⊠ *65 Baochao Hutong, Gulou Dongdajie, Gulou, Dongcheng District* ☎ *010/8404–4818* ⊕ *www.theorchidbeijing.com* ⬎ *10 rooms* ⦿| *Breakfast* Ⓜ *Guloudajie* ✛ *C2.*

$$ Park Plaza Beijing (北京丽亭酒店 *Běijīng Lìtíng jiǔdiàn*). Known
HOTEL for its attentive service, the Park Plaza has good amenities for business
travelers—the beige rooms are equipped with executive-size desks and
wireless Internet connections; the garden is perfect for open-air dining,
offering tranquility in the center of a bustling city. **Pros:** close to the Forbidden City; relaxing garden. **Cons:** lobby is small and dark. ⑤ *Rooms from: Y1350* ⊠ *97 Jinbao St., Dongcheng District* ☎ *010/8522–1999* ⊕ *www.parkplaza.com/beijingcn* ⬎ *216 rooms, 16 suites* ⦿| *No meals* Ⓜ *Dengshikou* ✛ *E5.*

$$$ Peninsula Beijing (王府半岛酒店 *Wángfǔ Bàndǎo jiǔdiàn*). Guests
HOTEL at the Peninsula Beijing enjoy an impressive combination of modern
Fodor's Choice facilities and traditional luxury—guest rooms are a little small for
★ this sort of hotel, but are superlatively well appointed, with teak and
rosewood flooring, colorful rugs, and high-tech touches like custom

bedside control panels that let you adjust lighting, temperature, and the flat-screen TVs; the service is excellent, as is the spa. **Pros:** close to sightseeing, restaurants, and shopping; rooms are impeccable; near the Forbidden City. **Cons:** lobby is squeezed by the surrounding luxury shopping mall; hectic atmosphere; rooms could be bigger. ⑤ *Rooms from: Y1800* ⊠ *8 Jinyu Hutong, Wangfujing, Dongcheng District* ☎ *010/8516–2888* ⊕ *www.peninsula.com* ↘ *525 rooms, 59 suites* ��❂ *No meals* Ⓜ *Dengshikou* ✛ *D5.*

$ ⌂ **Pentahotel Beijing** (贝尔特酒店 *Běi'ertè jiǔdiàn*). Formerly known

HOTEL as the Courtyard, this hotel recently changed hands and received a much-needed refurbishment—meaning more modern facilities, faster Wi-Fi, and decor switched to the "right side" of this millennium. **Pros:** business-friendly; good meeting rooms; next to the subway. **Cons:** in a traffic-clogged area; not much around for tourists. ⑤ *Rooms from: Y750* ⊠ *3 Chongwenmenwai Dajie, Dongcheng District, Beijing, China* ☎ *010/6708–1188* ⊕ *www.pentahotels.com* ↘ *307 rooms, 15 suites* � *Breakfast* Ⓜ *Chongwenmen* ✛ *D6.*

$$$$ ⌂ **Raffles Beijing Hotel** (北京饭店莱佛士 *Běijīng fàndiàn Láifóshì*).

HOTEL Raffles is an iconic brand in Asia and this property certainly doesn't

Fodor's Choice disappoint; in 2006, Singaporean designer Grace Soh transformed half

★ of what used to be the Beijing Hotel into a vivid, modern space (crystal chandeliers in the lobby; a grand white staircase enveloped in a royal-blue carpet) while retaining its history—service is excellent, and the location, for tourism purposes, is flawless. **Pros:** within easy walking distance of the Forbidden City; nifty location for sightseeing; switched-on staff; spacious rooms. **Cons:** pricey restaurants; not in the right part of town for business travelers; occasional problems with the pool. ⑤ *Rooms from: Y2500* ⊠ *33 Dongchang'an Jie, off Wangfujing Dajie, Dongcheng District* ☎ *010/6526–3388* ⊕ *www.raffles.com/beijing* ↘ *171 rooms, 24 suites* ⑩❂ *No meals* Ⓜ *Wangfujing* ✛ *D5.*

$ ⌂ **Red Capital Residence** (新红资客栈 *Xīnhóngzī kèzhàn*). Each of the

HOTEL four rooms at this boutique courtyard hotel—located in a carefully

Fodor's Choice restored home in Dongsi Hutong—are decorated with antiques and

★ according to different themes, such as the Chairman's Suite, in playful homage to Mao, and the two Author's Suites (one inspired by Edgar Snow, a 1930s U.S. journalist who lived in Beijing, and the other by Han Suyin, the Japanese novelist who wrote *Love is a Many-Splendored Thing*, among others); there is a cigar lounge where you can sit on original furnishings used by China's early revolutionary leaders, as well as a wine bar in a Cultural Revolution–era bomb shelter. **Pros:** Fodorites rave about the friendly service, unique atmosphere, and intimate feel. **Cons:** small rooms; limited facilities; quaint more than comfortable; dysfunctional website. ⑤ *Rooms from: Y1050* ⊠ *9 Dongsi Liutiao, Dongcheng District* ☎ *010/6402–7150* ⊕ *www.redcapitalclub.com.cn* ↘ *4 rooms* ⑩❂ *Breakfast* Ⓜ *Zhangzizhonglu* ✛ *E4.*

$$$$ ⌂ **The Regent** (北京丽晶酒店 *Běijīng Lìjīng jiǔdiàn*). Some of the

HOTEL most suavely elegant guest rooms in the city, an excellent location—

Fodor's Choice a block from the Wangfujing shopping district—and an imposing,

★ soaring glass-walled lobby are just some reasons why the Regent is a top choice for the rich and famous (and those getting there). **Pros:**

convenient location; close to the subway; spacious rooms. **Cons:** unimpressive breakfast; occasional blemishes in some rooms; check-in can be slow. $ *Rooms from: Y2250* ⊠ *99 Jinbao St., Dongcheng District* ☎ *010/8522–1888* ⊕ *www.regenthotels.com* ↘ *500 rooms, 25 suites* ⊘ *No meals* Ⓜ *Dengshikou* ✛ *E5.*

$$ 🅃 **Sheraton Beijing Dongcheng Hotel** (北京金隅喜来登酒店 *Běijīng*
HOTEL *Jīnyú Xǐláidēng jiǔdiàn*). The crisp new Sheraton Dongcheng, with its cubic glass facade, great-value lunch deals, and spacious, clean, and up-to-date rooms, can feel a little out on a limb near the post–Beijing 2008 Olympic area. **Pros:** lots of dining opportunities; close to the Bird's Nest and Water Cube; plenty of taxis and easy subway access. **Cons:** out of the way; not much to do nearby. $ *Rooms from: Y1400* ⊠ *36 N. 3rd Ring Rd. E, Dongcheng District* ☎ *010/5798–8888* ⊕ *sheraton.com/beijingdongcheng* ↘ *441 rooms, 70 suites* ⊘ *No meals* Ⓜ *Hepingxiqiao* ✛ *D1.*

$ 🅃 **Zhuyuan Hotel** (竹园宾馆 *Zhúyuán bīnguǎn*). The charming "Bam-
HOTEL boo Garden" was actually once the residence of Kang Sheng, a sinister
FAMILY character responsible for "public security" during the Cultural Revolution, who nevertheless had fine taste in Chinese art and antiques (some of which are still on display) but, as the hotel's English name suggests, the beautiful and peaceful grounds are the real highlight here. **Pros:** traditional feel; interesting *hutong* neighborhood; free Wi-Fi. **Cons:** room quality is variable; pricey for what you get; not that close to the big-name sights. $ *Rooms from: Y880* ⊠ *24 Xiaoshiqiao Hutong, Jiugulou Dajie, Dongcheng District* ☎ *010/5852–0088* ⊕ *www.bbgh.com. cn* ↘ *40 rooms, 4 suites* ⊘ *No meals* Ⓜ *Gulou Dajie* ✛ *C2.*

XICHENG DISTRICT 西城区

Xicheng District lies to the west of Dongcheng. It makes up the other half of Beijing's inner core with the Forbidden City as its starting point. This area is home to many of Beijing's old hutong alleyways and is a great place stroll around the neighborhood's famous lake.

$$ 🅃 **DoubleTree by Hilton Beijing** (北京希尔顿逸林酒店 *Běijīng Xī'ěrdùn*
HOTEL *yìlín jiǔdiàn*). Soaring 22 stories into the air, the DoubleTree is a solid
FAMILY hotel with perks beyond its station, from the warm chocolate-chip cookies in the lobby to the alluring oasis of the terraced outdoor swimming pool. **Pros:** gorgeous pool area; decent value. **Cons:** a little too remote; lack of good dining options. $ *Rooms from: Y1250* ⊠ *168 Guang'anmenwai Dajie, Xicheng District* ☎ *010/6338–1888* ⊕ *www. beijing.doubletreebyhilton.com* ↘ *543 rooms, 118 suites* ⊘ *No meals* Ⓜ *Caishikou* ✛ *A6.*

$$$$ 🅃 **InterContinental Financial Street Beijing** (北京金融街洲际酒店 *Běijīng*
HOTEL *Jīnróngjiē zhōují jiǔdiàn*). The large rooms at this massive chain hotel have contemporary designs and hints of traditional Chinese art. Smart, smooth, and comfortable, think of this place as an exercise in corporate chic (apt, considering this InterContinental is in the heart of Financial Street), including a 24-hour business center, plus an indoor pool, spa, and state-of-the-art fitness center rounding out the package that should be perfect for traveling executives. **Pros:** convenient location within

Beijing's financial hub; great for business travelers; excellent facilities. **Cons:** no appealing quirks; lack of culture nearby; business vibe may put off families. ⑤ *Rooms from: Y2300* ✉ *11 Financial St., Xicheng District* ☎ *010/5852–5888* ⊕ *www.ichotelsgroup.com* ⤺ *318 rooms, 10 suites* ⍥ *No meals* Ⓜ *Fuchengmen (Exit C)* ✛ *A4.*

$ **HOTEL** Ⓣ **Minzu Hotel** (民族饭店 *Mínzú fàndiàn*). When it opened in 1959, the Minzu was labeled one of the Ten Great Buildings in Beijing—this paean to China's unity has welcomed many prominent dignitaries over the years but has since been renovated into yet another shiny pleasure dome, even though it has maintained its original local appeal. **Pros:** close to the Xidan shopping area; good quality for price; spacious. **Cons:** service can be lackluster; feels tired; lack of buzz. ⑤ *Rooms from: Y950* ✉ *51 Fuxingmennei Dajie, Xicheng District* ☎ *010/6601–4466* ⊕ *www.minzuhotel.cn* ⤺ *512 rooms, 40 suites* ⍥ *No meals* Ⓜ *Xidan* ✛ *A5.*

$$$$ **HOTEL** Ⓣ **Ritz-Carlton Beijing, Financial Street** (北京金融街丽思 卡尔顿酒店 *Běijīng Lìsīkǎ'ěrdùn jiǔdiàn*). With ample amounts of glass and chrome, the Ritz-Carlton could be mistaken for one of the many sleek financial buildings that crowd its business-like Financial Street area. The interior is equally swish and contemporary, with crystal mythological animals in place for good luck and smart East-meets-West decor that matches the Ritz standard. Its location, excellent amenities, and eager-to-please staff make it popular with tour groups and business folk. **Pros:** impeccable service; luxurious atmosphere; incredible Italian dining. **Cons:** far from the city's attractions; expensive; lobby lacks pizzazz. ⑤ *Rooms from: Y3500* ✉ *18 Financial St., Xicheng District* ☎ *010/6601–6666* ⊕ *www.ritzcarlton.com* ⤺ *253 rooms, 33 suites* ⍥ *No meals* Ⓜ *Fuchengmen* ✛ *A5.*

$$$$ **HOTEL** Ⓣ **Westin Beijing** (威斯汀酒店 *Wēisītīng jiǔdiàn*). One of the trio of big players on Financial Street—along with the InterContinental and The Ritz-Carlton—it's business as usual at this worthwhile spot: comfortable rooms with plush beds, neutral tones, and marble bathrooms; a plethora of amenities, including dining spots both formal and fun; and not forgetting the perhaps-to-be-expected, well-staffed executive lounge. **Pros:** sumptuous beds; high-tech gadgets; business location. **Cons:** glass between bathroom and bedroom not for the timid; gym could be bigger; not in a good spot for tourists. ⑤ *Rooms from: Y2800* ✉ *9B Financial St., Xicheng District* ☎ *010/6606–8866* ⊕ *www.westin.com/beijingfinancial* ⤺ *486 rooms, 25 suites* ⍥ *No meals* Ⓜ *Fuchengmen* ✛ *A3.*

CHAOYANG DISTRICT 朝阳区

Chaoyang District is outside the old city walls and extends east of Dongcheng, so there's little of historical interest here. This is, however, home to Beijing's more modern, urban center. As such, you'll find some of the city's best restaurants, bars, and shopping malls here. The nightlife hub of Sanlitun is of particular note and the Central Business District is also located here.

$$$$
HOTEL
China World Hotel (中国大饭店 *Zhōngguó dàfàndiàn*). Once placing high on lists of top Beijing hotels, this place now does opulence in a rather unsubtle way—gold highlights in the lobby; marble tubs in the luxe rooms; high-priced fine dining—but it more than lives up to its look: the service is top rate, the restaurants are excellent (Aria, serving contemporary European cuisine, is particularly special), and the attached mall/cinema offers a welcome escape. **Pros:** convenient location for business travelers; some superb restaurants; close to both the subway and shopping. **Cons:** the bustle here can overwhelm; big and impersonal; rooms are small for the price. ⑤ *Rooms from: Y2800* ✉ *1 Jianguomenwai Dajie, Chaoyang District* ☎ *010/6505–2266* ⊕ *www. shangri-la.com* ⇩ *716 rooms, 26 suites* Ⓜ *Guomao* ✛ *H5.*

$$$$
HOTEL
China World Summit Wing (北京国贸大酒店 *Běijīng Guómào dàjiǔdiàn*). Towering over 1000 feet above the ground, the Summit Wing dominates the surrounding skyline as part of the tallest building in the city; guests are housed from levels 64 to 77, with floor-to-ceiling windows affording knee-trembling views of some of Beijing's more iconic sights, such as the Rem Koolhaas–designed CCTV headquarters—happily, if you need a drink to steady your nerves, the excellent 80th-floor cocktail bar makes a slick old-fashioned. **Pros:** jaw-dropping views; close to the CBD; Grill 79 does a great steak. **Cons:** traffic in the area is hellish; dining can be very pricey; lack of culture nearby. ⑤ *Rooms from: Y3500* ✉ *1 Jianguomenwai Ave., Chaoyang District* ☎ *010/6505–2299* ⊕ *www.shangri-la.com* ⇩ *278 rooms, 17 suites* ⑩ *No meals* Ⓜ *Guomao* ✛ *H5.*

$$
HOTEL
Courtyard by Marriott Beijing Northeast (北京人济万怡酒店 *Běijīng Rénjì wànyí jiǔdiàn*). More an option for business travelers than casual tourists—meaning it's not too far from the airport and a number of work hubs—this hotel near Wangjing High Tech Park thankfully understands that a functional location needn't engender an altogether utilitarian aesthetic: a 24-hour fitness center; modern, well-equipped guest rooms; plus a handy café and decent breakfasts may not match the heights of five-star living, but they're unlikely to disappoint. **Pros:** good value; well located for doing business in Beijing's northeast; reliable. **Cons:** extremely far from the tourist hot spots or downtown; little to do nearby; more for work than pleasure. ⑤ *Rooms from: Y1300* ✉ *101 Jingmi Lu, Chaoyang District* ☎ *010/5907–6666* ⊕ *courtyardbeijingnortheast.com* ⇩ *258 rooms, 43 suites* ⑩ *No meals* Ⓜ *Sanyuanqiao* ✛ *H1.*

$$
HOTEL
Crowne Plaza Beijing Chaoyang U-Town (北京朝阳悠唐 皇冠假日酒店 *Běijīng Cháoyáng yōutáng huángguàn jiàrì jiǔdiàn*). This hotel's name may be a bit awkward, but everything else runs smoothly: modern, good-size guest rooms; a great pool and gym; a sparkling marble lobby; and

let's not forget the integrated U-Town mall (hence the clunky title), which provides a plethora of other dining options, as well as the usual shopping and entertainment—even a German-themed bar that brews its own beers. **Pros:** still shiny new; conveniently attached to a buzzing mall; nicely functional. **Cons:** not close to tourism; lacks unique features; no strong identity. $ *Rooms from: Y1200* ✉ *3 Sanfeng N Area, Chaoyangmen Waidajie, Chaoyang District* ☎ *010/5909–6688* ⊕ *www.crowneplaza. com* ⤵ *360 rooms, 13 suites* ⦿ *No meals* Ⓜ *Chaoyangmen* ✛ *F4.*

$$ ⬚ **EAST, Beijing** (北京东隅 *Běijīng Dōngyú*). Launched in 2012, EAST is
HOTEL the latest attempt by the people behind the Opposite House (a luxurious
Fodor'sChoice boutique wonder) to create a business hotel with style, a place to do
★ business without the stiffness—note the communal networking space in the café-inspired lounge. **Pros:** a business hotel with style; impeccable service; great in-house dining and drinking. **Cons:** far from the main tourist sights (other than 798); nearby subway yet to open; adjacent park area still in development. $ *Rooms from: Y1250* ✉ *22 Jiuxianqiao Lu, Jiangtai, Chaoyang District* ☎ *010/8426–0888* ⊕ *www.east-beijing. com* ⤵ *346 rooms, 23 suites* ⦿ *No meals* ✛ *H1.*

$$$$ ⬚ **Fairmont Beijing** (北京华彬费尔蒙酒店 *Běijīng Huábīn fèi'ěrméng*
HOTEL *jiǔdiàn*). Surrounded by high-end office buildings, Fairmont Beijing is like a debutante fenced in by eager beaux, but it courts the diplomatic and commercial district with a gentle grace. **Pros:** handy for business and shopping; great executive lounge; excellent spa facilities. **Cons:** traffic can be grueling; breakfast is mediocre; surrounded by offices rather than the arts. $ *Rooms from: Y2300* ✉ *8 Yong An Dong Li, Chaoyang District* ☎ *010/8511–7777* ⊕ *www.fairmont.com* ⤵ *222 rooms* ⦿ *Breakfast* Ⓜ *Yong An Li* ✛ *G6.*

$$$$ ⬚ **Four Seasons Hotel Beijing** (北京四季酒店 *Běijīng Sìjì jiǔdiàn*). When
HOTEL it comes to hospitality it's fair to say that the Four Seasons has become
Fodor'sChoice synonymous with service of a level that still somehow manages to
★ exceed expectations. **Pros:** some of the best service in the city; elegant rooms; impeccable attention to detail. **Cons:** extraordinarily expensive; not particularly close to key tourist hubs; lobby feels a little cramped. $ *Rooms from: Y3200* ✉ *48 Liangmaqiao Rd., Chaoyang District* ☎ *010/5695–8888* ⊕ *www.fourseasons.com/beijing* ⤵ *247 rooms, 66 suites* ⦿ *No meals* Ⓜ *Liangmaqiao* ✛ *H2.*

$ ⬚ **Grace Beijing** (格瑞斯北京 *Géruìsī Běijīng*). Formerly known as Yi
HOTEL House, this unique concept hotel was once home to a crystal factory;
Fodor'sChoice today, however, the redbrick Bauhaus structure has been transformed
★ into a stylish boutique hotel. **Pros:** unique art-themed hotel; on-site restaurant is excellent; perfect for visiting 798. **Cons:** far from everything else; no subway; no pool. $ *Rooms from: Y850* ✉ *D-Park, Jiuxianqiao Lu 2 Hao Yuan, 798 Art District, Chaoyang District* ☎ *010/6436–1818* ⊕ *www.gracebeijing.com* ⤵ *30 rooms* ⦿ *Breakfast* ✛ *H1.*

$$ ⬚ **Grand Millennium Beijing Hotel** (北京千禧大酒店 *Běijīng Qiānxǐ*
HOTEL *dàjiǔdiàn*). Deep in the heart of the Central Business District, this glass tower is essentially a business hotel; the spacious guest rooms are more on the simplistic side of chic, with little that would draw or jolt the eye, but are smart and contemporary enough. **Pros:** centrally located; near subway; close to the Silk Market. **Cons:** food outlets are expensive;

difficult to get a taxi; some rooms need sprucing up. [$] *Rooms from: Y1300* ✉ *7 Dongsanhuan Zhonglu, Chaoyang District* ☎ *010/8587–6888* ⊕ *www.millenniumhotels.com* ↳ *521 rooms, 118 suites* ⟐ *No meals* Ⓜ *Jintai Xizhao* ✛ *H5.*

$$$
HOTEL

⟐ **Great Wall Sheraton** (北京喜来登长城饭店 *Běijīng Xǐláidēng cháng-chéng fàndiàn*). One of the oldest luxury hotels in Beijing, the Great Wall Sheraton is still going strong because of its popularity with tour groups. **Pros:** in the embassy district; lovely views. **Cons:** location isn't convenient; service can be a bit hit and miss. [$] *Rooms from: Y1530* ✉ *10 Dongsanhuan Beilu, Chaoyang District* ☎ *010/6590–5566* ⊕ *www.sheraton.com/greatwall* ↳ *827 rooms, 98 suites* ⟐ *No meals* Ⓜ *Liangmaqiao* ✛ *H2.*

$$$
HOTEL

⟐ **Hilton Beijing** (北京希尔顿酒店 *Běijīng Xī'ěrdùn jiǔdiàn*). Rather out on a limb for a big-name hotel, the Hilton Beijing lies at the city's north-east corner; it's a good choice for those wanting easy access to the airport (just a handy 20-minute ride away) but quite a schlep from the main sights. **Pros:** not far from the airport; One East restaurant does a great roast; good service. **Cons:** far from the sights; neighborhood lacks charm; the bar's a bit much. [$] *Rooms from: Y1690* ✉ *1 Dongfang Lu, Dong-sanhuan Beilu, Chaoyang District* ☎ *010/5865–5000* ⊕ *www.beijing.hilton.com* ↳ *502 rooms, 52 suites* ⟐ *No meals* Ⓜ *Liangmaqiao* ✛ *H1.*

$$$
HOTEL
Fodor's Choice
★

⟐ **Hotel G** (北京极栈 *Běijīng Jízhàn*). Vibrant, stylish, and next to the Gongti nightclub strip, this trendy boutique hotel has a multi-colored facade that masks a slick interior, where mid-century modern design uses subtle Chinese accents to add an understated glamour. **Pros:** adjacent to one of the hottest nightlife areas; chic design; good restaurants. **Cons:** too colorful for some; can be noisy; no pool. [$] *Rooms from: Y1520* ✉ *7 Gongti Xilu, Chaoyang District* ☎ *010/6552–3600* ⊕ *www.hotel-g.com* ↳ *110 rooms* ⟐ *No meals* ✛ *G4.*

$
HOTEL
Fodor's Choice
★

⟐ **Hotel Kunlun** (北京昆仑饭店 *Běijīng Kūnlún fàndiàn*). With a mag-nificently spectacular series of restaurants, bars, and lounges, this hotel nearly trumps the Forbidden City for sheer magic and splendor. **Pros:** gorgeous decor throughout; well-finished, restful rooms; a good choice of dining. **Cons:** staff can be a little slow; not a top choice for sightseeing; quite business orientated. [$] *Rooms from: Y980* ✉ *2 Xinyuan Nanlu, Sanlitun, Chaoyang District* ☎ *010/6590–3388* ⊕ *www.hotelkunlun.com* ↳ *600 rooms, 50 suites* ⟐ *Breakfast* ✛ *H2.*

$$$
HOTEL

⟐ **Jianguo Hotel Beijing** (建国饭店 *Jiànguó fàndiàn*). With an interior that follows the usual model of business chic, the Jianguo has main-tained its friendly feel over the years and continues to attract diplomats, journalists, and business executives aplenty—all in all, this is a reason-ably priced alternative to the many high-priced options on Jianguom-enwai Dajie. **Pros:** central location; fairly reasonable rates for the area; welcoming. **Cons:** limited amenities; rooms are small; can be a little noisy. [$] *Rooms from: Y1485* ✉ *5 Jianguomenwai Dajie, Chaoyang District* ☎ *010/6500–2233* ⊕ *www.hoteljianguo.com* ↳ *459 rooms* ⟐ *No meals* Ⓜ *Yonganli* ✛ *G5.*

$
HOTEL

⟐ **Jinglun Hotel** (京伦饭店 *Jīnglún fàndiàn*). From the outside, there's little that's appealing about the blocky design of the Jinglun Hotel. **Pros:** straight to the point; budget value; great location. **Cons:** lack of facilities; it's seen better days. $ *Rooms from: Y710* ⊠ *3 Jianguomenwai Dajie, Chaoyang District* ☎ *010/6500–2266* ⊕ *www.jinglunhotel.com* ⤴ *642 rooms, 18 suites* ⦿ *No meals* Ⓜ *Yonganli* ✛ *G5.*

$$$
HOTEL

🏨 **JW Marriott Hotel Beijing** (北京JW万豪酒店 *Běijīng JW Wànháo jiǔdiàn*). One of the city's luxury hotels, the JW Marriott pampers its guests with palatial rooms, thick mattresses, fluffy pillows, and all the boons of a five-star hotel: a ballroom the size of a city block; a luxury spa; obligatory high-end shopping mall nearby; even a branch of world-famous sushi specialists Nobu—it's hard to find fault with what's on offer. **Pros:** sleek style; spectacular service; attention to detail. **Cons:** dark hallways; irritating glass walls in the bathrooms; traffic-clogged area. $ *Rooms from: Y1500* ⊠ *83 Jianguo Rd., Chaoyang District* ☎ *010/5908–6688* ⊕ *jwmarriottbeijing.com* ⤴ *586 rooms, 100 suites* ⦿ *No meals* Ⓜ *Dawanglu* ✛ *H6.*

$$
HOTEL

🏨 **Kempinski Hotel Beijing Lufthansa Center** (凯宾斯基饭店 *Kǎibīnsījī fàndiàn*). At around 20 years old, if the Kempinski were a man, it would just be starting out in the world. **Pros:** excellent service; a good bar; easy access to the airport. **Cons:** some areas are in need of renovation; far from the big tourist spots. $ *Rooms from: Y1290* ⊠ *50 Liangmaqiao Lu, Chaoyang District* ☎ *010/6465–3388* ⊕ *www.kempinski.com* ⤴ *526 rooms, 114 suites* ⦿ *No meals* Ⓜ *Liangmaqiao* ✛ *H2.*

$$$
HOTEL
FAMILY

🏨 **Kerry Centre Hotel** (北京嘉里中心饭店 *Běijīng Jiālǐ zhōngxīn fàndiàn*). An ongoing renovation has seen this Shangri-La-owned hotel get a new lease of life. **Pros:** reasonably priced luxury; great location; nearby shopping. **Cons:** smallish rooms; congested area; ridiculously expensive bar. $ *Rooms from: Y1403* ⊠ *1 Guang Hualu, Chaoyang District* ☎ *010/6561–8833* ⊕ *www.shangri-la.com/beijing/kerry* ⤴ *487 rooms, 23 suites* ⦿ *No meals* Ⓜ *Guomao* ✛ *H5.*

$
HOTEL
FAMILY

🏨 **Metropark Lido Hotel** (北京丽都维景酒店 *Běijīng Lìdū wěijǐng jiǔdiàn*). In a leafy northeastern suburb of Beijing lies Lido Place, an enormous commercial and residential complex in which you'll find both the Metropark Lido (formerly a Holiday Inn) and a sense of puzzlement—namely a British-style pub, a Tex-Mex joint, and a buffet restaurant that makes this feel like Anywheresville. **Pros:** plenty of alternative dining options nearby; quiet streets; not far from the airport. **Cons:** slightly sterile neighborhood; far from the sights; part of an expat enclave. $ *Rooms from: Y731* ⊠ *6 Jiangtai Lu, Chaoyang District* ☎ *010/6437–6688* ⊕ *www.hkctshotels.com/lidohotel* ⤴ *433 rooms, 89 suites* ⦿ *No meals* Ⓜ *Sanyuanqiao* ✛ *H1.*

$$
HOTEL

🏨 **New Otani Changfugong** (北京长富宫饭店 *Běijīng Chángfugōng fàndiàn*). This Japanese-run hotel is renowned for its crisp service and enjoys a great downtown location that makes it a reliable middle ground for businessmen and (largely Japanese) tour groups alike; not all of the guest rooms have been renovated yet, but at least they're squeaky clean, plus the hotel overlooks a delightful garden where guests can participate in morning exercises. ▮▮▮**TIP→** It's also accessible for people with disabilities—sadly, not always the norm for Beijing. **Pros:** close to the sights; efficient staff. **Cons:** pricey food; worn-out carpets. $ *Rooms from: Y1200* ⊠ *26 Jianguomenwai Dajie, Chaoyang District* ☎ *010/6512–5555* ⊕ *www.cfgbj.com* ⤴ *460 rooms, 18 suites* ⦿ *No meals* Ⓜ *Jianguomen* ✛ *F6.*

$$$
HOTEL
Fodor's Choice
★

The Opposite House (瑜舍 *Yúshě*). If you want a taste of 21st-century China then look no further than this place (located in the heart of the Sanlitun nightlife district), a prime contender for being Beijing's best boutique hotel: designed by award-winning Kengo Kuma, the look and feel of this place is unlike anywhere else, featuring a huge atrium and contemporary art in the stunning lobby, plus spacious and warm guest rooms kitted out with natural wood and Scandi-Asian minimalist chic along with a bevy of splendid restaurants and bars abuzz with the city's cool kids. Service is a delight. **Pros:** a design addict's dream; fantastic food and drink options (both within and around); unique experience. **Cons:** too trendy for those who thrive on formality; not super close to the tourist trail; beyond-awful traffic. $ *Rooms from: Y1725* ✉ *11 Sanlitun Lu, Chaoyang District* ☎ *010/6417–6688* ⊕ *www. theoppositehouse.com* ⤳ *98 studios, 1 penthouse* ⦿ *No meals* ✛ *H3.*

$$$$
HOTEL
Fodor's Choice
★

Park Hyatt Beijing (北京柏悦酒店 *Běijīng Bòyuè jiǔdiàn*). An easy-to-like (if costly) slice of luxury, this 63-store tower hotel offers plenty of pampering (just imagine your own spa-inspired bathroom with oversize rain shower, deep-soak tub, and heated floors), with large guest rooms that are a tad functional but packed with the obligatory mod cons. **Pros:** spectacular views of the city; the hotel's buzzing Xue bar has a fab rooftop terrace; centrally located. **Cons:** pricey; lacks intimacy; hard area to walk around. $ *Rooms from: Y2000* ✉ *2 Jianguomenwai Dajie, Chaoyang District* ☎ *010/8567–1234* ⊕ *beijing.park.hyatt.com* ⤳ *237 rooms, 18 suites.* ⦿ *No meals* Ⓜ *Guomao* ✛ *H6.*

$
HOTEL

Radisson Blu Hotel (北京皇家大饭店 *Běijīng Huángjiā dàfàndiàn*). A big box of a hotel located near the international exhibition center in northeast Beijing, this "high-end" hotel falls just short of the standards demanded by such a description: whether you choose a "Chinese" or "Italian" style room, both are a little ragged by modern standards and in need of renovation; the rates—moderate for a business hotel—reflect the slightly out-of-the-way location, but the Radisson Blu only really makes sense if you're staying here on business. **Pros:** decent dining options; handy for business travelers; good value. **Cons:** out-of-the-way location; congested traffic; in need of an update. $ *Rooms from: Y800* ✉ *6A Beisanhuan Donglu, Chaoyang District* ☎ *010/5922–3388* ⊕ *www.radissonblu.com* ⤳ *362 rooms, 16 suites* ⦿ *No meals* ✛ *G1.*

$$$$
HOTEL

The Ritz-Carlton, Beijing (北京丽思卡尔顿酒店 *Běijīng Lìsīkǎ'ěrdùn jiǔdiàn*). On Jianguo Lu, where couture practically spills out onto the street, this Ritz-Carlton feels rather at home surrounded by branches of Chanel, Ferragamo, et al; the dinky marble lobby, mahogany decorated rooms, excellent Italian restaurant (Barolo), and Davidoff-sponsored cigar bar feel like something from another age, which is no bad thing if you can afford it. **Pros:** superior service; great location; impressive dining options. **Cons:** dark public areas; expensive food; small lobby. $ *Rooms from: Y2040* ✉ *83A Jianguo Lu, Chaoyang District* ☎ *010/5908–8888* ⊕ *www.ritzcarlton.com* ⤳ *305 rooms* ⦿ *No meals* Ⓜ *Dawanglu* ✛ *H6.*

$
HOTEL

SciTech Hotel (赛特饭店 *Sàitè fàndiàn*). Partnered with the SciTech outlet mall (shuttle buses between the two run from the hotel), this hotel enjoys a privileged position on the busy Jianguomenwai Dajie; however,

Park Hyatt Beijing

St. Regis

aside from a few decent facilities—basic gym and pool; tennis courts; a rather bizarre bowling alley—there is little worthy of your attention here. **Pros:** exceptionally cheap for the location; easy access to public transportation; near restaurants. **Cons:** tobacco odors throughout; worn carpets; humdrum rooms. $ *Rooms from: Y428* ✉ *22 Jianguomenwai Dajie, Chaoyang District* ☎ *010/6512–3388* ⊕ *www.scitechhotel.com* ⤵ *294 rooms, 32 suites* ⊗*No meals* Ⓜ *Yonganli* ✛ *F6.*

$$ **Sofitel Wanda** (北京万达索菲特大饭店 *Běijīng Wàndá suǒfēitè*
HOTEL *dàfàndiàn*). Tang Dynasty style mixes with contemporary French flair at this plush hotel, where swanky rooms and suites are enlivened with subtle Asian motifs; a well-equipped fitness center boasts a 25-meter-long pool and state-of-the-art gym; hotel restaurant Le Pré Lenôtre dishes up fabulous French cuisine. **Pros:** good design; plenty of high-tech touches; near subway. **Cons:** traffic-clogged area; the view could be better; keen tourists may want to be closer to the sites. $ *Rooms from: Y1200* ✉ *97 Jianguo Rd., Tower C (Wanda Plaza), Chaoyang District* ☎ *010/8599–6666* ⊕ *www.sofitel-wanda-beijing.com* ⤵ *417 rooms, 43 suites* ⊗*No meals* Ⓜ *Dawanglu* ✛ *H6.*

$$$ **St. Regis** (北京国际俱乐部饭店 *Běijīng guójì jùlèbù fàndiàn*). A
HOTEL favorite of business travelers and dignitaries alike, the luxurious inte-
Fodor'sChoice riors here combine classic Chinese elegance with modern furnish-
★ ings, but it's the facilities that really stand out: the fine health club is equipped with a Jacuzzi that gets its water direct from a natural hot spring deep beneath the hotel, the glass-atrium swimming pool offers a sun-drenched backstroke, and the smart, wood-paneled Press Club Bar has the air of a private club. **Pros:** nice location; fantastic facili-ties; good Asian and European dining options. **Cons:** the little extras really add up; may look too formal for some; lack of local atmosphere. $ *Rooms from: Y1742* ✉ *21 Jianguomenwai Dajie, Chaoyang District* ☎ *010/6460–6688* ⊕ *www.stregis.com/beijing* ⤵ *156 rooms, 102 suites* Ⓜ *Jianguomen* ✛ *F5.*

$ **Swissôtel Beijing** (港澳中心瑞士酒店 *Gǎng'ao zhōngxīn ruìshì*
HOTEL *jiǔdiàn*). With easy access to the Second Ring Road and Line 2 of the subway, this well-run hotel provides something of a welcome hub for tourists: the marble lobby is impressive, guest rooms are of a high quality (decked out in a recognizably European style), and the health club has a large pool and tennis courts: while it'll never be one of the city's more glamorous hotels, it's a solid fit. **Pros:** regular jazz nights in the lobby; great amenities; easy access to the city. **Cons:** can be noisy; generally mediocre food; not next to the sites. $ *Rooms from: Y750* ✉ *2 Chaoyangmennei Dajie, Dongsishiqiao Flyover Junction (2nd Ring Rd.), Chaoyang District* ☎ *010/6553–2288* ⊕ *www.swissotel-beijing. com* ⤵ *430 rooms, 50 suites* ⊗*No meals* Ⓜ *Dongsishitiao* ✛ *F3.*

$$ **Traders Hotel** (国贸饭店 *Guómào fàndiàn*). A functional name for a
HOTEL pretty utilitarian hotel, Traders is located inside the China World Trade Complex, hence the prevalence of business travelers to be found staying here; its good-value, simple (think muted colors), efficient guest rooms hit the mark, as does its fine service and excellent health club (you'll want to eat out, though, but that's not always such a bad thing). **Pros:** moderate price for a business hotel; near the CBD; plenty of shopping.

Cons: a lack of good dining; not really for tourists; lobby could be bigger. $\[S\]$ *Rooms from: Y1150* ✉ *1 Jianguomenwai Dajie, Chaoyang District* ☎ *010/6505–2277* ⊕ *www.tradershotels.com* ⤴ *570 rooms, 27 suites* ¶◯¶ *No meals* Ⓜ *Guomao* ✢ *H5.*

$$$ 🛏 **Westin Beijing Chaoyang** (金茂北京威斯汀大饭店 *Jīnmào Běijīng*
HOTEL   *wēisīdtīng dàjiǔdiàn*). With 550 spacious guest rooms, the Westin Beijing Chaoyang isn't exactly a small affair, but what the hotel lacks in intimacy it more than makes up for in luxury: highlights include the heavenly beds and rain-forest showers, flat-screen interactive televisions, and welcoming guest rooms decorated with warm colors and contemporary furnishings. **Pros:** convenient location near the airport expressway; beautiful atrium-style swimming pool; great breakfast buffet. **Cons:** in northeast of the city far from tourist sites; not as shiny new as it used to be; check-in can sometimes be slow. $\[S\]$ *Rooms from: Y1600* ✉ *1 Xinyuan Nanlu, Chaoyang District* ☎ *010/5922–8888* ⊕ *www.westin.com/chaoyang* ⤴ *550 rooms* ¶◯¶ *No meals* Ⓜ *Liangmaqiao* ✢ *G1.*

$ 🛏 **Zhaolong Hotel** (兆龙饭店 *Zhàolóng fàndiàn*). This building was
HOTEL   gifted to the nation in 1985 by Hong Kong shipping magnate YK Pao; however, following a renovation in 2002, it's clear that little, if any, love has been lavished on it since: a glitzy lobby gives way to some rather modestly attired rooms, while sluggish staff and an overpriced (albeit excellent) Indian restaurant offer little incentive to eat in (in a weird way a blessing, as this hotel is ideally perched on the doorstep of Sanlitun, the buzzing heart of Beijing's nightlife scene). **Pros:** near restaurants and nightlife; close to shopping. **Cons:** uninspired decor; lackluster service. $\[S\]$ *Rooms from: Y1018* ✉ *2 Gongren Tiyuchang Beilu, Chaoyang District* ☎ *010/6597–2299* ⊕ *www.zhaolonghotel.com.cn* ⤴ *270 rooms, 16 suites* ¶◯¶ *No meals* Ⓜ *Tuanjiehu* ✢ *H3.*

HAIDIAN DISTRICT 海淀区

The Haidian District, in the far northwestern corner of Beijing, is where you'll find the university district, the city zoo, and numerous parks. The main attractions here for visitors are the Summer Palace and Old Summer Palace.

$$$$ 🛏 **Aman at Summer Palace** (北京颐和安缦 *Běijīng yíhé ānmàn*). The
HOTEL   epitome of blissful indulgence, this luxury hotel belonging to the famed
Fodor'sChoice Aman chain is spread out across a series of carefully renovated ancient
★   Qing Dynasty courtyards—it even has its own private entrance to the Summer Palace—with guest rooms decorated in restful earth tones (lovely traditional wooden screens and bamboo blinds) and grounds that are positively stunning. **Pros:** right next to the Summer Palace; restaurant Naoki serves fine *kaiseki* (Japanese) cuisine; beautiful setting. **Cons:** very pricey; extremely far from downtown; too isolated for some. $\[S\]$ *Rooms from: Y3820* ✉ *1 Gongmen Qian St., Summer Palace, Haidian District* ☎ *010/5987–9999* ⊕ *www.amanresorts.com* ⤴ *51 rooms, 33 suites* ¶◯¶ *Breakfast* Ⓜ *Yiheyuan* ✢ *A1.*

$ 🛏 **Friendship Hotel** (友谊宾馆 *Yǒuyì bīnguǎn*). The name is telling, as the
HOTEL   hotel was built in 1954 to house foreigners, mostly Soviets, who had come to help rebuild the nation; these days, it relies more on tour groups

and those who need to be close to the university area, since it remains far removed from most sights; still, this place retains a certain glory as one of the largest garden-style hotels in Asia, even if many of its rooms could do with the gentle caress of modernity. **Pros:** a bit of history; inexpensive; gardens are attractive. **Cons:** far from the city center; needs updating; not much to do nearby (unless you're a student in search of cheap drinks). $ *Rooms from: Y538* ⊠ *1 Zhongguancun Nandajie, Haidian District* ☎ *010/6849–8888* ⊕ *www.bjfriendshiphotel.com* ⤇ *1,700 rooms, 200 suites* ⫶ *No meals* Ⓜ *Renmin University* ✢ *A1.*

$$ ⚏ **Shangri-La Hotel, Beijing** (北京香格里拉饭店 *Běijīng Xiānggélǐlā*
HOTEL *fàndiàn*). With its landscaped gardens, luxury mall, and the addition of a more modern wing, the Shangri-La is a slice of charm for business travelers and those who don't mind being far from the city center; the service is spot-on throughout, from the pristine rooms to the efficient check-in, while the dining options are excellent (the pick of the bunch being the superb, if rather expensive, S.T.A.Y, a French restaurant from the brain of Michelin-loved, three-starred chef Yannick Alléno). **Pros:** nice gardens; excellent amenities; great restaurants. **Cons:** far from the city center; no subway; older wing not as good as the newer one. $ *Rooms from: Y1180* ⊠ *29 Zizhuyuan Lu, Haidian District* ☎ *010/6841–2211* ⊕ *www.shangri-la.com* ⤇ *670 rooms, 32 suites* ⫶ *Breakfast* ✢ *A1.*

FAR-FLUNG BEIJING

$ ⚏ **CITIC Hotel Beijing Airport.** (北京国都大饭店 *Běijīng Guódū dàfàndiàn*)
HOTEL Formerly known as the Sino-Swiss Hotel, this hotel has lost some of its
FAMILY Swiss efficiency in the handover (the staff here can be a little disinterested) but it thrives on its location, just five minutes from the airport (shuttle buses run to and fro). Rooms are a bit hit and miss—insist on one from the recently renovated top floor. The hotel's Mongolian Gher restaurant is worth a try, with entertainment and barbecue all served up under the canvas of a traditional yurt. There's also a rather lovely outdoor pool surrounded by trees, shrubs, and colorful umbrellas. **Pros:** decent dining options; near the airport. **Cons:** far from the city's sights and attractions; still undergoing renovation in places. $ *Rooms from: Y768* ⊠ *9 Xiao Tianzhu Nanlu, Beijing Capital International Airport, Shunyi District* ☎ *010/6456–5588* ⊕ *www.citichotelbeijing.com* ⤇ *408 rooms, 35 suites* ⫶ *No meals* ✢ *H1.*

$$$ ⚏ **Commune by the Great Wall** (长城脚下的公社 *Chángchéng jiǎoxià de*
RENTAL *gōngshè*). An hour from Beijing, Commune offers a dash of modernity
FAMILY amid the wild hills and scrubland of Badaling; there's certainly plenty of space, so it's an ideal spot for families and small groups, with Bamboo House and Suitcase House providing the pick of its bespoke villas (designed by renowned Asian architects), although each lodging offers stunning views of the Great Wall, as well as private access. **Pros:** rustic environment; comfortable accommodation; near the Great Wall. **Cons:** you will likely share the villa with other guests; sketchy service; not in the city. $ *Rooms from: Y1800* ⊠ *Exit 20 at Shuiguan, Badaling Hwy., Yanqing County* ☎ *010/8118–1888* ⊕ *www.communebythegreatwall. com* ⤇ *40 houses* ⫶ *Breakfast.*

$$$$ ⌂ **Grandma's Place (Schoolhouse Hotels)** (奶奶家 *Nǎinaijiā*). This two-
RENTAL   bedroom rental cottage is part of a project by Jim Spears, a long-term
FAMILY   resident of Mutianyu, called Schoolhouse Hotels, which offers gorgeous
self-catering stays in remote villages around the Great Wall; Grandma's
Place is the pick of the bunch, created using stones salvaged from Ming
and Qing Dynasty structures, as well as massive beams from an old
village house, featuring a cozy, traditional *kang*—a brick bed heated
from beneath—and a very private fruit garden and terrace that provides jaw-dropping views of the Great Wall. **Pros:** a wonderfully rustic
getaway with modern comforts; views of the Great Wall; The Schoolhouse restaurant is nearby. **Cons:** guests need a car to reach the property; no hotel services; outside Beijing. $ *Rooms from: Y2600* ⊠ *The
Schoolhouse, 12 Mutianyu Village, Huairou District* ☎ *010/6162–6282*
⊕ *www.grandmasplaceatmutianyu.com* ⤳ *2 rooms, 8 homes* ⊟ *No
credit cards* ❘⊙❘ *Breakfast.*

$$ ⌂ **Hilton Beijing Capital Airport** (北京首都机场希尔顿酒店 *Běijīng*
HOTEL   *Shǒudū jīchǎng xī'ěrdùn jiǔdiàn*). The number of worthwhile options
next to Beijing's airport has flourished in recent years, and the arrival
of the Hilton, in particular, has added that brand's usual five-star stan-
dards to the mix. **Pros:** easy access to the airport; good choice of res-
taurants; slick rooms. **Cons:** far from Beijing sights; a pain to get a
taxi from; not really geared towards tourism. $ *Rooms from: Y1398*
⊠ *1 San Jing Rd., Beijing Capital International Airport (Terminal 3)*
☎ *010/6458–8888* ⊕ *beijingairport.hilton.com* ⤳ *265 rooms, 57 suites*
❘⊙❘ *No meals* Ⓜ *Airport Express* ⟟ *H1.*

$$$ ⌂ **Langham Place, Beijing Capital Airport** (北京首都机场朗豪酒店 *Běijīng*
HOTEL   *Shǒudū jīchǎng lǎngháo jiǔdiàn*). Airport hotels have a reputation
Fodor's Choice   for being boring—not so with Langham Place, a fun and funky spot
★   next to Terminal 3 that screams style while whispering quiet comfort.
Pros: airport hotels are rarely this stylish; fantastic service; good facilities. **Cons:** far from the city center; overly long corridors; can feel too
quiet at times. $ *Rooms from: Y1608* ⊠ *1 Er Jing Rd., Beijing Capital
International Airport (Terminal 3)* ☎ *010/6457–5555* ⊕ *beijingairport.
langhamplacehotels.com* ⤳ *372 rooms, 67 suites* ❘⊙❘ *No meals* Ⓜ *Airport Express* ⟟ *H1.*

$ ⌂ **Shan Li Retreats** (山里逸居 *Shānlǐ Yìjū*). Sometimes you need to get
RENTAL   out of the city, and that's especially true for those living in China's capi-
FAMILY   tal, constantly crowded by 20 million other such souls. **Pros:** a truly
Fodor's Choice   bucolic escape from the city; good hikes nearby; beautifully restored
★   village homes. **Cons:** a car is required to get there; guests need to take
their own food; not open all year round. $ *Rooms from: Y900* ⊠ *Hu-
angyankou Cun, Beizhuang, Miyun County* ☎ *138/1171–6326* ⊕ *www.
shanliretreats.com* ⤳ *5 homes* ⊙ *Closed Nov.–Mar.* ❘⊙❘ *No meals.*

5

SHOPPING

Updated by
Gareth Clark

Large markets and malls are the lifeblood of Beijing. They generally open from 9 am to 9 pm, though hours vary from shop to shop. If a stall looks closed (perhaps the lights are out or the owner is resting), don't give up. Many merchants conserve electricity or take catnaps when business is slack. Just knock or offer the greeting *"ni hao"* and, more often than not, the lights will flip on and you'll be invited to come in and take a look. Shops in malls have more regular hours and will only be closed on a few occasions throughout the year, such as Chunjie (Chinese New Year) and October's National Day Golden Week.

Major credit cards are accepted in pricier venues but cash is the driving force here. Thankfully, ATMs abound, however it's worth noting that before accepting any Mao-faced Y100 notes, most vendors will hold them up to the light, tug at the corners, and rub their fingers along the surface. Counterfeiting is becoming increasingly sophisticated in China and banks are reluctant to accept responsibility for ATMs that dispense fake notes.

Shops frequented by foreigners often have at least one employee with some degree of fluency in English. But cold, hard cash remains the international language. In many situations—whether or not there's a common tongue—the shop assistant will still whip out a calculator and, in the case of most markets, look at you to see what they think you'll cough up before typing in a starting price. You're then expected to punch in your offer (start at one third of their valuation). The clerk will usually come down a surprisingly large amount, and so on and so on. Remember that the terms *yuan*, *kuai*, and *RMB* are interchangeable and to reserve your bargaining skills for the markets; you might be in China, but try playing hardball on the cost of your Starbucks latte and you'll find yourself wearing it home.

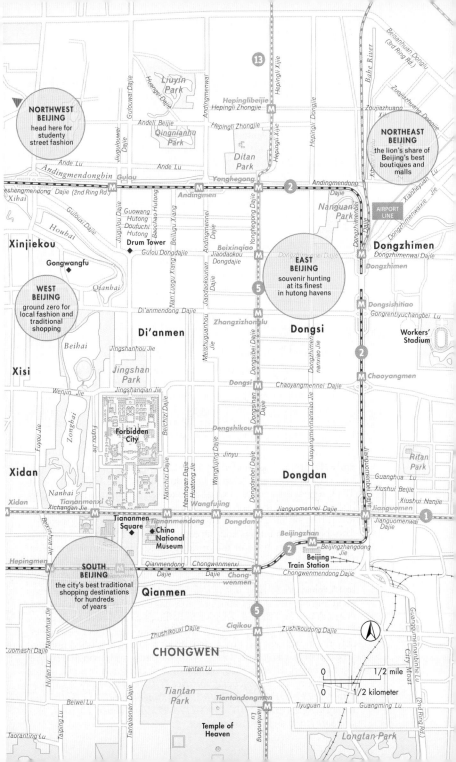

DONGCHENG DISTRICT 东城区

Strolling the old *hutong* (alleyways) of Dongcheng is one of the simplest pleasures to be found in Beijing. This area is rife with them and, despite a local council that's itching to modernize, many remain relatively unscratched. The effect has been the emergence of a thriving boutique culture. Nanluoguxiang was the first to blush at the attention of tourist dollars, with its bohemian mix of hipster-chic stores, silk shops, and old-China wares attracting huge interest; next to bask in the limelight was the quieter, but no less hip, Wudaoying Hutong, opposite Lama Temple. Today, both command high rents and almost as much attention as nearby Houhai. So, for some niche and truly unusual finds, try exploring some of the lesser-trod tributaries off Gulou Dongdajie, such as Baochao, Fangjia, and Beiluoguxiang instead.

ART AND ANTIQUES

Beijing Postcards (北京卡片 *Běijīng Kǎpiàn*). When historians Simon Gjeroe and Lars Ulrik Thom had the idea of turning their horde of old-Beijing photographs into a shop, they struck gold. Postcards, calendars, large prints, and antique maps dating from 1890 detail a way of life long since lost. Prices start at Y50; plus check out the website for details on talks and walking tours—some of the best and most informative in the city. ⊠ *85–1 Nanluoguxiang, Dongcheng District* ☎ *135/0109–8794* ⊕ *www.bjpostcards.com* ⊗ *Daily 10–10* Ⓜ *Zhangzizhonglu.*

⚠ **Deception is the only real "art" practiced by the charming "art students" who will approach you at tourist destinations and invite you to their college's art show. The artworks are, in fact, usually mass-produced copies. If you want to support Beijing's burgeoning art scene, explore the galleries of Dashanzi (798 Art District), Caochangdi, or drop by one of the galleries listed in Chapter 6.**

BOUTIQUES

Brand Nü (Brand 女, *Brand nü*). On the chic, hipster-splattered Wudaoying Hutong lies former "charity boutique" Brand Nü. At the tail end of 2012, it underwent something of a makeover; now its abiding theme is upcycling, with a focus on clothes, bags, and jewelry. As you'd expect, it can be a bit hit-and-miss, and the emphasis on "fashion" incorporates both the ambitious and the eccentric alike. The prices aren't too steep and a percentage of the profits goes to helping rural women in China. ⊠ *61 Wudaoying Hutong, Dongcheng District* ☎ *150/1115–3421* ⊕ *www.brandnuproject.com* ⊗ *Tues.–Sun. 10–10* Ⓜ *Yonghegong.*

Lost & Found (失物招领 *Shīwù zhāolǐng*). Tucked down a historic tree-lined hutong, this design boutique now has a second branch just a few doors down. Stylish and sensitive to Beijing's past, American designer Paul Gelinas and Chinese partner Xiao Miao salvage objects—whether they're chipped enamel street signs from a long-demolished hutong, a barbershop chair, or a 1950s Shanghai fan—and lovingly remove the dirt before offering them on sale in their treasure trove of a store. ⊠ *42 Guozijian, Dongcheng District* ☎ *010/6401–1855* ⊗ *Mon.–Thurs. 10:30–8, Fri.–Sun. 10:30–8:30* Ⓜ *Yonghegong* ⊠ *57 Guozijian, Dongcheng District* ☎ *010/6400–1174* ⊗ *Mon.–Thurs. 10:30–8, Fri. and Sat. 10:30–8:30* Ⓜ *Yonghegong.*

One of the many tea shops in Beijing

Mega Mega Vintage. In Gulou, the only real currency is "vintage"—it's the Krugerrand of Beijing fashion. Fresh-from-the-factory retro T-shirts have their place, but nothing can replace leafing through the racks at Mega Mega Vintage in search of gold. Distressed denim, classic tees, leather bags, and old-style dresses crown a collection that rises high above the "frumpery" peddled by countless copycat boutiques. ⊠ *241 Gulou Dongdajie, Dongcheng District* ☎ *010/8404–5637* ⊕ *www.douban.com/group/mmvintage/* ⊘ *Daily 2–9:30* Ⓜ *Beixinqiao.*

Plastered T-Shirts (Plastered T-恤, *Plastered T-xù*). Now over 15 years old, this store—originally called Plastered 8—has weathered well, with a second branch now open in 798 Art District. Stop here for T-shirt designs that capture the nostalgic days of Old Peking, as well as posters, notebooks, and traditional thermoses. Fun and kitschy, everything costs around Y100. This is a must-visit for anyone in search of that rarest of all things: a souvenir you'd actually use when home. ⊠ *61 Nanluoguxiang Hutong, Dongcheng District* ☎ *010/6407–8425* ⊕ *www.plasteredtshirts.com* ⊘ *Daily 9:30 am–11 pm* Ⓜ *Zhangzizhonglu* ⊠ *798 Art Zone, 4 Jiuxianqiao Lu, Chaoyang District* ☎ *136/7137–9896* ⊕ *www.plasteredtshirts.com* ⊘ *Daily 9:30 am–11 pm.*

Woo (妩 *Wǔ*). The gorgeous scarves displayed in the windows here lure in passersby with their bright colors and luxurious fabrics. In contrast to those of the vendors in the markets, the cashmere, silk, and bamboo used here are 100% natural. The design and construction are comparable to top Italian designers, while the prices are much more affordable. ⊠ *110/1 Nanluoguxiang, Dongcheng District* ☎ *010/6400–5395* ⊘ *Daily 9:30 am–10 pm* Ⓜ *Zhangzizhonglu.*

Wuhao Curated Shop (五号 *Wǔhào*). Part fashion gallery, part shop, all chic! Seasonal new designs are scattered in eccentric installations throughout this beautifully converted *siheyuan* (courtyard). Browsing is a pleasure, with international designers across the fields of art, fashion, jewelry, and ceramics on display. Thankfully, guests are encouraged to explore, although be warned: The prices are quite steep. ⊠ *35 Mao'er Hutong, Dongcheng District* ☎ *189/1135–5035* ⊕ *www. wuhaoonline.com* ⊘ *Wed.–Sun. 2–8* Ⓜ *Zhangzizhonglu.*

Zi'an Print & Graphics (子安版画 *Zǐ ān Bānhuà*). Exquisite Chinese and European prints (from Y50) decorate the shelves of this adorable little store on Fangjia Hutong. Owner Zi'an is an avid collector of graphic art, engravings, and *ex libris* (the small prints traditionally pasted into the front of books). Many of the works on display here date from the 19th century onwards and nearly all have links to China's past, depicting everything from life during the Three Kingdoms period to the Opium Wars. ⊠ *30 Fangjia Hutong, Dongcheng District* ☎ *131/4649–3917* ⊘ *Daily noon–6* Ⓜ *Beixinqiao.*

MALLS AND DEPARTMENT STORES

Malls at Oriental Plaza (东方广场购物中心 *Dōngfāng guǎngchǎng*). This enormous shopping complex originates at the southern end of Wangfujing where it meets Chang'an Jie and stretches a city block east to Dongdan Dajie. It's a true city within a city and certainly geared toward higher budgets. Some of the more upscale shops include Kenzo and Armani Exchange, while ladies should check out the boutique from iconic Chinese-American designer Anna Sui for clothes, accessories, and make-up. ⊠ *1 Dongchang'an Jie, Dongcheng District* ☎ *010/8518– 6363* ⊘ *Daily 10–10* Ⓜ *Wangfujing.*

MARKETS

FAMILY **Hongqiao Market** (红桥市场 *Hóngqiáo shìchǎng*). Hongqiao, or Pearl Market, is full of tourist goods, knockoff handbags, and cheap watches, but it's best known for its three stories of pearls. Freshwater, seawater, black, pink, white: The quantity is overwhelming and quality varies by stall. Prices also range wildly, though the cheapest items are often fakes. Fanghua Pearls (No. 4318), on the fourth floor, displays quality necklaces and earrings, with photos of Hillary Clinton and Margaret Thatcher shopping there to prove it. Fanghua has a second store devoted to fine jade and precious stones. Stallholders here can be pushy, but accept their haggling in the gamelike spirit it's intended. Or wear headphones to drown them out. ⊠ *9 Tiantan Lu, east of the northern entrance to Temple of Heaven, Dongcheng District* ☎ *010/6711–7630* ⊘ *Daily 9:30–7* Ⓜ *Tiantan Dongmen.*

SHOES

Pi'erman Maoyi (皮尔曼贸易公司 *Pí'ěrmàn màoyì gōngsī*). If you've always wanted to have shoes made just for you, this traditional cobbler is highly rated by Beijing expats. If you're in the city for a bit longer—he'll take two weeks—you can have a pair of shoes or boots made for very reasonable prices. Bring in a photo or a pair that you wish to copy, as the cobbler doesn't speak much English. ⊠ *37 Gulou Dongdajie, Dongcheng District* ☎ *010/6404–1406* ⊘ *Daily 10–10.*

⚠ Fakes abound—everything from jade, cashmere, pashminas, silk, and leather to handbags, antiques, and Calvin Klein underwear. Many foreign tourists and local people buy fakes, but keep in mind that the low price generally reflects poor quality, often in ways that aren't immediately apparent. Never buy fake beauty products or perfumes, as these can often cause serious skin irritation, and reserve your big purchases for accredited shops or merchants who can prove the quality of their product. Some countries limit the number of knockoffs you can bring back through customs, so don't go overboard on the handbags or DVDs. If you're buying authentic antiques, just ask the vender for a receipt (or "fapiao" 发票), embossed with an official red seal.

SILK AND FABRICS

Daxin Textiles Co. (大新纺织 *Dàxīn fǎngzhī*). For a wide selection of all types of fabrics, from worsted wools to sensuous silks, head to this shop. It's best to buy the material here and find a tailor elsewhere, as sewing standards can be shoddy. ⊠ *Northeast corner of Dongsi, Dongcheng District* ☎ *010/6403–2378* ⊘ *Daily 9–7:30* Ⓜ *Dongsi.*

XICHENG DISTRICT 西城区

Xicheng is still perhaps best known as the home of the Forbidden City, but it also has a few choice shopping areas. Located to the south of Tiananmen Square, Qianmen might not rank high on the authenticity scale, thanks to a pre-Olympics renovation, but it still offers plenty of color (as well as brand names), while a ride on the tram down what is one of the city's oldest shopping streets is a must. To the east lies the similarly spruced-up Dashilar area, a series of shiny *hutong* (alleyways) that are a bit too clean to be real but house old-school Chinese medicine stores, silk shops, and "ancient" souvenirs aplenty.

Head northwest of the Forbidden City and you'll find Beijing's lake district of Shichahai, comprising Qianhai, Xihai, and Houhai. The latter is surrounded by a morass of hutong that include Yandai Xiejie, a sidestreet packed with stores and hawkers pushing jewelry, clothes, Mao-shape oddities, and plenty of stuff you don't need but simply can't resist. Meanwhile, farther west of here lies Xidan, a giant consumer playground swarming with high-rise malls as well as basement markets stuffed with knockoffs and obscure Chinese brands. Joy City is probably the best (certainly the largest) shopping center here, although a new Galeries Lafayette was opening at the time of going to press. Alternatively, elbow past both to discover some cheap chic clustered along **Xidan Beidajie,** just north of the Xidan subway stop.

CHINESE MEDICINE

Tongrentang (同仁堂 *Tóngréntáng*). A first-time consultation with a Chinese doctor can feel a bit like a reading with a fortune-teller. With one test of the pulse, many traditional Chinese doctors can describe the patient's medical history and diagnose current maladies. China's most famous traditional Chinese medicine shop, Tongrentang, is one of the oldest establishments on Dashilan Street. Hushed and dimly illuminated, this 300-year-old shop even smells healthy. Browse the glass displays of deer antlers and pickled snakes, dried seahorses and frogs, and delicate tangles of roots with precious price tags of Y48,000. If you don't speak Chinese and wish to have a consultation with a doctor, consider bringing along a translator. ⊠ *24 Dashilan, Qianmen, Exit C, Xicheng District* ☎ *010/6701–5895* ◷ *Daily 8:30–5* Ⓜ *Qianmen.*

⚠ Chinese medicine is wonderful, but not when practiced by lab-coated "doctors" sitting behind a card table on the street corner. If you're seeking Chinese medical treatment, visit a local hospital, Tongrentang medicine shop, or ask your hotel concierge for a legitimate recommendation.

> ### THE ART OF THE HAGGLE
>
> If you have an idea of the value of what you're buying, start at two-thirds of that amount and slowly build up to it. Should you allow the stall-owner to name an amount, they'll open negotiations at an outrageous figure (particularly in Yashow). If so, let them come down a bit in price before lowballing them with an equally opportunistic sum, and start from there. Pretend to walk away if negotiations are stalling, but the bottom line is: pay what you think is fair.

MALLS AND DEPARTMENT STORES

Seasons Place (金融街购物中心 *Jīnróngjiē gòuwùzhōngxīn*). This ritzy mall is farther west in Beijing's Financial Street area. If you're staying at one of the business hotels nearby, Seasons Place will fulfill your shopping needs—as long as you're not on a budget. Designer labels like Louis Vuitton, Gucci, and Versace are here, as well as the Beijing branch of Hong Kong's fab department store, Lane Crawford. ⊠ *2 Jinrong Jie, Xicheng District* ☎ *010/6622–0088* ⊕ *www.seasonsplace.com* ◷ *Daily 11–8:30* Ⓜ *Fuxingmen.*

CHAOYANG DISTRICT 朝阳区

The vast Chaoyang District is *the* area to shop in Beijing, although given it's the size of most cities, that is somewhat understating things. It stretches all the way from downtown to the airport, encompassing 798 Art District, Sanlitun, and the Central Business District areas. But its consumer joys lie mainly in its collection of labyrinthine markets and ever-more futuristic malls, with a smattering of boutiques nestled in between. Indeed, Chaoyang is seemingly in the midst of an almighty game of architectural "chicken" with regard to its shopping centers. The new Galaxy SOHO (unfinished at the time of writing) and Parkview Green are just some of the more breathtaking examples of the many cathedrals to consumerism that dot the new-look China.

The Ultimate Shopping Tour

Day 1 (weekend): Can't sleep from jet lag? No worries. Rise before dawn and join the hordes at **Panjiayuan** antiques market for Beijing Shopping 101. Spend some time on a reconnaissance tour of its vast collection of stores before making any purchases. Bags in tow, head directly across the street to furniture market **Zhaojia Chaowai** and hit the fourth floor for ceramics and more old-China trinkets. Next, direct a pedicab driver to **Beijing Curio City** for all manner of kitsch memorabilia. From here, take a cab to haggle hard for knockoffs and cheap silk garments at **Silk Alley**. Have lunch, then make the trek to **Qianmen and Dashilan** for a walk down old streets newly renovated for modern shoppers. Travel their length on foot (or take the Qianmen tram); by this time of day its shops will begin to close and it's time to head back to your hotel.

Day 2: Kick off the day by sampling tea from the seemingly infinite number of vendors pedaling their wares on Maliandao **Tea Street**. Buy clay or porcelain service sets and loose tea leaves galore. Then take a cab to Qing Dynasty–style shopping street **Liulichang** for calligraphy, scrolls,

paintings, and more. Linger here a while before returning to modernity and heading to **Wangfujing**. Then, if its mix of malls, snack shops, and souvenir stalls doesn't wipe you out, take a cab to **Hongqiao Market** for a pearl-shopping spree.

Day 3: Start the day in the heart of Beijing's lake district on the picturesque **Yandai Xiejie**, beside Houhai. Ethnic garments and Communist "maorabilia" litter its stores. Afterwards, stretch your legs along the nearby, boutique-packed Gulou Dongdajie until you reach Nanluoguxiang, the popular shopping hutong. Affordable local designs, cute and ironic T-shirts, and gorgeous scarves abound. After one lap, continue east until you reach Yonghegong Dajie; here, you'll find the quieter Guozijian and Wudaoying hutong, and plenty more stores to sate your lust for trinkets. From here, grab a taxi and hit Sanlitun for a visit to **Yashow Market** and, next door, **Sanlitun Village**. Designer boutiques and chic malls scatter what used to be just a bar district. Shop, shop, shop, and then drop—wherever you land, a waiter will appear to offer you an ice-cold *jianyi kele* (Diet Coke) or Tsingtao beer.

Elsewhere, shopping highlights include Panjiayuan Antique Market, Silk Alley, the indie stores of 798, and the local capitalist's mecca that is Sanlitun Village.

BOOKS

The Bookworm (书虫 *Shūchóng*). Book lovers, hipsters, and aspiring poets take note: This lending library and bookstore offers a spacious second-story reading room with a full café and bar. All are welcome to browse: the magazine and new-books section are a stupendous sight for English-starved travelers. The store frequently hosts poetry readings and lectures, as well as an annual literary festival in March. ⊠ *4 Sanlitun Nan lu, set back slightly in an alley 165 feet south of the Gongti Beilu junction, Chaoyang District* ☎ *010/6586–9507* ⊕ *www. beijingbookworm.com* ⊙ *Daily 9 am–midnight* Ⓜ *Tuanjiehu.*

Crowded souvenir stalls on the Dashilan Shopping Street

Timezone 8 (东八时区 *Dōngbā Shíqū*). This bookstore-café is a welcome pit stop for those with brows higher than the average. A nice selection of Belgian brews and a recently added sushi bar makes it a lunchtime gem, but literati should flock here for its overflowing collection of up-to-date local art and fashion books, as well as magazines and monographs in both English and Mandarin. ⊠ *798 Art District, 4 Jiuxianqiao Lu, Chaoyang District* ☎ *010/5978–9917* ⊕ *www.timezone8.com.cn* ⊙ *Daily 8:30 am–2 am.*

COMPUTERS AND ELECTRONICS

Beijing Huashiweiye CD DVD Shop (北京华实伟业CD DVD商店 *Běijīng Huáshíwěiyè CD DVD Shāngdiàn*). Easily the most reliable DVD store in the city, this store has plenty of oldies as well as the usual "just released in cinemas" Hollywood blockbusters. Occasionally, the police raid it (which shouldn't be too arduous for them, as it's only a 10-second walk from the nearest station); in which case you'll find largely bare shelves with nothing but the odd black-and-white classic on display. But normal service is usually resumed pretty fast. DVDs start at Y10 each; box sets range from Y60 to Y500. ⊠ *Shop 3, E. Yashow Market, 58 Gongti Beilu, Chaoyang District* ☎ *010/6417–8633* ⊙ *Daily 9 am–10 pm* Ⓜ *Tuanjiehu.*

Buy Now Computer Shopping Mall (百脑会电脑广场 *Bǎinǎohuìdiànnǎo guǎngchǎng*). Buy Now (or Bainaohui) is home to hundreds of stalls shilling laptops, PCs, iPods, speakers, phones, and just about any electrical malarkey you can imagine. However, both real and knockoff goods tend to be mixed in with each other, so choose wisely. Some stall owners will bargain, others won't, but it's always worth a try. ⊠ *10 Chaoyangmenwai Dajie, Chaoyang District* ☎ *010/6599–5912* ⊙ *Daily 9–8* Ⓜ *Hujialou.*

EXPLORING TEA STREET

Tea Street (马连道茶叶批发市场 *Mǎliándào cháyè chéng*). Maliandao hosts the ultimate tea party every day of the week. Literally a thousand tea shops perfume the air of this prime tea-shopping district, west of the city center. Midway down this near-mile-long strip looms the **Teajoy Market**, the Silk Alley of teas. Unless you're an absolute fanatic, it's best to visit a handful of individual shops, crashing tea parties wherever you go. Vendors will invite you to sit down in heavy wooden chairs to nibble on pumpkin seeds and sample their large selections of black, white, oolong, jasmine, and chrysanthemum teas. Prices range from a few kuai for a decorative container of loose green tea to thousands of yuan for an elaborate gift set. Tea Street is also the place to stock up on clay and porcelain teapots and service sets. Green and flower teas are sold loose; black teas are sold pressed into disks and wrapped in natural-colored paper. Despite the huge selection of drinking vessels available, you'll find that most locals prefer to drink their tea from a recycled glass jar. ✉ *Located near Guanganmen Waidajie, Xicheng District* ⏱ *Times vary* Ⓜ *Xuanwumen.*

MARKETS

Baoguosi Temple Antiques Market (报国寺收藏品市场 *Bàoguósì shōucángpǐn shìchǎng*). This little-known market, atmospherically set in the picturesque grounds of Baoguosi Temple, is a smaller, more manageable version of Panjiayuan. It sees very few foreigners and no one will speak English, but armed with a calculator, stallholders will get their point across. As well as memorabilia from the Cultural Revolution, look out for stalls that sell original photos, ranging from early-20th-century snaps to people posing with their first TVs in the 1970s. ✉ *Guanganmennei Dajie, Xicheng District* ☎ *010/8223–4583* ⏱ *Daily 9–4:30.*

SILK AND FABRICS

Beijing Silk Shop (北京谦祥益丝绸商店 *Běijīng qiānxiángyì sīchóu shāngdiàn*). Since 1830, the Beijing Silk Shop has been supplying the city with quality bolts of silks and fabrics. There are tailors on-site to whip up something special and the second floor has ready-to-wear clothing. To reach the shop, walk all the way down Dashilan then head directly onto Dashilan West Street. ✉ *50 Dashilan Xijie, Xicheng District* ☎ *010/6301–6658* ⏱ *Daily 9–7:30* Ⓜ *Qianmen.*

TOYS

Three Stones Kite Store (三石斋风筝店 *Sān dàn zhāifēng zhēngdiàn*). For something more traditional, go fly a kite. But not the run-of-the-mill type you see anywhere. Here, for three generations, the same family has hand-painted butterflies and birds onto bamboo frames to delight adults and children alike. ✉ *25 Di'anmen Xidajie, Xicheng District* ☎ *010/8404–4505* ⏱ *Daily 10–5* Ⓜ *Zhangzizhonglu.*

5

FASHION DESIGNERS AND BOUTIQUES

Candy & Caviar. Chinese-American fashion designer Candy Lin owns and operates this gem. In just two years her label has attracted a celebrity following, including Will.i.am from the Black Eyed Peas and Taiwanese superstar Jay Chou. From her peaceful and professional store, she designs for both men and women. Expect lots of sharp tailoring, stark colors, and relatively high prices. ✉ *921, Bldg. 16, China Central Place, 89 Jianguo Lu, Chaoyang District* ☎ *010/5203–6581* ⊕ *www. candyandcaviar.com* ⏱ *Weekdays 9–5:30* Ⓜ *Guomao.*

Dong Liang Studio (栋梁工作室 *Dòngliáng Gōngzuòshì*). Prices begin at steep and climb to positively perpendicular at this boutique. A visit here is key for anyone wanting to get under the skin of the local fashion scene. Its stock reads like a who's who of rising Chinese designers, including clothes by Vega Wang, He Yan, Manchit Au, and more. ✉ *Shop 102, Bldg. 2, Central Park, 6 Chaoyangmenwai Dajie, Chaoyang District* ☎ *010/8404–7648* ⏱ *Daily 11–9* Ⓜ *Yong'anli.*

Fei Space (飞 *Fēi*). In the 798 Art District, Fei Space more than holds its own against its neighboring galleries with a funky interior design and eclectic selection of clothes and housewares. Some of the fashion brands stocked (including the first foray into China by Topshop and Topman) are unique to the store, and all are uniformly stylish—and expensive. ✉ *B-01, 798 Art District, 4 Jiuxiangqiao Lu, Chaoyang District* ☎ *010/5978–9580* ⏱ *Daily noon–7.*

Heyan'er (何燕服装店 *Héyán fúzhuāng diàn*). He Yan's design philosophy is stated in her label: "*bu yan bu yu*" or "no talking." Her linen and cotton tunics and collarless jackets speak for themselves. From earth tones to aubergine hues and peacock patterns, He Yan's designs echo traditional Tibetan styles. ✉ *15–2 Gongti Beilu, Chaoyang District* ☎ *010/6415–9442* ⏱ *Daily 9:30–9:30* Ⓜ *Dongsishitiao* ✉ *Holiday Inn Lido, 6 Fangyuan Xilu* ☎ *010/6437–6854* ⏱ *Daily 9:30–9:30* Ⓜ *Sanyuanqiao.*

Middle Kingdom Design Suite. This private store, the brainchild of the niece and nephew of acclaimed architect I.M. Pei (of Louvre pyramid fame), is a secret gem packed with handmade regional Chinese art, jewelry, rugs, and gifts. Prices start from around Y200 and rise quite steeply. Remember: visits are by appointment only, so book a time and make the most of it. ✉ *Suite 21, 2nd floor, Bldg. 8, Qi Jia Yuan Diplomatic Residence Compound, 9 Jianguomenwai Dajie, Chaoyang District* ☎ *138/1063–3376* ⏱ *By appointment only* Ⓜ *Yong'anli.*

UCCA Design Store (东八时区 *UCCA Shèjì Shāngdiàn*). The 798 Art District is home to a burgeoning collection of housewares, fashion, and design shops. The most innovative of these, however, is an offshoot of the Ullens Center for Contemporary Art (UCCA), located just one door down from the gallery. Clothes, posters, ingenious knickknacks, and artist Sui Jianguo's iconic (if pricey) "Made in China" plastic dinosaurs make it a must-visit for anyone in the area. ✉ *798 Art District, 4 Jiuxianqiao Lu, Chaoyang District* ☎ *010/5780–0228* ⊕ *ucca.org.cn/ en/uccastore* ⏱ *Daily 10–6:30.*

CLOSE UP

You Can Judge a Pearl by Its Luster

All the baubles of Beijing could be strung together and wrapped around the Earth 10 times over—or so it seems with Beijing's abundance of pearl vendors. It's mind-boggling to imagine how many oysters it would take to produce all those natural pearls. But, of course, not all are real: some are cultured and others fake.

The attentive clerks in most shops are eager to prove their product quality. Be wary of salespeople who don't demonstrate, with an eager and detailed pitch, why one strand is superior to another. Keep in mind the following tips as you judge whether that gorgeous strand is destined to be mere costume jewelry or the next family heirloom.

■ **Color:** Natural pearls have an even hue, whereas dyed pearls vary in coloration.

■ **Good Luster:** Pick only the shiniest apples in the bunch. Pearls should have a healthy glow.

■ **Shape:** The strand should be able to roll smoothly across a flat surface without wobbling.

■ **Blemishes:** We hate them on our faces and we hate them on our pearls.

■ **Size:** Smaller pearls are obviously less expensive than larger ones, but don't get trapped into paying more for larger poor-quality pearls just because they're heftier.

The cost of pearls varies widely. A quality strand will generally run around US$50 to $200, but it's possible to buy good-looking but lower-quality pearls much more cheaply. As with any purchase, choose those pearls you adore most, and only pay as much as you think they warrant. After all, we could all use an extra strand of good-looking fakes. Also, if you plan on making multiple purchases and you have time to return to the same shop, go ahead and establish a "friendship" with one key clerk. Each time you return, or bring a friend, the price will miraculously drop.

HOUSEWARES

Spin (旋 *Xuán*). This trendy ceramics shop near the 798 Art District features the work of several talented Shanghainese designers who take traditional plates, vases, and vessels and give them a unique and delightful twist. Prices are surprisingly inexpensive. ✉ *6 Fangyuan Xilu, Lido, Chaoyang District* ☎ *010/6437–8649* ⊙ *Daily 10–7.*

JEWELRY

Shard Box Store (慎 德阁 *Shèndégé*). The signature collection here includes small to midsize jewelry boxes fashioned from the broken shards of antique porcelain. Supposedly the shards were collected during the Cultural Revolution, when scores of antique porcelain pieces were smashed in accordance with the law. Birds, trees, pining lovers, and dragons decorate these affordable ceramic-and-metal containers, which range from Y20 to Y200. ✉ *1 Ritan Beilu, Chaoyang District* ☎ *010/8561–3712* ⊙ *Daily 10–10* Ⓜ *Yong'anli* ✉ *2 Jiangtai Lu, near the Holiday Inn Lido* ☎ *010/5135–7638* ⊙ *Daily 10–10* Ⓜ *Sanyuanqiao.*

MALLS AND DEPARTMENT STORES

China World Mall (国贸商城 *Guómào Shāngchéng*). Nothing embodies Beijing's lusty embrace of luxury goods quite like China World Mall. Home to a giant branch of Hong Kong designer emporium Joyce, the average spend at this mall runs into millions of yuan. However, for smaller budgets, the cinema is decent, there's a good ice rink for kids, and Page One is the most comprehensive English-language bookstore in the city. ✉ *1 Jianguomenwai Dajie, Chaoyang District* ☎ *010/8535–1698* 🌐 *www.cwtc.com/cwtc/mall/emall.jsp* ☯ *Daily 10 am–9:30 pm* Ⓜ *Guomao.*

Indigo (颐堤港 *Yítígǎng*). This new complex, located just on the edge of Dashanzi (798 Art District), is among a raft of recent additions to the city's now impressive litany of "super malls." Light, airy, and currently still finding its feet, new stores will open over the course of 2013, but at the time of going to press the likes of GAP, H&M, Sephora and a branch of the excellent Page One bookstore were the main draws. The indoor garden isn't much to write home about, but its gigantic outdoor park area will be when it's finished. ✉ *18 Jiuxianqiao Lu, Chaoyang District* ☎ *010/8426–0898* 🌐 *www.indigobeijing.com* ☯ *Daily 10–10.*

Parkview Green, Fangcaodi (芳草地 *Fāngcǎodì*). Scattered in and around this giant, green pyramid-shape "biodome" is a boutique hotel, a mall that doubles as a walk-through gallery, and (most bizarrely of all) the largest private collection of Salvador Dali works on display outside Spain. For shoppers, stores by designers Stella McCartney and Roberto Cavalli rub shoulders with the likes of GAP; meanwhile a branch of the world-famous Taiwanese dumpling-slingers Din Tai Fung is always worth a visit. Even if designer knickknacks aren't your thing, stopping by just to gawp at the sheer Charles Foster Kane-esque hubris of it all comes highly recommended. ✉ *9 Dongdaqiao Lu, Chaoyang District* ☎ *010/5690–7000* 🌐 *www.parkviewgreen.com/eng* ☯ *Daily 10–8* Ⓜ *Yong'anli.*

The Place (世贸天阶 *Shìmào tiān jiē*). Shopping-wise you'll find all the usual suspects here—Zara, JNBY, et al—even if a lack of good dining spots ensures that you won't linger too long. However, visitors largely flock to The Place to witness its eye-wateringly gigantic LED skyscreen, which bursts into life every hour and shows some pretty stunning mini-movies (the meteorites are the best!) before lapsing back into screensavers and commercials. ✉ *9 Guanghua Lu, Chaoyang District* ☎ *010/6587–1188* 🌐 *www.theplace.cn* ☯ *Daily 10–10* Ⓜ *Jintaixizhao.*

Sanlitun Village (三里屯 Village *Sānlìtùn Village*). The default destination for all expats, this fashionable complex, split into two zones, is the place to shop thanks to its great range of stores at all price points, cool architecture, and fun people-watching. Village South houses the biggest Adidas store in the world, as well as branches of Uniqlo, Steve Madden, I.T, and the busiest Apple store you'll *ever* see. The newer and more exclusive Village North has high-end designer stores such as Alexander Wang and Emporio Armani. There's also a good cinema and some great restaurants and bars. ✉ *19 Sanlitun Jie, Chaoyang District* ☎ *010/6417–6110* 🌐 *www.sanlitunvillage.com* ☯ *Daily 10–10* Ⓜ *Tuanjiehu.*

Inspecting the goods at the Panjiayuan Antiques Market

Solana Lifestyle Shopping Park (蓝色港湾 *Lánsè Gǎngwān*). This California-style, outdoor shopping complex has a rather enviable location, nestled alongside Chaoyang Park, Asia's biggest man-made green zone. It's certainly something Solana's impressive lakeside strip of wine bars and terraces takes full advantage of. As to the shopping, it pulls in a decent list of names, from H&M, Zara, and Stradivarius to branches of Muji and Demeter's always-interesting Scent Library—"wet dirt" fragrance anybody? ✉ *6 Chaoyang Gongyuan Lu, Chaoyang District* ☎ *010/5905–6663* ⊕ *www.solana.com.cn* ☽ *Daily 10–10* Ⓜ *Tuanjiehu.*

MARKETS

Beijing Curio City (北京古玩城 *Běijīng gǔwán chéng*). This complex has four stories of kitsch and curio shops and a few furniture vendors, some of whom may be selling authentic antiques. Prices are high (driven up by free-spending tour groups), so don't be afraid to lowball your offer. Ignore the overpriced duty-free shop at the entrance. ✉ *21 Dongsanhuan Nan Lu, Chaoyang District* ☎ *010/6774–7711* ☽ *Daily 10–6* Ⓜ *Jinsong.*

Fodor's Choice ★ **Panjiayuan Antiques Market** (潘家园市场 *Pānjiāyuán shìchǎng*). Every day the sun rises over thousands of pilgrims rummaging in search of antiques and the most curious of curios, though the biggest numbers of buyers and sellers is on the weekends. With more than 3,000 vendors crowding an area of 160,000 feet, not every jade bracelet, oracle bone, porcelain vase, and ancient screen is authentic, but most people are here for the reproductions anyway. Behold the bounty: watercolors, scrolls, calligraphy, Buddhist statues, opera costumes, old Russian SLR cameras, curio cabinets, Tibetan jewelry, tiny satin lotus-flower

shoes, rotary telephones, jade dragons, antique mirrors, and infinite
displays of "maorabilia." If you're
buying jade, first observe the Chinese customers, how they hold a
flashlight to the milky-green stone
to test its authenticity. As with all
Chinese markets, bargain with a
vengeance, as many vendors inflate
their prices astronomically for *wai-
guoren* ("outside country people").
A strip of enclosed stores forms a
perimeter around the surprisingly
orderly rows of open-air stalls.
Check out photographer Xuesong
Kang and his **Da Kang** store (No.
63-B) for some fascinating black-
and-white snaps of Beijing city life
dating from the start of the 20th

> ## A QUICK CHAT ABOUT CURRENCY
>
> The official currency unit of China
> is the yuan or renminbi (literally,
> "the people's currency"). Infor-
> mally, the main unit of currency
> is called kuai (using "kuai" is the
> equivalent of saying a "buck" in
> the United States). On price tags,
> renminbi is usually written in its
> abbreviated form, RMB, and yuan
> is abbreviated as ¥.
>
> 1 RMB = 1 Renminbi = 1 Yuan
> = 1 Kuai = 10 Jiao = 10 Mao =
> 100 Fen

century up to the present day. Also be sure to stop by the **Bei Zhong Bao
Pearl Shop** (No. 7-A) for medium-quality freshwater pearls cultivated
by the Hu family. Also here are a sculpture zoo, a book bazaar, repro-
duction-furniture shops, and an area stashing propaganda posters and
Communist literature. ⊠ *18 Huaweili, Panjiayuan Lu, Chaoyang District* ☎ *010/6774–1869* ☉ *Weekdays 8:30–6, weekends 6–6* Ⓜ *Jinsong.*

Ritan Office Building Market (日坛商务楼 *Rìtán shāngwù loú*). Don't let
the gray-brick and red-trim exterior fool you: The three stories of offices
inside the Ritan Building are strung with racks of brand-name dresses
and funky-fab accessories. Unlike the tacky variations made on knockoff labels and sold in less expensive markets, the collections here, for the
most part, retain their integrity—perhaps because many of these dresses
are actually designer labels. They're also more expensive and bargaining is discouraged. The **Ruby Cashmere Shop** (No. 1009) sells genuine
cashmere sweaters and scarves at reduced prices, while **Fandini** (No.
1011) serves up a modern selection of typically "street" womenswear.
⊠ *15A Guanghua Lu, just east of the south entrance to Ritan Park,
opposite the Vietnam Embassy, Chaoyang District* ☎ *010/6502–1528*
☉ *Daily 10–7* Ⓜ *Yong'anli.*

Fodor's Choice **Silk Alley Market** (秀水市场 *Xiùshuǐ shìchǎng*). Once a delightfully cha-
★ otic sprawl of hundreds of outdoor stalls, the Silk Alley Market is now
corralled inside a huge shopping center. The government has been cracking down on an increasing number of certain copycat items, so if you
don't see that knockoff Louis Vuitton purse or Chanel jacket, just ask;
it might magically appear from a stack of plastic storage bins. You'll
face no dearth, however, of knockoff Pumas and Nikes or Paul Smith
polos. Chinese handicrafts and children's clothes are on the top floors.
Bargain relentlessly, check carefully the quality of each intended purchase, and guard your wallet against pickpockets. ⊠ *8 Xiushui Dongjie,
Chaoyang District* ☎ *010/5169–9003* ⊕ *www.xiushui.com.cn* ☉ *Daily
9:30–9* Ⓜ *Yong'anli.*

Yashow Market (雅秀市场 *Yǎxiù shìchǎng*). Especially popular among younger Western shoppers, Yashow is yet another indoor arena stuffed to the gills with low-quality knockoff clothing and shoes. Prices are slightly cheaper than Silk Alley, but the haggling no less cruel— don't pay any more than Y50 for a pair of "Converse" sneakers. Also, don't be alarmed if you see someone sniffing the shoes or suede jackets:

they're simply testing if the leather is real. On the third floor, **Wendy Ya Shi** (No. 3066) is the best of the many tailors on offer, with a basic suit usually starting out at around Y1,500 (including fabric) after a good haggle. ▓TIP➜ The Lily Nails salon on the first floor offers inexpensive manicures and foot rubs if you need a break. ✉ *58 Gongti Beilu, Chaoyang District* ☎ *010/6416–8699* ⊗ *Daily 9:30–9* Ⓜ *Tuanjiehu.*

Zhaojia Chaowai Market (朝外市场 *Cháowài shìchǎng*). Beijing's best-known venue for affordable antiques and reproduction furniture houses scores of independent vendors who sell everything from authentic Qing Dynasty–era chests to traditional baskets, ceramics, carpets, and curios. Be sure to bargain; vendors routinely sell items for less than half their starting price. ✉ *43 Huawei Bei Li, Chaoyang District* ☎ *010/6776–5318* ⊗ *Daily 9:30–7* Ⓜ *Jinsong.*

HAIDIAN DISTRICT 海淀区

If you're in Haidian, the chances are that you're either a student, Korean, or both. An abundance of universities and a large Korean population around Wudaokou make this a rather bustling, fun area, although not worth the journey for that alone—unless you have a penchant for kimchi, cheap shots, and overcrowded dance floors. But, if you're on your way to the Summer Palace or Beijing Zoo, it's worth stopping by. Inexpensive and cheerful boutiques aimed at students are commonplace, while the plentiful (and incredibly cheap) Korean massage joints make winding down at the end of the day a treat.

Ai Jia Gu Dong Market (犸爱家红木大楼 *Aìjiā hóngmù dàgúanlóu*). For something more refined, collectors of antiques can spend hours perusing the quiet halls of Ai Jia Gu Dong Market, a large antiques and jade market, hidden just under the South Fourth Ring Road beside the Big Bell Museum. It's open daily, but shops close early on weekdays. ✉ *Chengshousi Lu, Beisanhuan Xilu, Haidian District* Ⓜ *Zhichunlu.*

ARTS AND
NIGHTLIFE

Updated by
Ami Li

Beijing has blossomed. China is now a global superpower, and between the frenzied lead-up to the 2008 Summer Olympics and today, the city has become a mecca for nightlife, culture, and the arts. The traditional options still endure: Peking opera, acrobatics, classical music, marital arts, and more. However, more and more exciting contemporary events and locations are appearing every day.

From avant-garde plays and modern music to world-class cocktail bars and international talent performing in the hottest clubs, Beijing has ascended to the world stage. The performing arts, led by the programming at the National Centre for the Performing Arts (aka "the Egg") are thriving with talent from as far as the United States and as close as two blocks away taking over the stage nightly. With concerts by the likes of Elton John, the city has become a must-stop destination on all international tours. There's a bar for every type of boozer out there, from microbrewery to classy lounge to vampire-themed. No matter what your interest, Beijing awaits.

PLANNING

CITY LISTINGS
The best way to find out what's on or where to party is to pick up one of the free listing magazines found at many bars and restaurants. The best ones are the monthly *The Beijinger, Time Out Beijing,* and *That's Beijing,* as well as the biweekly *City Weekend:* all have frequently updated websites and give bilingual addresses in their listings.

WHAT TO WEAR
A rapidly expanding middle class and runaway economic growth means that the local population has developed an insatiable appetite for international luxury brands such as Prada and Louis Vuitton, and it shows in many of the classiest venues in Beijing. That being said, there's no strictly enforced dress code and you're just as likely to see the pajamas-and-sweat pants crowd out and about at the aforementioned places.

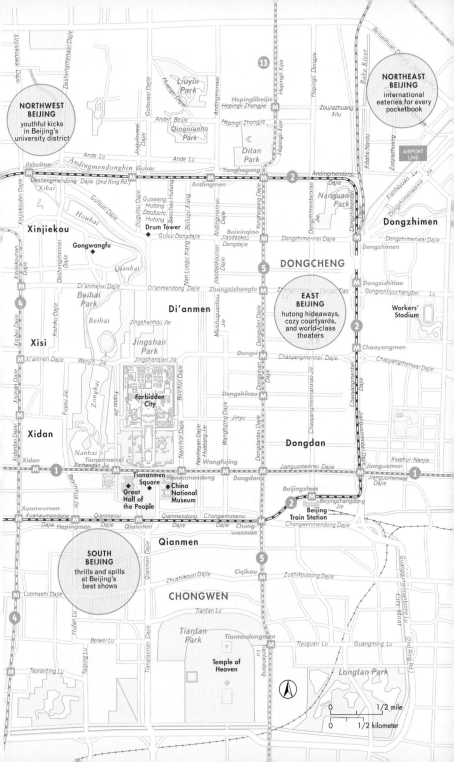

Just remember that on a whole Beijing is more about substance than image, and that the uneven sidewalks have ruined many a pair of nice heels before yours.

GETTING AROUND SAFELY

Most of the bars and clubs are clumped together in districts, so you can amble from pub to wine bar to cocktail lounge on foot. Your best bet is to rely on taxis to get back to your hotel—make sure you pick up a business card from your hotel to show the driver. Hailing cabs is generally not an issue except for in the busiest areas. Watch out for unlicensed cabbies who drive plain cars but often display a light similar to official cars. Beijing's public transportation system shuts down for the most part after 11 pm. Fares rise by 20% after 11 pm.

Watch out for fake alcohol at many of the cheap bars clustered around Sanlitun Back Street—your head will thank you in the morning.

LAST CALL

After-hours is where Beijing is still playing catch-up to the rest of the world. Though there are a handful of 24-hour joints and the bleary-eyed punters who populate them. Even the hardest partiers in the city wind down around 3 or 4 am and decamp to 24-hour dim sum joints to recover. If you're a true night owl, check out the Den, a sports bar with a 6 am breakfast deal.

SMOKING

Smoking inside bars and clubs is still de rigueur in Beijing. There are a handful of nonsmoking bars such as Mao Mao Chong off Nanluoguxiang and nearby Great Leap Brewing, which prohibits smoking inside while allowing smokers to light up in the courtyard, but partygoers should be prepared for a heavy dose of secondhand smoke at most venues.

COVERS

Next to no bars charge cover in Beijing. Live music clubs such as Yugong Yishan and MAO Live House, however, will charge for audiences to see a foreign or local band. The dance clubs clustered around Worker's Gymnasium will sometimes invite marquee international DJs to spin at night and charge suitable prices for their services as well.

THE ARTS

The arts in China took a long time to recover from the Cultural Revolution (1966–76), and political works are still generally avoided. Recently, names such as Kevin Spacey and the Royal Shakespeare Company have alighted on Beijing, reinforcing the capital's reputation as an arts destination. For culture vultures, there are a plethora of options from avant-garde plays to chamber music to traditional Peking opera and acrobatics shows.

As most of the stage is inaccessible to non-Chinese speakers, visitors to Beijing are more likely to hunt out the big visual spectacles, such as Beijing opera or kung fu displays. These long-running shows are tailored for travelers: Your hotel will be able to recommend performances and venues and will likely be able to help you book tickets.

DID YOU KNOW?

Chinese acrobatics has existed for more than two thousand years. Like vaudeville in the West, acrobatic performances in old China were considered low class; they were even banned from theaters. Many of the acts used props such as chairs, tables, and plates. Today you'll see amazing feats like traditional group gymnastics, springboard stunts, and gymnastics on double-fixed poles.

ACROBATICS AND KUNG FU

Chaoyang Theater (朝阳剧场 *Cháoyáng jùchǎng*). This space is the queen bee of acrobatics venues, especially designed to unleash oohs and ahhs. Spectacular individual and team acrobatic displays involving bicycles, seesaws, catapults, swings, and barrels are performed here nightly. It's touristy but fun. ⊠ *36 Dongsanhuan Beilu, Chaoyang District* ☎ *010/6507–2421* Ⓜ *Hujialou.*

Fodor'sChoice ★ **The Red Theatre** (红剧场 *Hóng jùchǎng*). If it's Vegas-style stage antics you're after, the *Legend of Kung Fu* show is what you want. Extravagant martial arts—performed by dancers, not martial artists—are complemented by neon, fog, and heavy-handed sound effects. Shows are garish but also sometimes glorious. ⊠ *44 Xingfu Dajie, Dongcheng District* ☎ *010/5165–1914* ⊕ *www.redtheatre.cn* Ⓜ *Tiantan Dong Men.*

Tianqiao Acrobatic Theater (天桥乐茶馆). The Beijing Acrobatics Troupe of China is famous for weird, wonderful shows. Content includes a flashy show of offbeat contortions and tricks, with a lot of high-wire action. There are two shows per night, at 5:30 and 7:15 pm. ⊠ *30 Beiwei Lu, Xicheng District* ☎ *010/6303–7449.*

ART GALLERIES

Chambers Fine Art. Named after noted British architect Sir William Chambers, Chambers Fine Art Beijing opened in 2007 in the art village of Caochangdi. Situated in a redbrick gallery complex designed by Chinese contemporary artist Ai Weiwei, Chambers consistently puts on exhibitions of young native Chinese artists. ⊠ *Red No. 1-D, Caochangdi, Chaoyang District* ☎ *010/5127–3298* ⊕ *www.chambersfineart.com.*

Pace Beijing (佩斯北京 *Pèisīběijīng*). This Beijing branch of the famed Pace Gallery operates with an independent program focusing on Chinese contemporary artists. ⊠ *No. 2 Jiuxianqiao Lu, 798 Art District, Chaoyang District* ☎ *010/5978–9781.*

Pékin Fine Arts. Founded by expatriate Bostonian Meg Maggio, who has lived in Beijing for 20 years, Pékin Fine Arts focuses on contemporary artists from around Asia, emphasizing individuals working across different media and with both international and domestic exhibition experience. ⊠ *No. 241 Caochangdi, Cuigezhuang Village, Chaoyang District* ☎ *010/5127–3220* ⊕ *pekinfinearts.com.*

Red Gate Gallery. This gallery, one of the first to open in Beijing, displays and sells contemporary Chinese art in the extraordinary location of the old Dongbianmen Watchtower, which dates back to the 16th century. The venue is worth a visit even if you're not interested in the art. Be aware that the subway stop listed here is about a 25-minute walk from the gallery. ⊠ *1st and 4th floors, Dongbianmen Watchtower, Chongwenmen Dongdajie* ☎ *010/6525–1005* ⊕ *www.redgategallery. com* Ⓜ *Jianguomen.*

798 Art District Dashanzi in the Chaoyang District

BEIJING OPERA

Chang'an Grand Theater (长安大戏院 *Cháng'ān dàxìyuàn*). In this new theater specializing in Chinese opera, spectators can choose to sit either in the traditional seats or at cabaret-style tables. Besides Peking-style opera, the theater also puts on performances of other regional styles, such as *yueju* (from Guangdong) and *chuanju* (from Sichuan). ✉ *7 Jianguomennei Dajie, Dongcheng District* ☏ *010/6510–1309* ⊕ *www.changantheater.com.*

Huguang Guild Hall (湖广会馆 *Húguǎng huìguǎn*). Built in 1807, the Huguang Guild Hall was at its height one of Beijing's "Four Great" theaters. In 1925, the Guild Hall hosted Dr. Sun Yat-sen at the founding of the Chinese Nationalist Party (KMT). Today, the Guild Hall has been restored to its former glory and hosts regular opera performances. The venue also hosts a small museum of Peking opera artifacts. ✉ *3 Hufangqiao, Xicheng District* ☏ *010/6351–8284.*

Lao She Teahouse (老舍茶馆 *Lǎoshě cháguǎn*). Named for famed Beijing author Lao She, this teahouse in the pedestrianized Qianmen area plays host to a variety of traditional performances including acrobatics, opera, and vaudeville shows. Dinner is served on the premises and reservations are required one day in advance for the shows, which occur at 7:15 pm nightly. ✉ *Bldg. 3, 3 Qianmenxi Dajie, Xicheng District* ☏ *010/6303–6830.*

Fodor's Choice   **Liyuan Theater** (梨园剧场 *Líyuán jùcháng*). Unabashedly touristy, it's
★   still a great time. You can watch performers put on makeup before the show (come early) and then graze on snacks and sip tea while

Fringe Art: The Dashanzi 798 Art District

798 Art District. Chinese contemporary art has exploded in the past decade, and to see some of the finest examples of the scene look no further than 798 Art District, located in the northeast corner of the city. Experimenting with classical mediums such as paint and printmaking as well as forays into new and digital media, installation, and performance art, young Chinese artists are caught between old and new, Communism and capitalism, urban and rural, rich and poor, and East and West. These conflicts set the stage and color their artistic output, with varying results. Although more and more Chinese artists are achieving international recognition, 798 still abounds with cheap knockoffs of bad Western art and tacky Socialist Realist portraits. Nevertheless the area remains the hub of contemporary creative arts in Beijing and is definitely worth a visit, especially if you're interested in the state of the arts in China.

Built in the 1950s, this factory district was a major industrial project by East German architects backed by Soviet aid. All but abandoned by the 1980s, the complex was rediscovered in the late 1990s by a small group of Beijing artists who had just been evicted from their previous haunts and were looking for a new place to set up working and living spaces. Initially a completely DIY affair similar to the squats of the East Village in the 1980s and East

Berlin of the 1990s, the quality of art produced and international media attention starting from the early 2000s meant that the district government took notice. Eventually the area was declared a protected arts district, paving the way for commercial galleries, cafés, and souvenir shops. Priced out of their original studios, many working artists have decamped farther afield to the Caochangdi and Songzhuang neighborhoods. Both of these smaller areas are worth visiting, though neither is easily accessible except via taxi. Ask your hotel concierge for a detailed map or, better yet, call ahead to the galleries you're interested in visiting and get driving instructions.

798 is more accessible, however, and eminently walkable. Keep in mind that cabs are prohibited from driving into the complex and much of the area is pedestrianized. Though it's open on weekdays (except for Monday), most people visit on the weekend, when throngs of locals and foreigners congregate to see what's on display.

Many of the galleries there now are hit or miss, but establishments such as the Ullens Center for Contemporary Arts (UCCA) and Galleria Continua always put on informative, challenging exhibitions. If you need to refuel, stop by At Cafe, billed as the first café in 798 and still co-owned by Huang Rui, one of the district's cofounders. ✉ 2–4 Jiuxianqiao Rd., Dashanzi, Chaoyang District.

watching English-subtitled shows. Glossy brochures complement the crooning. ✉ 1st floor, Qianmen Hotel, 175 Yong'an Lu, Xicheng District ☎ 010/6301–6688 ⊕ www.qianmenhotel.com/en/liyuan.html.

Tianqiao Theater (天桥 Tiānqiáolè cháguǎn). A traditional theater that hosts everything from contemporary dance performances to ballet, folk music, and cross-talk revues. ✉ 30 Beiwei Rd., Xicheng District ☎ 010/8315–6300.

MUSIC

Beijing Concert Hall (北京音乐厅 *Běijīng yīnyuètīng*). Beijing's main venue for Chinese and Western classical-music concerts also hosts folk dancing and singing, and many celebratory events throughout the year. The 1,000-seat venue is the home of the China National Symphony Orchestra. ⊠ *1 Bei Xinhuajie, Xicheng District* ☎ *010/6605–7006* Ⓜ *Tiananmen West.*

Forbidden City Concert Hall (北京中山 *Zhōngshān gōngyuán yīnyuètáng*). One of the nicest venues in Beijing, the 1,400-seat Forbidden City Concert Hall plays host to a variety of classical, chamber, and traditional music performances in plush surroundings and world-class acoustics. Though the facilities are completely modern, concertgoers are treated to a moonlit walk through Zhongshan Park, a former imperial garden dotted with historical landmarks. ⊠ *In Zhongshan Park, Xichang'an Jie, Xicheng District* ☎ *010/6559–8285* ⊕ *www.fcchbj.com* Ⓜ *Tiananmen West.*

MAO Live House. With the finest acoustics in the city and live music almost every night of the week, this is the place to experience the vibrant local music scene. ⊠ *111 Gulou Dongdajie, Dongcheng District* ☎ *010/6402–5080* ⊕ *www.maolive.com* Ⓜ *Gulou Dajie.*

Poly Plaza International Theater (保利剧院 *Bǎolì jùyuàn*). This is a modern shopping-center-like complex on top of Dongsishitiao subway station. One of Beijing's better-known theaters, the Poly hosts Chinese and international concerts, ballets, and musicals. ▮▮**TIP→** If you're seeking a performance in English, this is your best bet. ⊠ *1st floor, Poly Plaza, 14 Dongzhimen Nandajie, Dongcheng District* ☎ *010/6408–2666* Ⓜ *Dongsishitiao.*

Yugong Yishan (愚公移山 *Yúgōngyíshān*). Housed in a Republican-era courtyard, Yugong Yishan is the city's other premier destination for live music by both local rock bands and touring foreign acts. If you're in the mood to catch a good show, check local listings or the venue website to see who's playing when you're visiting Beijing. ⊠ *3–2 Zhangzizhong Lu, Dongcheng District* ☎ *010/8402–8477* ⊕ *www.yugongyishan.com.*

THEATER

Beijing Exhibition Theater (北京展览馆剧场 *Běijīng zhǎnlǎnguǎn jùchǎng*). Chinese plays, Western and Chinese operas, and ballet performances are staged in this Soviet-style building that's part of the exhibition center complex. Talk about a wide range of shows: In 2010 the Michael Jackson musical *Thriller* was staged here, followed closely by some traditional folk art performances. ⊠ *135 Xizhimenwai Dajie, Xicheng District* ☎ *010/6835–4455* Ⓜ *Xizhimen.*

Capital Theater (首都剧场 *Shǒudū jùchǎng*). This is a busy, modern theater near Wangfujing shopping street. It often has performances by the respected Beijing People's Art Theatre and various international acts such as British troupe TNT. ⊠ *22 Wangfujing Dajie, Dongcheng District* ☎ *010/6525–0996* ⊕ *www.bjry.com* Ⓜ *Wangfujing.*

The National Centre for Performing Arts

FAMILY **China National Puppet Theater** (中国木偶剧院 *Zhōngguó guójiā mùǒujùyuà*). The shadow and hand-puppet shows at this theater convey traditional stories—it's lively entertainment for children and adults alike. This venue also attracts overseas performers, including the Moscow Puppet Theater. ✉ *1 Anhuaxili, Chaoyang District* ☎ *010/6424–7888.*

Fodor'sChoice **National Centre for Performing Arts** (国家大剧院. *Guójiā dàjùyuàn*).
★ Architecturally, the giant silver dome of this performing arts complex is stunning, and its interior holds a state-of-the-art opera house, a music hall, and a theater. The "Egg" offers a world-class stage for national and international performers. If you don't wish to see a show, you can tour the inside of the building by paying for an entrance ticket. ✉ *2 Xi Chang'anjie, Xicheng District* ☎ *010/6655–0000* ⊕ *www.chncpa.org* Ⓜ *Tiananmen West.*

NIGHTLIFE

Now quite the international nightlife destination, there's something for everyone in Beijing. From intimate bars and world-class cocktail lounges to pumping dance halls, sports bars, and proper English-style pubs, Beijing (almost) has it all. Establishments seemingly rise up overnight, and can disappear just as quickly in the breakneck pace of development that Beijingers have become used to ever since the Olympics.

BARS

DONGCHENG AND XICHENG DISTRICTS (INCLUDING HOUHAI)

Fodor's Choice
★

Amilal (按一拉尔 *Àn yī lā'ěr*). If you have the patience to track this cozy courtyard bar down a tiny alley, you'll be rewarded with one of the city's hidden gems. Grab a seat at one of the rough wooden tables, listen to the low-key live music that's often playing, and enjoy the laid-back hutong vibe that's so unique to Beijing. ⊠ *48 Shoubi Hutong, off Gulou Dongdajie, Dongcheng District.*

Bed. Bed earned its place as a trendy bar through its clever name, and built-in pickup line, "Do you want to go to Bed with me?" Although this courtyard bar has cute nooks and crannies and a relaxed feel, it's a bit cold in both senses of the word. The beds are all sharp concrete and the shadows are chilly. We'll admit it's worth a one-night stand if you're new to the city. ⊠ *17 Zhangwang Hutong, Xicheng District* ☏ *010/8400–1554* Ⓜ *Gulou.*

Cu Ju (蹴鞠 *Cùjū*). Cu Ju is Beijing's first hutong sports bar–cum–rum-tasting room. Proprietor Badr is a Moroccan expat who's lived in the city for many years and the bar is the culmination of all his many passions, such as rum, Moroccan food, and sporting events. ⊠ *28 Xiguan Hutong, Dongcheng District* ☏ *010/6407–9782* ⊕ *www.cujubeijing.com.*

Drum & Bell Bar (鼓钟咖啡馆 *Gǔzhōng kāfēiguǎn*). Situated in the Drum and Bell Tower plaza, this bar is a local and tourist favorite with one of Beijing's nicest views from its roof deck. An all-you-can-drink Sunday brunch only sweetens the deal. ⊠ *41 Zhonglouwan Hutong, Dongcheng District* ☏ *010/8403–3600.*

El Nido (方家小酒馆59号 *Fāngjiāxiǎojiǔguǎnwǔshíjiǔhào*). Little more than a hole in the wall, this hutong gem is stuffed to the gills with rare imported beers, fine cheeses and charcuterie, and the owner's home-made infused liquors. In the summer, it's a little roomier as overflow crowds spill onto picnic tables set up in the front. El Nido is a great first stop of the night or if you aren't feeling the crowds, grab some bottles to go and sip on the streets with the rest of the Beijng old-timers. Thank your lucky stars for the lack of open container laws. ⊠ *No. 59 Fangjia Hutong, Andingmennei Dajie, Dongcheng District* ☏ *158/1038–2089.*

4Corners (肆角餐吧 *Sìjiǎocānba*). Tucked inside a tiny hutong near the western end of Houhai, 4Corners boasts a working fireplace in the winter and breezy patio in the summer. There's inventive, pan-Asian cuisine from its Vietnamese-Canadian chef-owner, delicious cocktails, and refreshing beer such as Vedett White on tap. ⊠ *No. 27 Dashibei Hutong, Gulou Xidajie, Dongcheng District* ☏ *010/6401–7797.*

Great Leap Brewing (大跃啤酒 *Dàyuèpíjiǔ*). Beijing's first microbrewery, Great Leap Brewing's beers utilize unique ingredients such as tea and Sichuan peppercorns. The courtyard operation also hosts weekly movie screenings and the odd special event. Don't miss the bar peanuts—spicy and salty, they'll keep you going back to the bar for just one more brew. ⊠ *No. 6 Doujiao Hutong, Dongcheng District* ☏ *010/5717–1399* ⊕ *www.greatleapbrewing.com* ☾ *Closed Mon.*

6

Gulou Gems

Within the Second Ring Road, you can experience the best views, drinks, and even dance clubs Beijing has to offer.

SPORTS AND RUM

Beijing's first hutong sports bar and rum-tasting room **Cu Ju** is run by a long-term expat with myriad interests. Cu Ju has HD satellite televisions that show everything including soccer (football), American football, rugby, baseball, cricket, tennis, and more. While you're watching, sip one of proprietor Badr's hand-selected aged rums or snack on the bar's delicious merguez (sausage) sandwiches.

COZY HUTONG HIDEAWAYS

Weeknights are the perfect time to grab a quiet drink in one of the area's many small courtyard bars. Local favorite **Amilal** boasts a postage stamp-size outdoor courtyard, excellent whiskey selection, and two elusive cats. The back room of **4Corners** has a real fireplace, and **Bed** is known equally for its reclining seating and refreshing mojitos.

PIZZA, COCKTAILS, AND CANVASES

Mao Mao Chong is known for their infused cocktails, such as chili-infused vodka Bloody Marys and Sichuan peppercorn Moscow Mules.

MICROBREWERIES AND MORE

One of the hottest new trends in Beijing is microbreweries—beer brewed right in the city and flavored with local ingredients such as Chinese tea and spices. **Great Leap Brewing** calls a hutong home, while the **Slow Boat Brewery Taproom** has heated floors—quite a luxury during Beijing's frigid winters. If you're more into the bottled stuff, hole-in-the-wall gem **El Nido** has over 60 varieties of European, American, and Australian beers, with an emphasis on obscure Belgian brews.

DANCE THE NIGHT AWAY

Gulou even has a club to call its own. **Dada Bar**, a Shanghai import, bills itself as a "DJ bar" but features local and some international talent behind the decks almost every night of the week. Drinks are cheap and strong, and the music ranges from drum 'n bass and dubstep to dance hall, retro, and indie rock. There's sometimes a cover on weekends if the name is big.

ROOFTOP DRINKING

Summers in Beijing are long and hot, but respite comes in the form of lazy afternoons spent on breezy rooftops. Take in Gulou's best view on the balcony at **Drum & Bell Bar**, overlooking the namesake towers. Or spend a leisurely Sunday lounging on the roof deck of local hangout **Alba**.

Mao Mao Chong (毛毛虫 *Máomáochóng*). This bar is known for infused cocktails, included a chili-infused vodka Bloody Mary and Sichuan peppercorn Moscow Mule. ✉ *No. 12 Banchang Hutong, Dongcheng District* ☎ *159/9264–6024* ⊕ *www.maomaochongbeijing.com.*

Slow Boat Brewery Taproom. A sleek yet cozy taproom nestled in the hutong, the Slow Boat is another addition to the rapidly growing number of microbreweries in the capital city. There are at least a dozen beers on tap at any given moment, from all-weather tipples such as pale ales and IPAs, to seasonal specialties including warming stouts in the winter and refreshing citrusy brews come summertime. ✉ *56–2 Dongsi Batiao, Dongsi Beidajie, Dongcheng District* ☎ *010/6538– 5537* ⊕ *www.slowboatbrewery. com* ⊙ *Closed Mon.* Ⓜ *Zhangzi-zhong Lu (Line 5).*

CHAOYANG DISTRICT

Apothecary (药剂员 *Yào ji yuán*). Like an old-fashioned pharma-cist doling out carefully concocted medicinals, the mixologists at this low-key venue artfully blend all of your favorite ingredients into cock-tails that will soothe the soul. Mixologist-in-chief Leon Lee is something of a local celebrity for good reason. The location, in the trendy Nali Patio complex, and the New Orleans–style bar food are bonuses. ✉ *3rd floor, Nali Patio, 81 Sanlitun Beilu, Chaoyang District* ☎ *010/5208– 6040* Ⓜ *Tuanjiehu.*

China Bar (北京亮酒吧 *Běijīng liàng jiǔbā*). Perched atop the 65-story Park Hyatt, this upmarket cocktail bar offers bird's-eye views of the city, smog and all! Dark and sultry, the modern Asian decor is mini-malist so as not to distract from the views, or the drinks. Cocktails are expertly mixed and Scotch purists can choose from a list of 23 single malts. ✉ *Park Hyatt, 2 Jianguomenwai Dajie, 65th floor, Chaoyang District* ☎ *010/8567–1838.*

The Den. This old-school dive's attraction is sports on wide-screen TVs. The owner runs the city's amateur rugby club, so you'll find players and their supporters drinking rowdily. Open 24 hours a day, it's guaranteed to be buzzing every night, especially during happy hour, when you can grab half-price drinks and pizza until 10 pm. ✉ *4 Gongti Donglu, next to the City Hotel, Chaoyang District* ☎ *010/6592–6290* Ⓜ *Tuanjie Hu.*

D.Lounge. Raising the bar for bars in Beijing, this New York–style lounge is swank, spacious, and has an innovative drink list. At the moment, it's the place to rub elbows with the city's *it* crowd, and occasionally the doormen restrict entry to the more dapperly dressed. It's a bit tricky to find: Walk behind Salsa Caribe and head south. ✉ *Courtyard 4, Gongti Beilu, behind the Bookworm, Chaoyang District* ☎ *010/6593–7710.*

Face (飞色 *Fēi sè*). Stylish without being pretentious, Face is justifiably popular, especially with the mature, well-heeled crowd. The complex has a multitude of restaurants, but the real gem is the bar. Grab a lounge bed sur-rounded by silky drapes, take advantage of the happy-hour drink specials, and enjoy some premier people-watching. ✉ *26 Dongcaoyuan, Gongti Nanlu, Chaoyang District* ☎ *010/6551–6788* ⊕ *www.facebars.com.*

First Floor (壹楼 *Yīlóu*). An unpretentious bar perfect for a night out with friends, First Floor is fast becoming the "Cheers" of Beijing, where everyone—especially gregarious owner Jack Zhou—knows your name. ✉ *Tongli Studio, Sanlitun Houjie, 1st floor, Chaoyang District* ☎ *010/6413–0587.*

6

One of the many drinking establishments in Sanlitun

Ichikura (一藏 *Yī cāng*). This tiny Japanese bar is the place to go if you're a discerning whiskey drinker. The dimly lighted interior, red decor, and hushed conversation give it an air of exclusivity. If James Bond was in Beijing, this is where he'd come. Drinks are taken very seriously here and it shows in both the quality of the alcohol and the professionalism with which it's mixed by the all-Japanese bar staff. The entrance is via stairs at the south wall of the Chaoyang Theatre. ⊠ *Chaoyang Theatre, 36 Dongsanhuan Beilu, 2nd floor, Chaoyang District* ☎ *010/6507–1107* Ⓜ *Hujialou.*

Mokihi. Tucked behind an Italian-fusion restaurant with a Japanese chef on an unassuming strip mall of establishments near Chaoyang Park, Mokihi is a perfect oasis from the hustle and bustle of everyday Beijing. Have the Japanese-trained bartenders mix up one of their signature cocktails and nibble on exquisite hors d'oeuvres while engaging in quiet conversation with your drinking companions. ⊠ *C12, Haoyun Jie (Lucky St.), 3rd floor, Chaoyang District* ☎ *010/5867–0244.*

Fodor's Choice
★
Q Bar. Echo's cocktails—strong, authentic, and not superexpensive—are a small legend here in Beijing. This tucked-away lounge off the main Sanlitun drag is an unpretentious option for an evening out. Don't be put off by the fact that it's in a bland, 1980s-styled motel; in the summer the terrace more than makes up for that. ⊠ *Top floor of Eastern Inn Hotel, 6 Baijiazhuang Lu, Chaoyang District* ☎ *010/6595–9239* Ⓜ *Tuanjie Hu.*

The Tree. For years now, expats have crowded this bar for its Belgian beer, wood-fired pizza, and quiet murmurs of conversation. It does, however, get a bit smoky; if you're sensitive you may want to give this

GAY AND LESBIAN NIGHTLIFE

Although Beijing is no Berlin, there are several bars and clubs that woo gays and lesbians. *Time Out Beijing* has a regular gay and lesbian column that includes events and news. Since the scene changes quickly—bars open, close, and reopen at new locations—you should also check online resources. Try ⊕ *www.utopia-asia.com* for updates, or the Beijing LGBT Center's Facebook page.

Here are some popular venues:

Alfa (餐吧 *Alfa cānba*). Home of Beijing's greatest, most nostalgia-fueled theme nights, including ⊠80s and disco, Alfa is a hopping little dance spot popular with gay men in Beijing. ⊠ *No. 6 Xingfu Yicun, opposite the north gate of Worker's Stadium, Chaoyang District* ☎ *010/6413–0086.*

Destination (目的地 *Mùdìdì*). The city's best and most popular gay club has a bouncy dance floor, energetic DJs, and a small lounge area. It gets extremely packed on weekends and attracts a varied crowd of almost all male expats and locals. There's a cover charge on weekends. ⊠ *7 Gongti Xilu, Chaoyang District* ☎ *010/6551–5138* Ⓜ *Dongsi Shitiao.*

6

venue a pass. For pasta instead of pizza, its sister restaurant Nearby the Tree is, well, nearby, at 330 feet to the southeast. ⊠ *43 Sanlitun Beijie, Chaoyang District* ☎ *010/6415–1954* Ⓜ *Tuanjie Hu.*

Twilight (暮光 *Mùguāng*). Opened by the same partners who operate Apothecary in Sanlitun, Twilight is an oasis of calm in the otherwise hectic Central Business District (CBD). Have the bartender make you a perfect old-fashioned, which you can wash down with one of the bar's tasty pizzas. ⊠ *Bldg. 5, Jianwai SOHO, 39 Dongsanhuan Zhonglu, 3rd floor, Chaoyang District* ☎ *010/5900–5376.*

CHAOYANG WEST GATE

The World of Suzie Wong (苏西黄俱乐部 *Sūxīhuáng jùlèbù*). It's no coincidence that this bar is named after a 1957 novel about a Hong Kong prostitute. Come here late at night and you'll find a healthy supply of modern Suzie Wongs and a crowd of expat clients. The sleaze factor is enhanced by its 1930s opium-den design, with China-chic beds overrun with cushions. Suzie Wong's, however, has a reputation for mixing a more-than-decent cocktail and good music. ⊠ *1A S. Nongzhanguanlu, Chaoyang West Gate, Chaoyang District* ☎ *010/6593–6049.*

HAIDIAN DISTRICT

Lush. The go-to hangout in the university district of Wudaokou, Lush is a home-away-from-home for many a homesick exchange student. With weekly pub quizzes, open-mic nights, and large, strong drinks, Lush is an excellent place to start the night. ⊠ *2nd floor, Bldg. 1, Huaqing Jiayuan, across the street from the Wudakou light-rail station, Haidian District* ☎ *010/8286–3566* ⊕ *www.lushbeijing.com.*

The Red House (色家 *Hóng jiā*). A simple, no-frills exterior reflects the bar as a whole—bare walls warmed by a roaring fire, friendly bar staff, and a loyal crowd looking for a home away from home to booze

BARROOM WITH A VIEW

Although some people go to bars to be seen, you'll be richly rewarded if you check out those venues that actually have a *scene*. Beijing is glorious observed from above—with a drink in hand, it's even better. Along with the newest arrival on the sky-high scene, China Bar in the Park Hyatt, here are three of our other favorite spots which may be nearer the ground, but they still have killer views:

East Shore Live Jazz Café (东岸咖啡 *Dōng'àn kāfēi*). There's no competition: This place has the most fabulous views of Houhai Lake, hands-down, and authentic jazz on stage every night. ⊠ *2nd floor, 2 Qianhai Nanyanlu, west of the post office on Di'anmen Waidajie, Xicheng District* ☎ *010/8403-2131.*

Yin (饮 *Huángjiā Yìzhàn*) (皇家驿栈屋顶). The Emperor Hotel's rooftop terrace bar certainly has the "wow" factor. It overlooks the Forbidden City—perhaps the finest view in all Beijing—and there's even a hot tub if you need to relax. Unsurprisingly, drink prices are high, but it's a fabulous place to show visitors. Befitting the stylishness of the hotel, red lanterns and fashionably outfitted staff add to the classiness of the experience. If only service standards were as high. ⊠ *33 Qihelou, Dongcheng District* ☎ *010/6523-6877* Ⓜ *Tiananmen East.*

in peace. The pizza oven never stops churning out tasty pies, a good accompaniment to the beers on tap. ⊠ *Wudaokou, Wangzhuang Lu, Haidian District* ☎ *010/6291–3350* Ⓜ *Wudaokou.*

DANCE CLUBS

DONGCHENG DISTRICT

Dada Bar. A chilled-out place where you can dance, Dada is like the club your cool older cousin snuck you into in a foreign country. Talented resident and guest DJs from all over the world perform, and you can expect industrial-chic decor and cheap, strong drinks. It's a great final destination of a night out, and beloved by both long-term expats and local scenesters alike. ⊠ *Room 101, Bldg. B, 206 Gulou Dongdajie, Dongcheng District* ☎ *183/1108–0818.*

Tango (糖果 *Tángguǒ*). This warehouse-style space is way more interesting than the competition. Without the usual gaudy decor, Tango is roomy enough to take the crowds, and often plays some very loud but good music. Beijing's best midsize live-music venue is on the third floor and (unimaginatively) called Tango 3F. ⊠ *79 Hepingli Xijie, Dongcheng District* ☎ *010/6428–2288* Ⓜ *Yonghegong.*

CHAOYANG DISTRICT

Cargo Club. Fierce promotions have attracted some top-name international DJs. And in spite of the smallish dance floor, many expats consider Cargo the best club along Gongti Xilu. Perhaps it's the 1980s kitsch. ⊠ *6 Gongti Xilu, Chaoyang District* ☎ *010/6551–6898.*

BEST SIDE TRIPS

Including the Great Wall and
Thirteen Ming Tombs

WELCOME TO RURAL CHINA

TOP REASONS TO GO

★ **A Great Big Wall:** Postcard views of large sections of the restored wall rise majestically around you. The sheer scope of this ancient project boggles the mind. Watch out for areas off-limits due to redevelopment; Simatai has been officially closed since 2010 and talk of a reopening date in late 2013 is still just rumor.

★ **Ming and More:** It's easy to arrange a tour or your own transportation to the Great Wall and the Thirteen Ming Tombs—especially if you go to the Badaling section of the wall.

★ **The Adventure:** Traveling through rural China, even for a day trip, is always something of an adventure. Endless greenery peppered with ramshackle villages and roadside fruit stalls ensure that short stops along the way are a must rather than an inconvenience.

★ **Meet the Locals:** People in rural China can be extremely kind, inviting you to their homes for tea, a meal. If you accept an invite, a small gift is always appreciated.

1 Thirteen Ming Tombs. The grandeur of the final resting place for 13 Ming Dynasty emperors gives you an idea of the importance of ancestor worship in ancient China.

2 Fahai Temple and Jietai Temple. Li Tong, a favorite eunuch in Emperor Zhengtong's court, built Fahai; its frescos are considered some of the finest examples of Buddhist mural art from the Ming Dynasty. Jietai, China's most ancient Buddhist site, is located just west of Beijing.

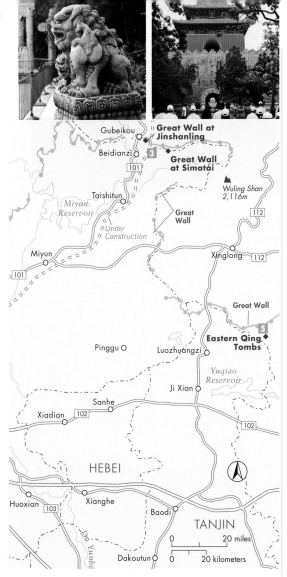

GETTING ORIENTED

By either train or taxi, it's easy to get out of Beijing. The major sites are no more than 80 km (50 miles) outside the city, with the exception of farther-flung sections of the Great Wall and the Eastern Qing Tombs (126 km [78 miles]). If you take a taxi, set a price beforehand; the metered fare can add up quickly (generally, rides start at Y10 for the first 3 km (2 miles), with an additional Y2 for each additional km and another Y2 per every five minutes of waiting time). If you go by train, most hotels will help you buy tickets up to four days in advance for a fee (typically Y5 to Y15 per ticket). There are also small train-ticket windows scattered around the city. Look for the China Railways logo—although if you plan to travel by fast-train, tickets must be purchased from the station.

3 The Great Wall.
The longest man-made structure on Earth is one of the country's most accessible and cosmopolitan attractions. This UNESCO World Heritage Site is home to hikers, hawkers, marathon runners, and sightseers alike; plus it makes for a surprisingly exacting workout.

4 The Mountain Resort, Chengde. Once an excuse for Ming emperors to escape the summer heat of Beijing and hunt some deer, today its sprawling gardens and surrounding temples offer a prosaic escape for those seeking a weekend getaway.

5 Yunju Temple and Eastern Qing Tombs. Don't miss the 14,278 delicately carved Buddhist tablets at Yunju. The Eastern Tombs were modeled after the Thirteen Ming Tombs, but these are even more extravagant and much less touristy.

Updated by
Gareth Clark

From the 15th century until the collapse of the Qing Dynasty, Beijing was a walled city, its horizons framed by nine gates that ushered in camel trains of supplies. These days, it can sometimes feel like they were never pulled down. Aside from an obligatory day trip to the Great Wall, many fail to explore beyond the old inner and outer city limits, shuttling from Forbidden City to Temple of Heaven and back again with predictable ease. All of which is a shame because Beijing's outskirts and the surrounding Hebei Province offer not only a powerful insight into the forming of an empire, but also adventures galore.

Of course, The Great Wall is a good starting point for any exploration, and while it isn't (as the old propagandist myth goes) visible to the naked eye from space, it's nonetheless an awesome sight. It might have failed to prevent the Manchus from invading, but as soaring testimonies to human endeavor go, there are few more visually rewarding. You needn't stop there, though. Why not go horseback riding at Yesanpo, or explore the imperial summer home in Chengde? Buddhist temples and ancient tombs, as well as beaches and anthropological digs, are all located within a few hours of Beijing, so don't let your horizons end with the city limits.

PLANNING

GETTING THERE

Taxis, which in Beijing are both plentiful and reasonably priced, are a good way to get to sights outside the city. At the time of writing, a Y3 fuel surcharge is added for all trips exceeding 3 km (2 miles). A small surcharge is also added between 11 pm and 5 am. If taking a taxi outside the city, try to agree on a fixed price for the trip beforehand; also make

TO MING OR NOT TO MING?

The Ming Tombs often get a bad rap by visitors, which is unfair. A leisurely stroll down the Sacred Way, inspecting the series of charming larger-than-life statues of imperial officials and animals, is a great way to spend an hour or two. Most combine a visit with a longer excursion, usually to the Badaling section of the Great Wall, which is found off the same expressway. The tombs themselves, of which only three (Changling, Dingling,

and Zhaoling) are open to the public, can disappoint those expecting more. Dingling, especially, is little better than a grim concrete bunker from which anything of note has long since been removed and replaced by irritatingly cheap-looking replicas. So, to get the most out of a visit, set aside time to hike around the unrestored tombs, found farther along the valley. These are usually quieter and altogether more rewarding.

sure that this covers the return journey, or face the prospect of haggling with illegal cab drivers on the way back—and they will fleece you!

Private-car services are available in Beijing, and even if they aren't always cheap, they're in most cases worth the investment. **Beijing Limo** rents a variety of cars and buses, complete with English-speaking drivers, from US$29 for a two-hour basic package (plus 20% service charge). ☎ 010/6546–1588 ✍ reservations@beijinglimo.com ⊕ www.beijinglimo.com/english ☯ Weekdays 9–6.

Rail travel is comparatively cheap in China for the distances covered. Some sites, such as Yesanpo, Tianjin, Chengde, Beidaihe, and Shanhaiguan, are accessible by train. Plan to get to the station at least 30 minutes before your train leaves, as they are huge and often confusing for visitors. It's easy to buy train tickets once there, but these sell out fast on peak dates, so if you're on a tight schedule and can't afford a delay, buy a ticket beforehand.

TIMING

It'll take you several days to see all the sights outside of Beijing. If you only have time for one, go to the **Great Wall.** If you have two days, head to **Fahai Temple,** about an hour's drive from the center, on the second day. Afterward you can see the **Jietai Temple** and the **Tanzhe Temple** before returning to the city in the afternoon. If you have more time to see the sights outside the city, check out the **Eastern Qing Tombs** on your third day. Wear walking shoes and bring a lunch.

If you have three days or more, and you're looking for a little summertime relaxation, take a day and a night (or, for real relaxation, two days) at **Beidaihe,** to bask on the beach, chow down on seafood, or see where the Great Wall meets the sea at Shanghaigan.

WHAT TO WEAR

The weather in Beijing and neighboring areas is notoriously fickle, so make sure you dress appropriately. In the summer it's hot; travel with sunglasses, sunscreen, and a wide-brimmed hat. It gets terribly cold in the winter, so dress in layers and pack gloves, a hat, and a scarf. And if you plan to do any hiking, make sure to bring sturdy, comfortable shoes.

Also, checking the weather forecast before an excursion is always a good idea for last-minute wardrobe changes. ■TIP→ Don't carry too much cash or expensive jewelry. Other things to bring along? A camera, a change of clothes if you're staying overnight, and your common sense.

THIRTEEN MING TOMBS
(明十三陵 *MÍNG SHÍSĀNLÍNG*)

48 km (30 miles) north of Beijing.

A narrow valley just north of Changping is the final resting place for 13 of the Ming Dynasty's 16 emperors (the first Ming emperor was buried in Nanjing; the burial site of the second one is unknown; and the seventh Ming emperor was dethroned and buried in an ordinary tomb in northwestern Beijing). Ming monarchs once journeyed here each year to kowtow before their clan forefathers and make offerings to their memory. These days, few visitors can claim royal descent, but the area's vast scale and imperial grandeur do convey the importance attached to ancestor worship in ancient China.

The road to the Thirteen Ming Tombs begins beneath an imposing stone portico that stands at the valley entrance. Allow ample time for a hike or drive northwest from Changling to the six fenced-off **unrestored tombs,** a short distance farther up the valley. Here, crumbling walls conceal vast courtyards shaded by pine trees. At each tomb, a stone altar rests beneath a stele tower and burial mound. In some cases the wall that circles the burial chamber is accessible on steep stone stairways that ascend from either side of the altar. At the valley's terminus (about 5 km [3 miles] northwest of Changling), the **Zhaoling tomb** rests beside a traditional walled village that's well worth exploring.

Picnics amid the ruins have been a favorite weekend activity among Beijingers for nearly a century; if you picnic here, be sure to carry out all trash. ⌂ *Changping County* ☎ *010/6076–1888, 010/6076–1424* ✉ *Y30 (for Zhaoling tomb)* ☉ *Zhaoling tomb Apr.–Oct., daily 8–5:30; Nov.–Mar., daily 8:30–5.*

Shendao (神 道*Shéndào*). Beyond the entrance, the Shendao (or Sacred Way) passes through an outer pavilion and between rows of stone sculptures depicting elephants, camels, lions, and mythical beasts that scatter the length of its 7-km (4½-mile) journey to the burial sites. This walk is not to be missed and is a route that was once reserved only for imperial travel. ✉ *Y30 (Y20 Nov.–Mar.)* ☉ *Apr.–Oct., daily 8–5:30; Nov.–Mar., daily 8–5.*

Changling (长陵 *Chánglíng*). The spirit way leads to Changling, the head tomb built for Emperor Yongle in 1427. The designs of Yongle's great masterpiece, the Forbidden City, are echoed in this structure. ☎ *010/6076–1888, 010/6076–1424* ✉ *Y45 (Y40 Nov.–Mar.)* ☉ *Apr.–Oct., daily 8–5; Nov.–Mar., daily 8:30–4:30.*

BEIDAIHE & YESANPO

Beidaihe (北戴河 *Běidàihé*). Chairman Mao and the party's favorite spot for sand, sun, and seafood, Beidaihe (250 km [170 miles] northeast of Beijing) is one of China's few beach resorts (though it's definitely no Bali). This crowded spot is just 2½ hours by train from Beijing station. Nearly every building in town has been converted to a hotel, and every restaurant has tanks of pick-your-own seafood lining the street. ⊠ *West of Beidaihe District, Qinhuangdao.*

Yesanpo (野三坡 *Yěsān pō*). Yesanpo (150 km [90 miles] northeast of Beijing) is a sleepy village between Beijing and neighboring Hebei Province. Go here if you're craving a slower-paced scene and some outdoor fun. The accommodations aren't first class, but there are plenty of great things to do. Leave Beijing from Beijing West station for the two-hour ride. Traditionally, locals have houses with extra rooms for guests, and owners will strive to make your stay as comfortable as possible. A clean room with two beds and an air-conditioner should run you no more than Y150. There are also a few hotels on the main street by the train station with rooms running approximately Y200. This scenic town is nestled in a valley. The area is best toured on horseback, and horses are available for rent for Y300 per day (with a guide), or Y100 for an hour or so. Yesanpo is also known for its whole barbecued lamb. Train No. 6437 leaves Beijing Weststation at 8:29 pm and arrives at 8:29 pm. Return train 6438 leaves at 9:35 am daily.

7

Dingling (定陵 *Dìnglíng*). Changling and a second tomb, Dingling, were rebuilt in the 1980s and opened to the public. Both complexes suffer from over-restoration and overcrowding, but they're worth visiting if only for the tomb relics on display in the small museums at each site. Dingling is particularly worth seeing because this tomb of Emperor Wanli is the only Ming Dynasty tomb that has been excavated. Unfortunately, this was done in 1956 when China's archaeological skills were sadly lacking, resulting in irrecoverable losses. Nonetheless, it's interesting to compare this underground vault with the tomb of Emperor Qianlong at Qingdongling. ☎ *010/6076–1888, 010/6076–1424* 🔁 *Y60 (Y40 Nov.–Mar.)* ⊙ *Apr.–Oct., daily 8–5; Nov.–Mar., daily 8:30–5.*

FAHAI TEMPLE (法海寺 *FǍHǍI SÌ*)

20 km (12 miles) west of Beijing.

The stunning works of Buddhist mural art at Fahai Temple, which underwent extensive renovation and reopened in 2008, are among the most underappreciated sights in Beijing. Li Tong, a favored eunuch in the court of Emperor Zhengtong (1436–49), donated funds to construct Fahai Temple in 1443. The project was highly ambitious: Li Tong invited only celebrated imperial and court painters to decorate the temple. As a result, the murals in the only surviving chamber of that

Continued on page 206

THE GREAT WALL

For some people, the Great Wall is the main reason for a trip to China; for any visitor to Beijing, it's a must-see. Originally intended to keep foreigners out, the world's most famous wall has become the icon of an increasingly open nation. One of the country's most accessible attractions, the Great Wall promises both breathtaking scenery and cultural illumination.

Built by successive dynasties over two millennia, the Great Wall isn't one structure built at one time, but a series of defensive installations that shrank and grew. Especially vulnerable spots were more heavily fortified, while some mountainous regions were left un-walled altogether. The actual length of the wall remains a topic of considerable debate: at its longest, some estimates say the protective cordon spans 6,437 km (4,000 mi)—a distance wider than the United States. Although attacks, age, and pillaging (not to mention today's tourist invasion) have caused the crumbling of up to two-thirds of its length, new sections are being uncovered even today.

As kingdoms scrambled to protect themselves from marauding nomads, portions of wall cropped up, leading to a motley collection of northern borders. It was the first emperor of a unified China, Qin Shi-huang (circa 259–210 BC), founder of the Qin Dynasty, who linked these fortifications into a single network. By some accounts, Qin mustered nearly a million people, or one-fifth of China's workforce, to build this massive barricade, a mobilization that claimed countless lives and gave rise to many tragic folktales.

The Ming Dynasty fortified the wall like never before: for an estimated 5,000 km (3,107 mi), it stood 26 feet tall and 30 feet wide at its base. However, the wall failed to prevent the Manchu invasion that toppled the Ming in 1644. That historical failure hasn't tarnished the Great Wall's image, however. Although China once viewed it as a model of feudal oppression, the Great Wall is now touted as the national symbol. "Love China, Restore the Great Wall," declared Deng Xiaoping in 1984. Since then large sections have been repaired and opened to visitors, turning it also into a symbol of the tension between preservation and restoration in China.

AN ETERNAL WAIT

One legend concerns Lady Meng, whose husband was kidnapped on their wedding night and forced to work on the Great Wall. She traveled to the work site to await his return, believing her determination would bring him back. She waited so long that, in the end, she turned into a rock, which to this day stands at the head of the Great Wall in the beautiful seaside town of Qinhuangdao.

■ During the 2nd century BC, the wall was largely composed of packed earth and piled stone.

■ Some sections, like those in the Taklimakan Desert, were fortified with twigs, sand, and even rice (the jury's still out on whether workers' remains were used as well).

■ The more substantial brick-and-mortar ruins that wind across the mountains north of Beijing date from the Ming Dynasty (14th–17th centuries). Some Ming mortar kilns still exist in valleys around Beijing.

YOUR GUIDE TO THE GREAT WALL

As a visitor to Beijing, you simply must set aside a day to visit one of the glorious Great Wall sites just outside the capital. The closest, Badaling, is just an hour from the city's center—in general, the farther you go, the more rugged the terrain. So choose your adventure wisely!

BADALING and **JUYONGGUAN** are the most accessible sections of the Great Wall, is where most tours go. This location is rife with Disney-like commercialism, though: from the cable car you'll see both the heavily reconstructed portions of wall and crowds of souvenir stalls.

If you seek the wall less traveled, book a trip to fantastic **MUTIANYU**, which is about the same distance as Badaling from Beijing. You can enjoy much more solitude here, as well as amazing views from the towers and walls.

Mutianyu

Badaling

90 km; 1.25 hours by car

70 km; 1 hour by car

✪ BEIJING

TRANSPORTATION

CARS: The easiest and most comfortable way to visit the wall is by private car. Though taxis are occasionally willing to make the trip to more accessible sections like Badaling and Mutianyu, most hotels can arrange a four-passenger car and an English-speaking driver for 8 hours at around Y500–Y700. Settle details in advance, and remember that it's polite to invite your driver to eat meals with you. To ensure your driver doesn't return to Beijing without you, pay after the trip is over.

TOURS: In addition to the tour buses that gather around Tiananmen Square, most hotels and tour companies offer trips (in comfortable, air-conditioned buses or vans) to Badaling, Mutianyu, Juyongguan, and Jinshanling. ■ TIP➔ Smaller, private tours are generally more rewarding than large bus trips. Trips will run between Y400 and Y1,500 per person, but costs vary depending on the group size, and can sometimes be negotiated. Wherever you're headed, book in advance.

TOUR OPERATORS

OUR TOP PICKS

■ **CITS (China International Tour Service)** runs bus tours to Badaling and private tours to Badaling, Mutianyu, and Juyongguan. (Y500–Y1,700 per person) ⊠ 1 Dongdan Bei DAJIE, Dongcheng District ☎ 010/6522-2991 ⊕ www.cits.net

■ **Beijing Service** leads private guided tours by car to Badaling, Mutianyu, and Juyongguan (Y400–Y500 per person for small groups of 3-4 people). ☎ 010/5166-7026 ⊕ www.beijingservice.com

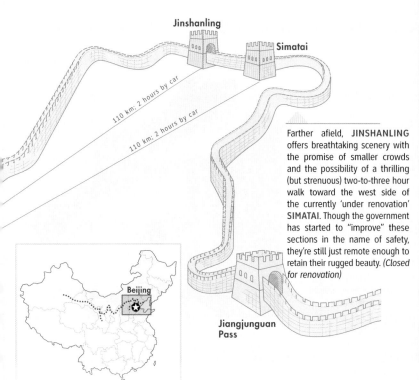

Farther afield, **JINSHANLING** offers breathtaking scenery with the promise of smaller crowds and the possibility of a thrilling (but strenuous) two-to-three hour walk toward the west side of the currently 'under renovation' **SIMATAI**. Though the government has started to "improve" these sections in the name of safety, they're still just remote enough to retain their rugged beauty. *(Closed for renovation)*

■ **Great Wall Adventure Club** organizes private bus and car trips to Jinshanling–Gubeikou (Y559–Y1,559) and Mutianyu (Y519–Y1,449). ☎ 138/1154–5162 ⊕ www.greatwalladventure.com

ADDITIONAL TOURS

■ **Bespoke Beijing** offers unique, tailor-made tours to the Wall at 'bespoke' prices. Call for details. ☎ 010/6400–0133 ⊕ www.bespoke-beijing.com

■ **Cycle China** runs good guided hiking tours of the unrestored Wall at Jiankou.

(Y450–Y700 for minimum of 5 people). ☎ 010/6402–5653, ⊕ www.cyclechina.com

■ **Beijing Hikers** arrange weekly day-treks to the wilder parts of the Great Wall (from Y350; see website) throughout the year, as well as personalized tours (from Y1,200). ☎ 010/6432–2786 ⊕ www.beijinghikers.com

■ **Stretch-A-Leg Travel** specialize in customizable, off-the-beaten-track tours of the wild Wall, usually accessed through someone's backyard or by hopping over

a fence. Perfect for escaping the crowds. Call for details. ☎ 010/6401–8933 ⊕ www.stretchalegtravel.com

■ **Wild China** arranges camping trips underneath the Great Wall, although it should be noted that the campsite is not actually on the wall, but next to it, so as to avoid damage. ☎ 010/6465–6602 ⊕ www.wildchina.com

GREAT WALL AT BADALING

GETTING THERE

Distance: 70 km (43 mi) northwest of Beijing, in Yanqing County

Tours: Beijing Service, CITS

By Train: Trains from Badaling Station (Y19–Y23) leave Beijing North Station almost every hour from 6.12 AM and take 1 hour 20 minutes. From there, it's just a 20-minute walk to the entrance to Badaling Great Wall.

By Car: A car for four people to Badaling should run no more than Y600 for five hours, sometimes including a stop at the Thirteen Ming Tombs.

Take Line 2 on the subway to Jishuitan and walk to Deshengmen bus terminus. From there, take Bus 919 to Badaling (Y12). Be warned: private taxis hang around the station will try and convince you that it's easier to go with them. It isn't. Stick to your guns and get on that bus.

FAST FACTS

Phone: 010/6912–1223

Hours: Daily 6:30 am–7 pm

Admission: Y45 Apr.–Oct.; Y40 Nov.–Mar.; cable car is an additional Y40 one-way, Y60 round-trip

Web Site: www.badaling. gov.cn

Only one hour by car from downtown Beijing, the Great Wall at Badaling is where visiting dignitaries go for a quick photo-op. Postcard views abound here, with large sections of the restored Ming Dynasty brick wall rising majestically to either side of the fort. In the distance, portions of the early-16th-century Great Wall disintegrate into more romantic but inaccessible ruins.

Badaling is convenient to the Thirteen Ming Tombs and outfitted with tourist-friendly facilities, so it's popular with tour groups and is thus often crowded, especially on weekends. ▥ TIP→ People with disabilities find access to the wall at Badaling better than elsewhere in the Beijing area. You can either take the cable car to the top, or you can walk up the gently sloping steps, relying on handrails if necessary. On a clear day you can see for miles across leafy, undulating terrain from atop the battlements. The admission price also includes access to the China Great Wall Museum and the Great Wall Circle Vision Theater.

▥ TIP→ Most tours to Badaling will take you to the Thirteen Ming Tombs, as well. If you don't want a stop at the tombs—or at a tourist-trapping jade factory or herbal medicine center along the way—be sure to confirm the itinerary before booking.

GREAT WALL AT MUTIANYU

GETTING THERE

Distance: 90 km (56 mi) northeast of Beijing, in Huairou County

Tours: CITS, Great Wall Adventure Club

By Car: A car to Mutianyu should cost no more than Y600 for the day—it takes about an hour to get there.

By Bus: Take Bus 916/936 from Dongzhimen to Huairou (Y5). From there take a minibus to Mutianyu (Y25–Y30) or hire a taxi to take you there and back to the bus station (about Y50 each way, Y100–Y150 round-trip after bargaining).

FAST FACTS

Phone: 010/6162–6506 or 010/6162–6022

Hours: Daily 8 am–4 pm

Admission: Y45 (students half-price); cable car, Y50 one-way, Y65 round trip with toboggan descent

★ Fodor's Choice Slightly farther from downtown Beijing than Badaling, the Great Wall at Mutianyu is more spectacular and, despite the occasional annoyances of souvenir stands, significantly less crowded. This long section of wall, first built during the Northern Qi Dynasty (6th century) and restored and rebuilt throughout history, can offer a solitary Great Wall experience, with unforgettable views of towers winding across mountains and woodlands. On a clear day, you'll swear you can see the deserts of Mongolia in the distance.

The lowest point on the wall is a strenuous one-hour climb above the parking lot. As an alternative, you can take a cable car on a breathtaking ride to the highest restored section (this is how President Bill Clinton ascended in 1998), from which several hiking trails descend. Take a gorgeous 1½-hour walk east to reach another cable car that returns to the same parking lot. Mutianyu is also known for its toboggan run.

▥ **TIP➜** For those taking a car, the road from Huairou, a suburb of Beijing, to Mutianyu follows a river upstream and is lined with restaurants selling fresh trout. In addition, Hongluo Temple is a short drive from the bottom of the mountain.

GREAT WALL AT JUYONGGUAN

GETTING THERE

Distance: At just 50 km (31 mi) northeast of Beijing, Juyongguan is the closest part of the wall to Beijing and lies not far from Badaling—although the crowds here are far more manageable.

Tours: Most hotels offer tours here, as do CITS and Great Wall Adventure Tour.

By Car: A taxi to Juyongguan should run to around Y450 for the return trip.

By Bus: Take Line 13 on the subway to Longze. From there, exit the station and walk to the bus stop across the street to take Bus 68 (Y12) to Juyongguan. Buses from here leave every 20 minutes until 4.30 PM and should take around two hours.

FAST FACTS

Phone: 010/6977 1665

Hours: Daily 7:30 am–5:30 pm

Admission: Y35 Nov.–Mar.; Y45 Apr.–Oct.

Juyongguan is a quick, easygoing alternative for those not willing to blow a whole day travelling to Mutianyu or Jinshanling, or brave the more testing, unrestored sites such as Jiankou. It's the part of the wall that runs closest to Beijing and once guarded a crucial pass to the city, repelling hordes of Mongol and, latterly, Japanese invaders. The section also lies not far from Badaling, essentially acting as an overflow for its oversubscribed neighbor. It certainly loses nothing in the comparison, boasting similarly impressive views but with far less abrasive crowds. However, Juyongguan has been heavily restored and does feel a little sterile and commercial as a result.

The main attraction here is the Cloud Platform (or "Crossing Street Tower"), which was built in 1342 during the Yuan Dynasty. In appearance, it now resembles a rather squat Arc de Triomphe. The three white Tibetan stupas that originally sat atop it were destroyed during the early Ming period, only to be replaced with a Buddhist Tai'an temple, which was later toppled by fire in 1702. Today, carvings on the inner portal depicting the Four Heavenly Kings (Buddhist gods who defend the four compass points) and some elegant script work make for fascinating viewing on the way up the pass.

GREAT WALL AT JINSHANLING

GETTING THERE

Distance: 110 km (68 mi) northeast from Beijing

Tours: CITS, Cycle China, Great Wall Adventure Club

By Car: A car should be no more than Y800; the ride is about two hours. If you plan to hike from Jinshanling to Simatai, be warned that the latter was undergoing renovation and closed at the time of going to press. While over half of this walk (which takes 2-3 hours one way) is still accessible, you won't be able to be picked up at Simatai until it reopens again.

By Bus: Take Bus 980 from Dongzhimen long-distance bus station to Miyun (Y8) and then change to a local bus or taxi.

FAST FACTS

Phone: 031/4883-0222 or 138/3144-8986

Hours: Daily 8 am-5 pm

Admission: Y65 Apr.-Oct.; Y55 Nov.-Mar.; Y398-Y598 for overnight stays.

Though it lacks the rugged adventure of Simatai, Jinshanling is perhaps the least restored of the major Great Wall sections near Beijing, as well as the least visited. Besides being the starting point for a fantastic four-hour hike to Simatai, Jinshanling also serves as one of the few sections of the Great Wall on which you can camp overnight.

A starry night here is gorgeous and unforgettable—go with a tour group such as Cycle China. Don't forget to pack a piece of charcoal and paper to make rubbings of bricks that still bear the stamp of the date they were made.

GREAT WALL MARATHON

Not for the faint of heart, the Great Wall Marathon (and half marathon) takes place each May. The marathon covers approximately 6.5 km (4 mi) of the Great Wall, with the rest of the course running through lovely valleys in rural Tianjin. 1,650 RMB per person.

⊕ www.great-wall-marathon.com

period, Daxiongbaodian (the Mahavira Hall), are considered the finest examples of Buddhist mural art from the Ming Dynasty. Sadly, statues of various Buddhas and one of Li Tong himself were destroyed during China's Cultural Revolution.

The most famous of the nine murals in Mahavira Hall is a large-scale triptych featuring Guanyin (the Bodhisattva of Compassion) and Wenshu (the Bodhisattva of Marvelous Virtue and Gentle Majesty) in the center, and Poxian (the Buddha of Universal Virtue) on either side. The depiction of Guanyin follows the theme of "moon in water," which compares the Buddhist belief in the illusoriness of the material world to the reflection of the moon in the water. Typically painted with Guanyin are her legendary mount Jin Sun and her assistant Shancai Tongzi. Wenshu is often presented with a lion, symbolic of the bodhisattva's wisdom and strength of will, while Poxian is shown near a six-tusked elephant, each tusk representing one of the qualities that leads to enlightenment. On the opposite wall is the *Sovereign Sakra and Brahma* mural, with a panoply of characters from the Buddhist canon.

The murals were painted during the time of the European Renaissance, and though the subject matter is traditional, there are comparable experiments in perspective taking place in the depiction of the figures, as compared with examples from earlier dynasties. Also of note is a highly unusual decorative technique; many contours in the hall's murals, particularly on jewelry, armor, and weapons, have been set in bold relief by the application of fine gold threads.

The temple grounds are also beautiful, but of overriding interest are the murals themselves. Visitors stumble through the dark temple with flashlights (free with your ticket). Viewing the murals in this way, it's easy to imagine oneself as a sort of modern-day Indiana Jones unraveling a story of the Buddha as depicted in ancient murals of unrivaled beauty. Fahai Temple is only a short taxi ride from Beijing's Pingguoyuan subway station. ⊠ *Moshikou Lu, Shijingshan District, Beijing* ⚓ *Take an approximate Y12 taxi ride from Pinguoyuan subway station directly to the temple* ☎ *010/8871–5776* 🎫 *Y20* ⌚ *Daily 9–4.*

Tian Yi Mu (田义幕 *Tiányì mù*)(北京宦官文化陈列馆). Eunuchs have played a vital role throughout Chinese history, frequently holding great sway over the affairs of state. Their importance, however, has often been overlooked, a reality which the **Beijing Eunuch Culture Exhibition Hall** and the tomb of the most powerful eunuch of all, **Tian Yi** (1534–1605), shows to be false. Tian Yi was only nine when he was voluntarily castrated and sent into the service of the Ming emperor Jiajing. During the next 63 years of his life, he served three rulers and rose to one of the highest ranks in the land. By the time he died, there were more than 20,000 eunuchs in imperial service. Thanks to their access to private areas of the palace, they became invaluable as go-betweens for senior officials seeking gossip or the royal ear, and such was Tian Yi's influence. It's said that upon his death The Forbidden City fell silent for three days.

Though not as magnificent as the Thirteen Ming Tombs, the final resting place of Tian Yi befits a man of high social status. Of special note are the intricate stone carvings around the base of the central burial mound. The four smaller tombs on either side belong to other eunuchs who wished to pay tribute to Tian Yi by being buried in the same compound as him. Elsewhere, the small exhibition hall at the front of the tomb complex contains the world's only "eunuch museum" and offers some interesting background (albeit mostly in Mandarin), particularly on China's last eunuch, Sun Yaoting (1902–96). It's worth visiting, if only to see the rather gruesome mummified remains of one unlucky castrati that holds center stage—you can still make out the hairs on his chin. Another equally squirm-inducing sight is the eye-watering collection of castration equipment; plus keep a look out for the ancient Chinese character meaning "to castrate," which resembles two knives, one inverted, side by side. The hall and tomb are a five-minute walk from Fahai Temple; just ask people the way to Tian Yi Mu. ⌂ *80 Moshikou Lu, Shijingshan District, Beijing* ☎ *010/8872-4148* 🚌 *Y8* ⊙ *Daily 9–4:30.*

JIETAI TEMPLE (戒台寺 JIÈTÁI SÌ)

35 km (22 miles) west of Beijing.

On a wooded hill west of Beijing, Jietai Temple is one of China's most famous ancient Buddhist sites. Its four main halls occupy terraces on a gentle slope up to Ma'an Shan (Saddle Hill). Originally built in AD 622, it's been used for the ordination of Buddhist novices since the Liao Dynasty. The temple complex expanded over the centuries and grew to its current scale in a major renovation conducted by devotees during the Qing Dynasty (1644–1912). The temple buildings, plus three magnificent bronze Buddhas in the Mahavira Hall, date from this period. There's also a huge potbellied Maitreya Buddha carved from the roots of what must have been a truly enormous tree. To the right of this hall, just above twin pagodas, is the Ordination Terrace, a platform built of white marble and topped with a massive bronze statue of Shakyamuni Buddha seated on a lotus flower. Tranquil courtyards, where ornate stelae and well-kept gardens bask beneath a scholar tree and other ancient pines, add to the temple's beauty. Many modern devotees from Beijing visit the temple on weekends. Getting to Jietai and the nearby Tanzhe Temple is easy using public transportation. Take subway Line 1 to its westernmost station, Pingguoyuan. From there, take the No.931 public bus to either temple—it leaves every half hour and the ride takes about 70 minutes. A taxi from Pingguoyuan to Jietai Temple should be Y50 to Y60; the bus fare is Y6. ⌂ *Mentougou County* ☎ *010/6980-6611* 🚌 *Y45* ⊙ *Daily 8:30–5.*

NEARBY

Tanzhe Temple (潭哲寺 *Tánzhè sì*). Farther along the road past Jietai Temple, Tanzhe Temple is a Buddhist complex nestled in a grove of *zhe* (cudrania) trees. Established around AD 400 and once home to more than 500 monks, Tanzhe was heavily damaged during the Cultural Revolution. It's since been restored, but if you look closely at some of the huge stone

tablets, or *bei*, littered around the site you'll see that many of the inscriptions have been destroyed. The complex makes an ideal side trip from Jietai Temple or Marco Polo Bridge. ✉ ***Mentougou County*** ✣ ***10 km (6 miles) northeast of Jietai Temple, 45 km (28 miles) west of Beijing*** ☎ ***010/6086-2500*** 🎫 ***Y55*** ⏲ ***Daily 7:30–5:30 (winter 8:30–4:30).***

MARCO POLO BRIDGE (卢沟桥*LÚGÔU QIÁO*)

16 km (10 miles) southwest of Beijing's Guanganmen Gate.

Built in 1192 and reconstructed after severe flooding during the Qing Dynasty, this impressive span—known as Marco Polo Bridge because it was allegedly praised by the Italian wayfarer—is Beijing's oldest bridge. Its 11 segmented-stone arches cross the Yongding River on what was once the Imperial Highway that linked Beijing with central China. The bridge's marble balustrades support nearly 485 carved-stone lions that decorate elaborate handrails. Note the giant stone slabs that comprise the bridge's original roadbed. Carved imperial stelae at either end of the span commemorate the bridge and surrounding scenery.

The Marco Polo Bridge is best remembered in modern times as the spot where invading Japanese armies clashed with Chinese soldiers on June 7, 1937. The assault began Japan's brutal eight-year occupation of eastern China, which ended with Tokyo's surrender at the end of World War II. The bridge has become a popular field-trip destination for Beijing students. On the Beijing side of the span is the **Memorial Hall of the War of Resistance Against Japan.** Below the bridge on the opposite shore, local entrepreneurs rent horses (the asking price is Y120 per hour, but you should bargain) and lead tours of the often-dry grassy riverbed. ✉ *Near Xidaokou, Fengtai District, Beijing* ☎ *010/8389-4614* 🎫 *Y20* ⏲ *Daily 7 am–8 pm.*Zhoukoudian Peking Man Site (周口店 北京人现场*Zhōukǒudiàn Běijīngrén xiànchǎng)*

48 km (30 miles) southwest of Beijing.

This area of lime mines and craggy foothills ranks among the world's great paleontological sites (and served as the setting for Amy Tan's *The Bonesetter's Daughter*). In 1929, anthropologists, drawn to Zhoukoudian by apparently human "dragon bones" found in a Beijing apothecary, unearthed a complete cranium and other fossils dubbed *Homo erectus pekinensis*, or Peking Man. These early remains, believed to be nearly 700,000 years old, suggest (as do similar *Homo erectus* discoveries in Indonesia) that humankind's most recent ancestor originated in Asia, not Europe (though today some scientists posit that humans evolved in Africa first and migrated to Asia). A large-scale excavation in the early 1930s further unearthed six skullcaps and other hominid remains, stone tools, evidence of fire, plus a multitude of animal bones, many at the bottom of a large sinkhole believed to be a trap for woolly rhinos and other large game. Sadly, the Peking Man fossils disappeared under mysterious circumstances during World War II, leaving researchers only plaster casts to contemplate. Subsequent digs at Zhoukoudian have yielded nothing equivalent to Peking Man, although archaeologists

Nearly 485 carved stone lions decorate the Marco Polo Bridge.

haven't yet abandoned the search. Trails lead to several hillside excavation sites. A small museum showcases a few (dusty) Peking Man statues, a collection of Paleolithic artifacts, two mummies, and some fine animal fossils, including a bear skeleton and a saber-toothed tiger skull. Because of the importance of Peking Man and the potential for other finds in the area, Zhoukoudian is a UNESCO World Heritage Site, but it may not be of much interest to those without a particular inclination for the subject. If you should find yourself here with little to do after your museum visit and the few dig locations, consider a little hike into the surrounding hills, which are named the Dragon Bone Mountains. ✉ *Zhoukoudian* ☎ *010/6930–1278* 🎫 *Y30* ⏱ *Daily 8:30–4:30.*

YUNJU TEMPLE (云居寺 *YÚNJŪ SÌ*)

75 km (47 miles) southwest of Beijing.

Yunju Temple is best known for its mind-boggling collection of 14,278 minutely carved Buddhist tablets. To protect the Buddhist canon from destruction by Taoist emperors, the devout Tang-era monk Jing Wan carved Buddhist scriptures into stone slabs that he hid in sealed caves in the cliffs of a mountain. Jing Wan spent 30 years creating these tablets until his death in AD 637; his disciples continued his work for the next millennium into the 17th century, thereby compiling one of the most extensive Buddhist libraries in the world. A small pagoda at the center of the temple complex commemorates the remarkable monk. Although the tablets were originally stored inside Shijing Mountain behind the temple, they're now housed in rooms built along the temple's southern perimeter.

The Eastern Qing Tombs are the most expansive burial grounds in China.

Four central prayer halls, arranged along the hillside above the main gate, contain impressive Ming-era bronze Buddhas. The last in this row, the Dabei Hall, displays the spectacular *Thousand-Armed Avalokiteshvara*. This 13-foot-tall bronze sculpture—which actually has 24 arms and five heads and stands in a giant lotus flower—is believed to embody boundless compassion. A group of pagodas, led by the 98-foot-tall Northern Pagoda, is all that remains of the original Tang complex. These pagodas are remarkable for their Buddhist reliefs and ornamental patterns. Heavily damaged during the Japanese occupation and again by Maoist radicals in the 1960s, the temple complex remains under renovation. ⊠ *Off Fangshan Lu, Nanshangle Xiang, Fangshan County* ☎ *010/6138–9612* ⊠ *Y40* ⊙ *Daily 8:30–5 (winter 8:30–4:30).*

EASTERN QING TOMBS
(清东陵 *QĪNGDŌNGLÍNG*)

125 km (78 miles) east of Beijing.

Fodor'sChoice
★   Modeled on the Thirteen Ming Tombs, the Eastern Qing Tombs replicate the Ming spirit ways, walled tomb complexes, and subterranean burial chambers. But they're even more extravagant in their scale and grandeur, and far less touristy. The ruins contain the remains of five emperors, 14 empresses, and 136 imperial concubines, all laid to rest in a broad valley chosen by Emperor Shunzhi (1638–61) while on a hunting expedition. By the Qing's collapse in 1911, the tomb complex covered some 46 square km (18 square miles) of farmland and forested hillside, making it the most expansive burial ground in all China.

The Eastern Qing Tombs are in much better repair than their older Ming counterparts—and considerably less crowded. Although several of the tomb complexes have undergone extensive renovation, none is overdone. Peeling paint, grassy courtyards, and numerous stone bridges and pathways convey a sense of the area's original grandeur. Often visitors are so few that you may feel as if you've stumbled upon an ancient ruin unknown beyond the valley's farming villages.

Of the nine tombs open to the public, two are not to be missed. The first is **Yuling**, the resting place of the Qing Dynasty's most powerful sovereign, Emperor Qianlong (1711–99), who ruled China for 59 years. Beyond the outer courtyards, Qianlong's burial chamber is accessible from inside Stela Hall, where an entry tunnel descends some 65 feet into the ground and ends at the first of three elaborately carved marble gates. Beyond, exquisite carvings of Buddhist images and sutras rendered in Tibetan adorn the tomb's walls and ceiling. Qianlong was laid to rest, along with his empress and two concubines, in the third and final marble vault, amid priceless offerings looted by warlords early in the 20th century.

Dingdongling was built for the infamous Empress Dowager Cixi (1835–1908). Known for her failure to halt Western-imperialist encroachment, Cixi once spent funds allotted to strengthen China's navy on a traditional stone boat for the lake at the Summer Palace. Her burial compound, reputed to have cost 72 tons of silver, is the most elaborate (if not the largest) at the Eastern Qing Tombs. Many of its stone carvings are considered significant because the phoenix, which symbolizes the female, is level with, or even above, the imperial (male) dragon—a feature, ordered, no doubt, by the empress herself. A peripheral hall paneled in gold leaf displays some of the luxuries amassed by Cixi and her entourage, including embroidered gowns, jewelry, imported cigarettes, and even a coat for one of her dogs. In a bow to tourist kitsch, the compound's main hall contains a wax statue of Cixi sitting Buddha-like on a lotus petal flanked by a chambermaid and a eunuch.

The Eastern Qing Tombs are a two- to three-hour drive from the capital. The rural scenery is dramatic, and the trip is one of the best full-day excursions outside Beijing. Consider bringing a bedsheet, a bottle of wine, and boxed lunches, as the grounds are ideal for a picnic. ⊠ *Near Malanguan, Hebei Province, Zunhua County* ☎ *0315/694–4467* 🎫 *Y120* ⏱ *Daily 8–5.*

THE LOCALS

The attention foreign travelers receive in rural China may seem overwhelming, but it's usually good-natured and best responded to with politeness. Locals can be extremely kind, inviting you to their homes for tea, a meal, or even to stay the night. If you wish to turn them down, do so politely. However, taking them up on their hospitality can be extremely rewarding. Those who invite you to their homes are doing it out of kindness (Confucius said: "To have friends come from afar, isn't that happiness?"). A gift of a small quantity of fruit or a bottle of *baijiu* (a Chinese spirit distilled from sorghum) is always appreciated.

7

CHINESE VOCABULARY

CHINESE	ENGLISH EQUIVALENT	CHINESE	ENGLISH EQUIVALENT
CONSONANTS			
b	boat	p	pass
m	mouse	f	flag
d	dock	t	tongue
n	nest	l	life
g	goat	k	keep
h	house	j	and yet
q	chicken	x	short
zh	judge	ch	church
sh	sheep	r*	read
z	seeds	c	dots
s	seed		
VOWELS			
ü	you	ia	yard
üe	you + e	ian	yen
a	father	iang	young
ai	kite	ie	yet
ao	now	o	all
e	earn	ou	go
ei	day	u	wood
er	curve	ua	waft
i	yield	uo	wall
i (after z, c, s, zh, ch, sh)	thunder		

WORD ORDER

The basic Chinese sentence structure is the same as in English, following the pattern of subject-verb-object:

He took my pen.   Tā ná le wǒ de bě.

s   v   o   s   v   o

NOUNS

There are no articles in Chinese, although there are many "counters," which are used when a certain number of a given noun is specified. Various attributes of a noun—such as size, shape, or use—determine which counter is used with that noun. Chinese does not distinguish between singular and plural.

a pen	yìzhī bǐ
a book	yìběn shū

VERBS

Chinese verbs are not conjugated, and they do not have tenses. Instead, a system of word order, word repetition, and the addition of a number of adverbs serves to indicate the tense of a verb, whether the verb is a suggestion or an order, or even whether the verb is part of a question. Tāzài ná wǒ de bǐ. (He is taking my pen.) Tā ná le wǒ de bǐ. (He took my pen.) Tā you méi you ná wǒ de bǐ? (Did he take my pen?) Tā yào ná wǒ de bǐ. (He will take my pen.)

TONES

In English, intonation patterns can indicate whether a sentence is a statement (He's hungry.), a question (He's hungry?), or an exclamation (He's hungry!). In Chinese, words have a particular tone value, and these tones are important in determining the meaning of a word. Observe the meanings of the following examples, each said with one of the four tones found in standard Chinese: mā (high, steady tone): mother; má (rising tone, like a question): fiber; mǎ (dipping tone): horse; and mà (dropping tone): swear.

PHRASES

You don't need to master the entire Chinese language to spend a week in China, but taking charge of a few key phrases in the language can aid you in just getting by.

COMMON GREETINGS

Hello/Good morning	Nǐ hǎo/Zǎoshàng hǎo
Good evening	Wǎnshàng hǎo
Good-bye	Zàijiàn
Title for a married woman or an older unmarried woman	Tàitai/Fūrén
Title for a young and unmarried woman	Xiǎojiě
Title for a man	Xiānshēng
How are you?	Nǐ hǎo ma?
Fine, thanks. And you?	Hěn hǎo. Xièxiè. Nǐ ne?
What is your name?	Nǐ jiào shénme míngzi?
My name is . . .	Wǒ jiào . . .

Nice to meet you	Hěn gāoxìng rènshì nǐ.
I'll see you later.	Huítóu jiàn.

POLITE EXPRESSIONS

Please	Qǐng.
Thank you	Xièxiè.
Thank you very much.	Duōxiè.
You're welcome.	Búkèqi.
Yes, thank you.	Shì de, xièxiè.
No, thank you.	Bù, xièxiè.
I beg your pardon.	Qǐng yuánliàng.
I'm sorry.	Hěn baòqiàn.
Pardon me.	Dùibùqǐ.
That's okay.	Méi shénme.
It doesn't matter.	Méi guānxi.
Do you speak English?	Nǐ shuō Yīngyǔ ma?
Yes.	Shì de.
No.	Bù.
Maybe.	Bù yī dìng.
I can speak a little.	Wǒ néng shūo yī diǎnr.
I understand a little.	Wǒ dǒng yì diǎnr.
I don't understand.	Wǒ bù dǒng.
I don't speak Chinese very well.	Wǒ Zhōngwén shūo de bù haǒ.
Would you repeat that, please?	Qǐng zài shūo yíbiàn?
I don't know.	Wǒ bù zhīdaò.
No problem.	Méi wèntí.
It's my pleasure.	Méi guānxi.

NEEDS AND QUESTION WORDS

I'd like . . .	Wǒ xiǎng . . .
I need . . .	Wǒ xūyào . . .
What would you like?	Nǐ yaò shénme?
Please bring me . . .	Qǐng gěi wǒ . . .

I'm looking for . . .	Wǒ zài zhǎo . . .
I'm hungry.	Wǒ è le.
I'm thirsty.	Wǒ kǐukě.
It's important.	Hěn zhòngyào.
It's urgent.	Hěn jǐnjí.
How?	Zěnmeyàng?
How much?	Duōshǎo?
How many?	Duōshǎo gè?
Which?	Nǎ yí gè?
What?	Shénme?
What kind of?	Shénme yàng de?
Who?	Shuí?
Where?	Nǎli?
When?	Shénme shíhòu?
What does this mean?	Zhè shì shénme yìsi?
What does that mean?	Nà shì shénme yìsi?
How do you say . . . in Chinese?	. . .yòng Zhōngwén zěnme shūo?

AT THE AIRPORT

Where is . . .	. . .zài nǎr?
customs?	Hǎigūan
passport control?	Hùzhào jiǎnyàn
the information booth?	Wènxùntái
the ticketing counter?	Shòupiàochù
the baggage claim?	Xínglǐchù
the ground transportation?	Dìmìan jiěotōng
Is there a bus service	Yǒu qù chéng lǐ de gōnggòng
to the city?	qìchē ma?
Where are . . .	. . .zài nǎr?
the international departures?	Guójì hángběn chūfě diǎn
the international arrivals?	Guójì hángběn dàodá diǎn.
What is your nationality?	Nǐ shì něi guó rén?

I am an American.	Wǒ shì Měiguó rén.
I am Canadian.	Wǒ shì Jiānádà rén.

AT THE HOTEL, RESERVING A ROOM

I would like a room . . .	Wǒ yào yí ge fángjiān.
for one person	yìjiān dānrén fáng
for two people	yìjiān shuāngrén fáng
for tonight	jīntiān wǎnshàng
for two nights	liǎng gè wǎnshàng
for a week	yí ge xīngqī
Do you have a different room?	Nǐ hái yǒu biéde fángjiān ma?
with a bath	dài yùshì de fángjiān
with a shower	dài línyù de fángjiān
with a toilet	dài cèsuǐ de fángjiān
with air-conditioning	yǒu kōngtiáo de fángjiān
How much is it?	Duōshǎo qián?
My bill, please.	Qǐng jiézhàng.

AT THE RESTAURANT

Where can we find a good restaurant?	Zài nǎr kěyǐ zhǎodào yìjiě hǎo cānguǎn?
We'd like a(n) . . . restaurant.	Wǒmen xiǎng qù yì gè . . . cānguǎn.
elegant	gāo jí
fast-food	kuàicān
inexpensive	piányì de
seafood	hǎixiān
vegetarian	sùshí
Café	kāfēi diàn
A table for two	Liǎng wèi
Waiter, a menu please.	Fúwùyuán, qǐng gěi wǒmen càidān.
The wine list, please.	Qǐng gěi wǒmen jiǔdān.
Appetizers	Kāiwèi cài
Main course	Zhǔ cài

Dessert	Tiándiǎn
What would you like?	Nǐ yào shénme cài?
What would you like to drink?	Nǐ yào shénme yǐnliào?
Can you recommend a good wine?	Nǐ néng tūijiàn yí ge hǎo jiǔ ma?
Wine, please.	Qǐng lǎi diǎn jiǔ.
Beer, please.	Qǐng lǎi diǎn píjiǔ.
I didn't order this.	Wǐ méiyǒu diǎn zhè gè.
That's all, thanks.	Jiù zhèxie, xièxie.
The check, please.	Qǐng jiézhàng.
Cheers!/Bottoms Up!	Gānbēi! Zhù nǐ shēntì
To your health!	jiànkāng.

OUT ON THE TOWN

Where can I find . . .	Nǎr yǒu . . .
an art museum?	yìshù bówùguǎn?
a museum of natural history?	zìránlìshǐ bówùguǎn?
a history museum?	lìshǐ bówugǔan?
a gallery?	huàláng?
interesting architecture?	yǐuqù de jiànzhùwù?
a church?	jiàotáng?
the zoo?	dòngwùyuán?
I'd like . . .	Wǒ xiǎng . . .
to see a play.	kàn xì.
to see a movie.	kàn diànyǐng.
to see a concert.	qù yīnyuèhuì.
to see the opera.	kàn gējù.
to go sightseeing.	qù guānguāng.
to go on a bike ride.	qí zìxíngchē.

SHOPPING

Where is the best place to go shopping for . . .	Mǎi . . . zuì hǎo qù nǎr?
clothes?	yīfu
food?	shíwù

souvenirs?	jìniànpǐn
furniture?	jiājù
fabric?	bùliào
antiques?	gǔdǐng
books?	shūjí
sporting goods?	yùndòng wùpǐn
electronics?	diànqì
computers?	diànnǎo

DIRECTIONS

Excuse me. Where is . . .	Duìbùqǐ . . . zài nǎr?
the bus stop?	Qìchēzhàn
the subway station?	Dìtiězhàn
the rest room?	Xǐshǐujiān
the taxi stand?	Chūzū chēzhàn
the nearest bank?	Zùijìn de yínháng
the hotel?	Lǚguǎn
To the right	Zài yòubiān.
To the left.	Zài zuǐbiān.
Straight ahead.	Wǎng qián zhízǐu.
It's near here.	Jìuzài zhè fùjìn.
Go back.	Wǎng húi zǔu.
Next to . . .	Jǐnkào . . .

TIME

What time is it?	Xiànzài jǐdiǎn?
It is noon.	Zhōngwǔ.
It is midnight.	Bànyè.
It is 9:00 a.m.	Shàngwǔ jǐu diǎn.
It is 1:00 p.m.	Xiàwǔ yì diǎn.
It is 3 o'clock.	Sān diǎn (zhōng).
5:15	Wǔ diǎn shíwǔ fēn.
7:30	Qī diǎn sānshí (bàn).

9:45	Jǐu diǎn sìshíwǔ.
Now	Xiànzài
Later	Wǎn yì diǎnr
Immediately	Mǎshàng
Soon	Hěn kuài

DAYS OF THE WEEK

Monday	Xīngqī yī
Tuesday	Xīngqī èr
Wednesday	Xīngqī sān
Thursday	Xīngqī sì
Friday	Xīngqī wǔ
Saturday	Xīngqī lìu
Sunday	Xīngqī rì (tiān)

MODERN CONNECTIONS

Where can I find . . .	Zài nǎr kěyǐ shǐ yòng . . .
a telephone?	dìanhuà?
a fax machine?	chuánzhēnjī?
an Internet connection?	guójì wǎnglù?
How do I call the United States?	Gěi Měiguó dǎ diànhuà zěnme dǎ?
I need . . .	Wǒ xūyào . . .
a fax sent.	fā chuánzhēn.
a hookup to the Internet.	yǔ guójì wǎnglù liánjiē.
a computer.	diànnǎo.
a package sent overnight.	liányè bǎ bāoguǐ jìchū.
some copies made.	fùyìn yìxiē wénjiàn.
a VCR and monitor.	lùyǐngjī he xiǎnshìqì.
an overhead projector and markers.	huàndēngjī he biěoshìqì.

EMERGENCIES AND SAFETY

Help!	Jiùmìng a!
Fire!	Jiùhuǐ a!
I need a doctor.	Wǒ yào kàn yīshēng.

Call an ambulance!	Mǎshàng jiào jiùhùchē!
What happened?	Fāshēng le shénme shì?
I am/My wife is/My husband is/	Wǒ/Wǒ qīzi/Wǒ Zhàngfu/
My friend is/Someone is . . . very sick.	Wǒ péngyǒu/Yǒu rén . . .
having a heart attack.	bìng de hěn lìhài.
choking.	yēzhù le.
losing consciousness.	yūndǎo le.
about to vomit.	yào ǒutùwù le.
having a seizure.	yòu fābìng le.
stuck.	bèi kǎ zhù le.
I can't breathe.	Wǒ bù néng hūxī.
I tripped and fell.	Wǒ bàn dǎo le.
I cut myself.	Wǒ gē shěng le.
I drank too much.	Wǒ jiǔ hē de tài duō le.
I don't know.	Wǒ bù zhīdào.
I've injured my . . .	Wǒ de . . . shòushěng le.
head	tóu
neck	bózi
back	bèi
arm	gē bèi
leg	tuǐ
foot	jiǎo
eye(s)	yǎnjīng
I've been robbed.	Wǒ bèi qiǎng le.

NUMBERS

0	Líng
1	Yī
2	Èr
3	Sān
4	Sì
5	Wǔ

6	Liù
7	Qī
8	Bā
9	Jiǔ
10	Shí
11	Shíyī
12	Shí'èr
13	Shísān
14	Shísì
15	Shíwǔ
16	Shíliù
17	Shíqī
18	Shíbā
19	Shíjiǔ
20	Èrshí
21	Èrshíyī
22	Èrshí'èr
23	Èrshísān
30	Sānshí
40	Sìshí
50	Wǔshí
60	Liùshí
70	Qīshí
80	Bāshí
90	Jiǔshí
100	Yìbǎi
1,000	Yìqiān
1,100	Yìqiān
2,000	Yìqiān
10,000	Yíwàn
100,000	Shíwàn
1,000,000	Bǎiwàn

TRAVEL SMART
BEIJING

GETTING HERE AND AROUND

Beijing has exploded over the past few decades thanks to China's economic boom. Five years ago that growth went into overdrive as the city prepared to host the 2008 Olympics. The city spent around $20 billion on infrastructure, erecting new expressways, subways, and modern-style buildings. Whole neighborhoods were demolished, constructed, or 'renovated' in a process that continues to this day. However, in a city where the ancient and the modern live side by side, Beijing's relentless march toward modernity has caused some controversy. Old neighborhoods such as Gulou's much-loved hutong (narrow lanes), near the Drum and Bell towers in north-central Beijing, has been preparing for the bulldozers for what seems like forever as prime property areas become scarcer. Old-timers can barely recognize many sections of the city, and maps go out of date almost overnight. It's a good idea to get the latest bilingual version on arrival.

The city's five concentric ring roads look like a target, with the Forbidden City in the bull's-eye. The Second Ring Road follows the line of the old city walls, consequently many of the stops have the suffix "men" (meaning "gate") as these were the original portals to the inner city. The circular subway Line 2 runs below it. Note that, oddly, there is no First Ring Road; this is commonly thought to be the original tramline that circled the Forbidden City until it was disbanded in the 1950s. The Third Ring Road passes through part of Beijing's Central Business District (CBD) and links up with the Airport Expressway. Traffic in Beijing can be a nightmare, especially at rush hour when the gridlock extends from the center of the city all the way out to the Fourth Ring Road. With the recent opening of a number of new subway lines and several more to follow by 2016, the subway is a good way to escape the jam. The Airport Express Line (20 minutes from the airport to the Dongzhimen subway stop at the northeast of the city center) and Beijing's electronic subway fare system—where all rides cost a flat Y2, or around $0.30, fare—have both proved to be transport boons.

The city's wide main streets are laid out on a grid system. Roads run north–south or east–west. These compass points often make up part of the street name, so *bei* (north), *dong* (east), *nan* (south), *xi* (west), and *zhong* (middle) are useful words to know. Networks of ancient lanes and alleys known as *hutongs* run between these main streets, though they are fast falling prey to developers and many have suffered the wrath of the wrecking ball.

Beijing's most important thoroughfare runs east–west along the top of Tiananmen Square. Generally known as Chang'an Jie or the "Avenue of Heavenly Peace," it actually changes names several times along its length (as do many other major streets).

The three remaining ring roads have equally unimaginative names (Fourth, Fifth, Sixth). Along the center of the north Fourth Ring Road is Olympic Park, where you'll find the impressive National Stadium ("the Bird's Nest") and the National Aquatics Center ("the Water Cube"). If you're sticking to central Beijing, these roads aren't much use, though fare-hungry taxi drivers would love you to believe otherwise.

▌ BY AIR

Beijing is one of China's three major international hubs, along with Shanghai and Hong Kong. The number of nonstop flights to Beijing has been increasing as China's air-travel industry continues to liberalize. You can catch a nonstop flight here from New York (13¾ hours), Washington, D.C. (13 hours), Chicago (13½ hours), Sydney (11½ hours), Los Angeles (13 hours), Seattle (11 hours), and London (11 hours). As new non-stop flights seem to be added every few months, check travel sites online or with your travel agent for details. Besides state-run stalwart Air China, carriers such as Hainan Airlines, China Southern, and China Eastern all have nonstop flights. Multiple-stop flights from other cities generally stop in Tokyo, Seoul, Hong Kong, or Vancouver.

Airlines and Airports Airline and Airport Links.com. Airline and Airport Links.com has links to many of the world's airlines and airports. ⊕ www.airlineandairportlinks.com.

Airline Security Issues Transportation Security Administration. Transportation Security Administration has answers for almost every question that might come up. ⊕ www.tsa.gov.

AIRLINE TICKETS

There are a number of Chinese cities included in the One World Alliance Visit Asia Pass. They include major destinations like Beijing, Shanghai, and Hong Kong, as well as interior stops such as Xi'an, Chengdu, Xiamen, Nanjing, Kunming, and Wuhan. Cities are grouped into zones and there is a flat rate for each zone. The pass does not include flights from the United States. Inquire through American Airlines, Cathay Pacific, or any other One World member. It won't be the cheapest way to get around, but you'll be flying on some of the world's best airlines.

If you are flying into Asia on a Sky Team airline (Delta, for example) you're eligible to purchase their Go Asia and South West Pacific or Go Greater China Pass. The China Pass allows travel to nearly 150 destinations and prices are based on zone structure. You'll have to book directly with one of the Sky Team airlines (such as China Eastern or China Southern) to get the discounted fares.

The Star Alliance China Airpass is a good choice if you plan to stop in multiple destinations within Mainland China (also including Macao and Hong Kong). With one ticket you can choose from 71

different locations, though the ticket is only good for 3 to 10 individual flights on Air China or Shenzhen Airlines. The catch? Bear in mind that Chinese domestic flight schedules can be changed or canceled at a moment's notice.

Air Pass Info China Airpass ☎ 800/241–6522 United ⊕ www.staralliance.com. **Go Greater China** ☎ 800/221–1212 **Delta** ⊕ www.skyteam.com. **Visit Asia Pass** ☎ 800/233–2742 Cathay Pacific, 800/433–7300 American ⊕ www.oneworld.com.

AIRPORTS

The efficient Beijing Capital International Airport (PEK) is 27 km (17 miles) northeast of the city center. There are three terminals, connected by walkways and a tram system. Departures and arrivals operate out of all of them; T1 serves mainly domestic flights, while T2 and T3 serve both domestic and international flights. If you can't find your flight on the departure board when you arrive, check that you're in the correct terminal. The best advice is to check with the airport website before you depart from Beijing, as you'll need to let the taxi driver know which terminal you need to be dropped off at.

Beijing's airport tax (officially known as a "civil aviation fee") is Y90 for international flights and Y50 for domestic. These taxes are incorporated into your ticket prices, replacing the old coupon system that Beijing used to operate.

Clearing customs and immigration can take a while depending on how busy the airport is. Make sure you arrive at least two hours before your scheduled flight time. Also be sure to fill out the departure card before getting in line at the immigration check or you'll have to leave the line, fill out the card, and get back in at the end.

Both Chinese and Western-style fast-food outlets are available if you hunt around. Most are open from around 7 am to 11 pm. Prices for food and drink have been standardized for the most part at the various concessions, but it's still overpriced for what it is.

The airport is open all day. There is an uninspiring transit lounge for T1 and T2 in which to while away the hours. T3's waiting area is a bit more comfortable. If you've got a long stopover and need a rest, consider buying a package from the Plaza Premium Traveler's Lounge, near Gate 11 in the international section of T2, or near Gate E13 in T3. Both have comfortable armchairs, Internet access, newspapers, and a buffet, although the former is closed between midnight and 6 am. The third-floor recreation center has traditional massage facilities and a hairdresser.

While wandering the airport, someone may approach you offering to carry your luggage, or even just to give you directions. Be aware that this "helpful" stranger will almost certainly expect payment.

Airport Information Beijing Capital International Airport (PEK) ☎ *010/96158* ⊕ *www.bcia.com.cn.*

GROUND TRANSPORTATION

The easiest way to get from the airport to Beijing is by taxi. In addition, most major hotels have representatives at the airport able to arrange a car or minivan. When departing from Beijing by plane, prebook airport transport through your hotel.

When you arrive, head for the clearly labeled taxi line just outside the terminal, beyond a small covered parking area. The (usually long) line moves quickly. Ignore offers from touts trying to coax you away from the line—they're privateers looking to rip you off. At the head of the line, a dispatcher will give you your taxi's number, useful in case of complaints or forgotten luggage. Prices per kilometer are displayed on the side of the cab. Insist that drivers use their meters, and do not negotiate a fare. If the driver is unwilling to comply, feel free to change taxis.

Most of the taxis serving the airport are large-model cars, with a flag-fall of Y10 (good for 3½ km [2½ miles]) plus Y2 per additional kilometer. The trip to the center of Beijing costs around Y80. Going to the airport, there is a Y10 toll; this is waived coming into the city. In light traffic it takes about 30 minutes to reach the city center; during rush hour expect a one-hour cab ride. After 11 pm, taxis impose a 20% late-night surcharge.

Another option is the Airport Express Subway Line, which departs from T2 and T3 and stops at Sanyuanqiao (northeast Third Ring Road) and Dongzhimen (northeast Second Ring Road) subway stations. The best thing about this: only 20 minutes travel time at a price of Y25. Air-conditioned airport shuttle buses are another cheap way of getting into town. There are six numbered routes, all of which leave from outside the arrivals area. Tickets cost Y16—buy them from the ticket booth just inside the arrival halls. Most services run every 15 to 30 minutes. There's a detailed route map on the airport website.

FLIGHTS

Air China is the country's flagship carrier. It operates nonstop flights from Beijing to various North American and European cities. Its safety record has improved dramatically, and it has been part of Star Alliance since 2007. China Southern is the major carrier for domestic routes. Like all Chinese carriers, it's a regional subsidiary of the Civil Aviation Administration of China (CAAC).

You can make reservations and buy tickets in the United States directly through airline websites or with travel agencies. It's worth contacting a Chinese travel agency like China International Travel Service (CITS) (⇨ *Visitor Information below*) to compare prices, as these can vary substantially. If you're in China and want to book flights to other cities in the country, the websites *www.ctrip.com* and *www.elong.com* are excellent options. Flights though this website are often much cheaper than if you book them through a foreign website.

The service on most Chinese airlines is more on par with low-cost American airlines than with big international carriers—be prepared for limited leg-room, iffy food, and possibly no personal TV. More important, always arrive at least two hours before departure, as chronic overbooking means latecomers lose their seats.

Airline Contacts **United Airlines**
☎ 800/864–8331 for U.S. reservations, 800/538–2929 for international reservations ⊕ www.united.com. **Air Canada** ☎ 400/811–2001 in Beijing, 888/247–2262 ⊕ www.aircanada.com. **British Airways** ☎ 010/6512–4070 in Beijing, 800/247–9297 US ⊕ www.britishairways.com.

▌BY BUS

TO BEIJING

China has plenty of long-distance buses with air-conditioning and movies (whether you want them or not). However, buying tickets can be complicated if you don't speak Chinese, and you may end up on a cramped school bus. Taking a train or an internal flight is often much easier. Buses depart from the city's several long-distance bus stations. The main ones are: Dongzhimen (Northeast); Muxiyuan (at Haihutun in the South); Beijiao, also called Dewai (North); and Majuan or Guangqumen (East).

Bus Information Note that information is not usually available in English at any of these phone numbers and sometimes the numbers don't even work. It's best to have your hotel or a travel agent make arrangements.

Beijiao ✉ A30 Huayan Beili, Dongcheng District ☎ 010/8284–6760. **Dongzhimen** ✉ 45 Dongzhimenwai Xiejie, Dongcheng District ☎ 010/6467–1346. **Majuan** ✉ 22 Guangqumenwai Dajie, Chaoyang District ☎ 010/6771–7620.**Muxiyuan** ✉ 199 Yongwai Haihutun, Fengtai District ☎ 010/6726–7149.

WITHIN BEIJING

Unless you know Beijing well, public buses aren't the best choice for getting around. There are hundreds of routes, which are hot and crowded in summer and cold and

---

crowded in winter. Just getting on and off can be, quite literally, a fight.

The Beijing Public Transportation Corporation is the city's largest bus service provider. Routes 1 to 199 are regular city buses and cost a flat fare of Y1. Routes in the 200s only run at night, costing Y2. Routes 300 to 799 go from downtown Beijing to suburban areas and fares (starting at Y1) depend on how far you're going—have your destination written in Chinese, as you have to tell the conductor so they can calculate your fare. The newer long-distance, air-conditioned buses in the 800s and 900s start at Y2 and increase depending on distance. If you bought an IC card for the subway, you can use it on buses. Most buses allow you to scan your card as you board. On the suburban buses you'll scan as you board and as you depart, calculating the fare. For buses that go even farther afield, there is a conductor onboard who will take your fare or scan your card.

Contact **Beijing Public Transportation Corporation** ✉ 29 Lianhuachi Xili, Fengtai District ☎ 010/6396–0008 ⊕ www.bjbus.com.

▎ BY CAR

In a nutshell, renting a car is not a possibility when vacationing in Beijing: neither U.S. licenses nor IDPs are recognized in China. Nevertheless, this restriction should be cause for relief, as the city traffic is terrible and its drivers manic. A far better idea, if you want to get around by car, is to put yourself in the experienced hands of a local driver and sit back and relax. All the same, consider your itinerary carefully before doing so—the expanded subway system can be far quicker for central areas. Save the cars for excursions outside the city.

The quickest way to hire a car and driver is to flag down a taxi and hire it for the day. After some negotiating, expect to pay between around Y600–Y 700, depending on the type of car. Most hotels can make arrangements for you, though they often charge you double that rate—you can probably guess whose pocket the difference goes into. Most drivers do not speak English, so it's a good idea to have your destination and hotel names written down in Chinese, as well as a few sentences telling them you'd like to rent their service for the day.

Another alternative is American car-rental agency Avis, which includes mandatory chauffeurs as part of all rental packages—although this can also be very expensive, with chauffeurs alone costing 230RMB per hour.

Contact Avis ☎ *400/882–1119* ⊕ *www.avischina.com.*

▎ BY SUBWAY

With street-level traffic often grueling, Beijing's quick and efficient subway system is an excellent way to get about town. After operating for years with only two lines, the network is growing exponentially, with eight lines servicing the inner city, a further eight heading out into the suburbs and several more due to open over the next few years.

At the time of writing, there are 16 lines open. Lines 1 and the newly expanded Line 6 run east–west across the city, stopping at tourist destinations such as Tiananmen Square and Beihai Park. The original circle line, or Line 2 runs roughly under the Second Ring Road. North–south Line 5, gives access to the Lama Temple and Temple of Heaven. Line 8 runs through the Olympic Village all the way down to Gulou in the heart of the hutong area. The Line 10 loop is now complete, running past destinations such as Sanlitun and the antiques market at Panjiayuan. In the west and south, Line 4 stops at the Summer Palace and also Beijing South station. The Airport Line connects the Dongzhimen interchange with the airport—now a 20-minute jaunt at about Y25. The remaining lines are mainly used by commuters and are less useful for sightseeing.

Subway stations are marked by blue signs with a "D" (for *ditie*, or subway) in a circle. Signs are not always obvious, so be prepared to hunt around for entrances or ask directions; *Ditie zhan zai nar?* (Where's the subway station?) is a useful phrase to remember. But sometimes simply saying *ditie* with an inquiring look may get you better results since native Chinese speakers are often confused by the mispronounced tones uttered by foreigners.

Stations are usually clean and safe, as are trains. Navigating the subway is very straightforward: station names are clearly displayed in Chinese and pinyin, and there are maps in each station. Once on board, each stop is clearly announced on a loudspeaker in Chinese and English.

▐ BY TAXI

Taxis are easy to spot and the most comfortable way to get around. Be aware that they tend to disappear during inclement weather, and rush-hour traffic can be infuriating. There's a flag-fall of Y10 for the first 3 km (2½ miles), then Y2 per kilometer thereafter. After 11 pm flag-fall goes up to Y11, and there's a 20% surcharge per kilometer.

Drivers usually know the terrain well, but most don't speak English; having your destination written in Chinese is a good idea. (Keep a card with the name of your hotel on it for the return trip.) Hotel doormen can also help you tell the driver where you're going. It's a good idea to study a map and have some idea where you are, as some drivers will take you for a ride—a much longer one—if they think they can get away with it.

▐ BY TRAIN

China's enormous rail network is one of the world's busiest. Trains are usually safe and run strictly to schedule. Although there are certain intricacies to buying tickets, once you've got one, trips are generally hassle-free. Beijing is a major rail hub. Services to the rest of China leave from its four huge stations. The Trans-Siberian Railway leaves from Beijing Zhan, the main station. Trains to Hong Kong and to areas in the west and south of China leave from Beijing Xi Zhan (West). Most of the Z-series trains (nonstop luxury services) come into these two stations. Lesser lines to the north and east of the country leave from Beijing Bei Zhan (North) and Beijing Dong Zhan (East). C-series and D-series trains (intercity nonstop rail) mostly go to Beijing Nan Zhan (South).

China's high-speed rail network is rapidly becoming one of the longest in the world, and new routes are debuting every year. Journeys that used to be overnight affairs, such as Beijing to Xian or Shanghai, now take around five hours. Smooth rides and few delays make rail travel a tempting

BIG TRAIN RIDES

Taking the Trans-Siberian railway is a serious undertaking. The two weekly services cover the 5,000 miles (8,050 km) between Moscow and Beijing. The Trans-Manchurian is a Russian train that goes through northeast China, whereas the Trans-Mongolian is a Chinese train that goes through the Great Wall and crosses the Gobi Desert. Both have first-class compartments with four berths (Y1,800), or luxury two-berth compartments (Y2,200), one-way. Keep in mind that you will have to obtain all the necessary visas before embarking on your journey.

alternative to domestic flights, even if the price is sometimes not too dissimilar. You can buy most tickets 10 days in advance (remember to bring your passport); 2 to 3 days ahead is usually enough time, except around the three national holidays—Chinese New Year (two days in mid-January to February, depending on the lunar calendar of that particular year), Labor Day (May 1), and National Day (October 1). If you can, avoid traveling then—tickets sell out weeks in advance. Slow-train tickets can be bought from ticket offices around the city, but high-speed rail tickets can only be bought from the station.

The cheapest rates are also found at the station and there are special, English-speaking ticket offices for foreigners at both the Beijing Zhan (first floor) and Beijing Xi Zhan (second floor). Most travel agents, including CITS, can book tickets for a small surcharge (Y20 to Y50), saving you the hassle of going to the station. You can also buy tickets for slow trains through online retailers like China Train Ticket. They'll deliver the tickets to your hotel (keep in mind you often end up paying more).

Overpriced dining cars serve meals that are often inedible, so you'd do better to make use of the massive thermoses of boiled water in each compartment or the taps in the carriage section and take along your own noodles or instant soup, as the locals do.

Trains are always crowded, but you are guaranteed your designated seat, though not always the overhead luggage rack. Note that theft on trains is increasing; on overnight trains, sleep with your valuables or else keep them on the inside of the bunk.

You can find out just about everything about Chinese train travel at Seat 61's fabulous website. China Highlights has a searchable online timetable for major train routes. The tour operator Travel China Guide has an English-language website that can help you figure out train schedules and fares.

Information Note that the information numbers at train stations are usually only in Chinese.

Beijing Bei Zhan ⊠ Xizhimen, Xicheng District ☎ 010/5182–6273. Beijing Nan Zhan ⊠ 12 Yongdingmenwai Dajie, Dongcheng District ☎ 010/6303–0031. Beijing Xi Zhan ⊠ 118 Lianhuachi Donglu, Fengtai District ☎ 010/6321–6253. Beijing Zhan ⊠ East side of Dongbianmen Gate, A13 Maojiawang Hutong, Dongcheng District ☎ 010/5101–9999. China Highlights ⊕ www.chinahighlights. com/china-trains/index.htm. Seat 61 ⊕ www.seat61.com/China.htm. Travel China Guide ⊕ www.travelchinaguide.com/china-trains/index.htm.

ESSENTIALS

▌ ACCOMMODATIONS

Opening a hotel seems quite the thing to do in Beijing these days. That said, it's not always easy to choose a hotel: the Chinese star system is a little unpredictable, and websites are often misleading. For lesser establishments, try to get recent personal recommendations: the forums on Fodors. com are a great place to start.

"Location, location, location" should be your mantra when booking a Beijing hotel, especially if you're only in town for a few days. It's a big city: there's no point schlepping halfway across it for one particular hotel when a similar option is available in a more convenient area. Consider where you'll be going (Summer Palace? Forbidden City? Great Wall?), then pick your bed.

APARTMENT AND HOUSE RENTALS

There's an abundance of furnished short- and long-term rental properties in Beijing. Prices vary wildly. The priciest are luxury apartments and villas, usually far from the city center and best accessible by (chauffeur-driven) car. Usually described as "serviced apartments," these often include gyms and pools; rents can be over $2,000 a month. There are a lot of well-located mid-range properties in the city. They're usually clean, with new furnishings; rents start at $500 a month. Finally, for longer, budget-friendly stays, there are normal local apartments. These are firmly off the tourist circuit and often cost only a third of the price of the mid-range properties. Expect mismatched furniture, fewer amenities, and—we won't lie—varying insect populations.

Property sites like Wuwoo, Move and Stay, Sublet, and Pacific Properties have hundreds of apartments all over town. For a bit of local flavor, check out the rental options on AirBnB.Com. These apartments are rented out by the owner and verified by the web-based service. Centrally located and reasonably priced, they are a worthy alternative to hotel living. The online classifieds pages in local English-language magazines such as *The Beijinger*, *City Weekend*, or the Craigslist Beijing page are good places to start.

ONLINE BOOKING RESOURCES

Contacts AirBnB.com ⊕ *www.airbnb.com.* **The Beijinger** ⊕ *www.thebeijinger.com.* **City Weekend** ⊕ *www.cityweekend.com.cn.* **Craigslist Beijing** ⊕ *beijing.craigslist. cn.* **Move and Stay** ⊕ *www.moveandstay. com/beijing.* **Sublet.com** ⊕ *www.sublet.com.* **Wuwoo** ☎ *010/5166–7126* ⊕ *www.wuwoo.com.*

HOMESTAYS

Single travelers can arrange homestays (often in combination with language courses) through China Homestay Club. Generally these are in upper-middle-class homes that are about as expensive as a cheap hotel—prices range from $150 to $180 a week. Nine times out of 10, the family has a small child in need of daily English conversation classes. ChinaHomestay.org is a different organization that charges a single placement fee of $300 for a stay of three months or less.

Organizations China Homestay Club ⊕ *www.homestay.com.cn.* **ChinaHomestay.org** ⊕ *www.chinahomestay.org.*

HOSTELS

Budget accommodation options are improving in Beijing. However, the term "hostel" is still used vaguely—the only thing guaranteed is shared dorm rooms; other facilities vary and some hostels do include private rooms, so it is worth checking into. There are several clean youth hostels downtown, including three HI–affiliated properties, but flea-ridden dumps are also common, so always ask to see your room before paying. Try to pick a hostel close to a subway, and avoid properties beyond the Third Ring Road.

A private room in a low-end hotel is often just as cheap as these so-called hostels; some guesthouses and hotels also have cheaper dorm beds in addition to regular rooms. Hostelworld.com is a good site to visit, especially for peer feedback on everything from service to cleanliness.

Information **Hostelling International—USA** ☎ *301/495–1240* ⊕ *www.hiusa.org.* **Hostelworld.com** ⊕ *www.hostelworld. com.* **Youth Hostel Association of China** ☎ *020/8751–3733* ⊕ *www.yhachina.com.*

▮ COMMUNICATIONS

INTERNET

Beijing is a very Internet-friendly place for travelers with laptop computers. Most mid- to high-end hotels have in-room Internet access—if the hotel doesn't have a server you can usually access a government-provided ISP, which only charges you for the phone call. Wi-Fi is growing exponentially. Café chains like Starbucks are good places to try.

Most hotels usually have a computer with Internet access that you can use. Internet cafés are ubiquitous (look for 网吧 signs); it's an unstable business and new ones open and close all the time—ask your hotel for a recommendation. Prices vary considerably. Near the northern university districts you could pay as little as Y2 to Y3 per hour; slicker downtown places could cost 10 times that.

⚠ Remember that there is strict government control of the Internet in China. Google and Gmail are accessible if toothgrindingly slow to use, but it is impossible to access some news and blogging sites without a VPN or proxy.

PHONES

The country code for China is 86; the city code for Beijing is 10 (omit the first "0"), and the city code for Shanghai is 21. To call China from the United States or Canada, dial the international access code (011), followed by the country code (86),

the area or city code, and the eight-digit phone number.

Numbers beginning with 800 within China are toll-free. Note that a call from China to a toll-free number in the United States or Hong Kong is a full-tariff international call.

CALLING WITHIN CHINA

The Chinese phone system is cheap and efficient. You can make local and long-distance calls from your hotel or any public phone on the street. Some pay phones accept coins, but it's easier to buy an IC calling card, available at convenience stores and newsstands (⇨ *See Calling Cards below*). Local calls are generally free from landlines, though your hotel might charge a nominal rate. Long-distance rates in China are very low. Calling from your hotel room is a viable option, as hotels can only add a 15% service charge.

Beijing's city code is 010, and Beijing phone numbers have eight digits. When calling within the city, you don't need to use "010." In general, city codes appear written with a 0 in front of them; if not, you need to add this when calling another city within China.

For directory assistance, dial 114, or 2689–0114 for help in English (though you may not get through). If you want information for other cities, dial the city code followed by 114 (note that this is considered a long-distance call). For example, if you're in Beijing and need directory assistance for a Shanghai number, dial 021–114. The operators do not speak English, so if you don't speak Chinese you're best off asking your hotel for help.

To make long-distance calls from a public phone you need an IC card (⇨ *See Calling Cards below*). To place a long-distance call, dial 0, the city code, and the eight-digit phone number.

Contacts **Local directory assistance** ☎ *114 in Chinese, 116–114 (Ext. 2) in English.* **Taxi booking** ☎ *96103 in English.* **Weather** ☎ *400/6000–121.*

LOCAL DO'S AND TABOOS

GREETINGS

Chinese people aren't very touchy-feely with one another, even less so with strangers. Keep bear hugs and cheek kissing for your next European trip and stick to handshakes.

Always use a person's title and surname until they invite you to do otherwise.

RULES AND RULE BREAKING

By and large, the Chinese are a rule-abiding bunch. Follow their lead and avoid doing anything signs advise against.

Beijing is a crowded city, and pushing, nudging, and line jumping are common-place. It may be hard to accept, but it has become the norm, so avoid reacting (even verbally) if you're accidentally shoved.

OUT ON THE TOWN

It's a great honor to be invited to someone's house, so explain at length if you can't go. Arrive punctually with a small gift for the hosts; remove your shoes outside if you see other guests doing so.

Tea, served in all Chinese restaurants, is a common drink at mealtimes, though many locals only accompany their food with soup.

Smoking is one of China's greatest vices. No-smoking sections in restaurants are becoming more prevalent, but people light up anywhere they think they can get away with it.

Holding hands in public is fine, but keep passionate embraces for the hotel room.

DOING BUSINESS

Time is of the essence when doing business in Beijing. Make appointments well in advance and be extremely punctual.

Chinese people have a keen sense of hierarchy in the office: the senior member should lead proceedings.

Suits are the norm in China, regardless of the outside temperature. Women should avoid plunging necklines, overly short skirts, or very high heels.

Respect silences in conversation and don't hurry things or interrupt.

When entertaining, local businesspeople may insist on paying: after a protest, accept.

Business cards are a big deal: not having one is a bad move. If possible, have yours printed in English on one side and Chinese on the other (your hotel can often arrange this). Proffer your card with both hands and receive the other person's in the same way.

Many gifts, including clocks and cutting implements, are considered unlucky in China. Food—especially presented in a showy basket—is always a good gift choice, as are imported spirits.

LANGUAGE

Learn a little of the local language. You need not strive for fluency; even just mastering a few basic words and terms is bound to make chatting with the locals more rewarding.

Everyone in Beijing speaks Putonghua ("the common language") as the national language of China is known. It's written using ideograms, or characters; in 1949 the government also introduced a phonetic writing system that uses the Roman alphabet. Known as pinyin, it's widely used to label public buildings and station names. Even if you don't speak or read Chinese, you can easily compare pinyin names with a map, but be warned: written pinyin is lost on taxi drivers, so always come prepared with your destination written in Chinese characters.

CALLING OUTSIDE CHINA

To make an international call from within China, dial 00 (the international access code within China) and then the country code, area code, and phone number. The country code for the United States is 1.

IDD (international direct dialing) service is available at all hotels, post offices, major shopping centers, and airports. By international standards prices aren't unreasonable, but it's vastly cheaper to use a long-distance calling card, known as an IP card (⇨ *See Calling Cards below*), whose rates also beat AT&T, MCI, and Sprint hands down.

CALLING CARDS

Calling cards are a key part of the Chinese phone system. There are two kinds: the IC card (integrated circuit; *àicei ka*), for local and domestic long-distance calls on pay phones; and the IP card (Internet protocol; *aipi ka*) for international calls from any phone. You can buy both at post offices, convenience stores, and street vendors.

IC cards come in values of Y20, Y50, and Y100 and can be used in any pay phone with a card slot—most Beijing pay phones have them. Local calls using them cost around Y0.30 a minute, and less on weekends and after 6 pm.

To use IP cards, you first dial a local access number. This is often free from hotels, however at public phones you need an IC card to dial the access number. You then enter a card number and PIN, and finally the phone number complete with international dial codes. When calling from a pay phone both cards' minutes are deducted at the same time, one for local access (IC card) and one for the long-distance call you placed (IP card). There are countless different card brands; China Unicom is one that's usually reliable. IP cards come with values of Y20, Y30, Y50, and Y100; however, the going rate for them is up to half that, so bargain vendors down.

CELL PHONES

If you have a multiband phone (some countries use different frequencies than what's used in the United States) and your service provider uses the world-standard GSM network (as do T-Mobile, AT&T, and Verizon), you can probably use your phone abroad. Roaming fees can be steep, however: 99¢ a minute is considered reasonable. And overseas you normally pay the toll charges for incoming calls. It's almost always cheaper to send a text message than to make a call, since text messages have a very low set fee (often less than 5¢).

If you just want to make local calls, consider buying a new SIM card (note that your provider may have to unlock your phone for you to use a different SIM card) and a prepaid service plan in the destination. You'll then have a local number and can make local calls at local rates. If your trip is extensive, you could also simply buy a new cell phone in your destination, as the initial cost will be offset over time.

▌▌▌TIP➔ If you travel internationally frequently, save one of your old cell phones or buy a cheap one on the Internet; ask your cell-phone company to unlock it for you, and take it with you as a travel phone, buying a new SIM card with pay-as-you-go service in each destination.

If you have a GSM phone, pick up a local SIM card (*sim ka*) from any branch of China Mobile or China Unicom. You'll be presented with a list of possible phone numbers, with varying prices—an "unlucky" phone number (one with lots of 4s) could be as cheap as Y50, whereas an auspicious one (full of 8s) could fetch Y300 or more. You then buy prepaid cards to charge minutes onto your SIM—do this straightaway, as you need credit to receive calls. Local calls to landlines cost Y0.25 a minute, and to cell phones, Y0.60. International calls from cell phones are very expensive. Remember to bring an adapter for your phone charger. You can also buy cheap handsets from China Mobile. If you're planning to stay even a couple of days this is probably cheaper than renting a phone.

Beijing Limo rents cell phones, which they can deliver to your hotel or at the airport. Renting a handset starts at $5 a day, and you buy a prepaid package with a certain amount of call time; prices start at $50. Beijing Impression travel agency rents handsets at similar rates, and you buy a regular prepaid card for calls. For that money, you may as well buy your own pay-as-you-go cell phone once you arrive (the cheapest Nokia handset goes for around Y220). Cell phone shops are plentiful, though you may need an interpreter to help you deal with the people behind the counter and to reset the language.

Contacts Beijing Impression ☎ 010/6400–0300 ⊕ www.beijingimpression.cn. **Beijing Limo** ☎ 010/6546–1588 ⊕ www.beijinglimo. com/english. **Cellular Abroad.** Cellular Abroad rents and sells GMS phones and sells SIM cards that work in many countries. ☎ 800/287–5072 ⊕ www.cellularabroad.com. **China Mobile.** China Mobile is China's main mobile-service provider. ☎ 10086 English-language assistance ⊕ www.chinamobileltd. com. **China Unicom.** China Unicom is China's second-largest main mobile-phone company. ☎ 010/116–114 English-language assistance ⊕ www.chinaunicom.com. **Planet Fone.** Planet Fone rents cell phones, but the per-minute rates are expensive. ☎ 888/988–4777 ⊕ www.planetfone.com.

▌ CUSTOMS AND DUTIES

Except for the usual prohibitions against narcotics, explosives, plant and animal materials, firearms, and ammunition, you can bring anything into China that you plan to take away with you. Cameras, video recorders, GPS equipment, laptops, and the like should pose no problems. However, China is very sensitive about printed matter deemed seditious, such as religious, pornographic, and political items, especially articles, books, and pictures on Tibet. All the same, small amounts of English-language reading matter aren't generally a problem. Customs officials are for the most part easy-going, and visitors are rarely searched. It's not necessary to fill in customs declaration forms, but if you carry in a large amount of cash, say several thousand dollars, you should declare it upon arrival.

On leaving, you're not allowed to take out any antiquities dating to before 1795. Antiques from between 1795 and 1949 must have an official red seal attached.

U.S. Information U.S. Customs and Border Protection ⊕ www.cbp.gov.

▌ EATING OUT

In China, meals are a communal event, so food in a Chinese home or restaurant is always shared. Although cutlery is available in many restaurants, it won't hurt to brush up on your use of chopsticks, the utensil of choice. The standard eating procedure is to hold the bowl close to your mouth and eat the food. Noisily slurping up soup and noodles is also the norm. It's considered bad manners to point or play with your chopsticks, or to place them on top of your rice bowl when you're finished eating (place the chopsticks horizontally on the table or plate). Avoid, too, leaving your chopsticks standing up in a bowl of rice—this is said to resemble the practice of burning two incense sticks at funerals and is considered disrespectful.

If you're invited to a formal Chinese meal, be prepared for great ceremony, endless toasts and speeches, and a grand variety of elaborate dishes. Your host will be seated at the "head" of the round table, which is the seat that faces the door. Wait to be instructed where to sit. Don't start eating until the host takes the first bite, and then simply help yourself as the food revolves around on a lazy Susan, but don't take the last piece on a platter. Always let the food touch your plate before bringing it up to your mouth; eating directly from the serving dish is bad form.

Beijing's most famous dish is Peking duck. The roast duck is served with thin pancakes, in which you wrap pieces of the meat, together with spring onions, vegetables, and plum sauce. Hotpot is another local trademark: you order different meats and vegetables, which you cook in a pot of stock boiling on a charcoal burner. *Baozi* (small steamed buns filled with meat or vegetables) are particularly good in Beijing—sold at stalls and in small restaurants everywhere, they make a great snack or breakfast food.

MEALS AND MEALTIMES

Food is a central part of Chinese culture, and so eating should be a major activity on any trip to Beijing. Breakfast is not a big deal in China—congee, or rice porridge (*zhou*), is the standard dish. Most mid- and upper-end hotels do big buffet spreads, whereas Beijing's blooming café chains provide lattes and croissants all over town.

Snacks are a food group in themselves. There's no shortage of steaming street stalls selling baozi, spicy kebabs (called *chuan'r*), savoury pancakes (*bing*), hot sweet potatoes, and bowls of noodle soup. Pick a place where lots of locals are eating to be on the safe side.

The food in hotel restaurants is usually acceptable but overpriced. Restaurants frequented by locals always serve tastier fare at better prices. Don't shy from trying establishments without an English menu— a good phrase book and lots of pointing can usually get you what you want.

Lunch and dinner dishes are more or less interchangeable. Meat (especially pork) or poultry tends to form the base of most Beijing dishes, together with wheat products like buns, pancakes, and noodles. Beijing food is often quite oily, with liberal amounts of vinegar; its strong flavors come from garlic, soy sauce, and bean pastes. Food can often be extremely salty and loaded with MSG. If you can manage it, try to have the waitress tell the cooks to cut back. Vegetables—especially winter cabbage and onions—and tofu play a big role in meals. As in all Chinese food, dairy products are scarce. Chinese meals usually involve a variety of dishes, which are always ordered communally in restaurants. Eat alone or order your own dishes and you're seriously limiting your food experience.

If you're craving Western food, rest assured that Beijing has plenty of American fast-food chains, as well as Western-style restaurants on the east side of town. Most higher-end restaurants have a Western menu, but you're usually safer sticking to the Chinese food.

Meals in China are served early: breakfast until 9 am, lunch between 11 and 2, and dinner from 5 to 9. Unless otherwise noted, the restaurants listed in this guide are open daily for lunch and dinner. Restaurants and bars catering to foreigners may stay open longer hours.

PAYING

At most restaurants you ask for the bill at the end of the meal. At cheap noodle bars and street stands you pay up front. Only very upmarket restaurants accept payment by credit card. (⇨ *For guidelines on tipping see Tipping below.*)

RESERVATIONS AND DRESS

In some places (Hong Kong, for example), making a prior reservation is expected. Beijing is less formal, although for popular restaurants, it's wise to book ahead, and reconfirm as soon as you arrive. (Large parties should always call ahead to check the reservations policy.) Few restaurants require a strict dress code, although smart casual dress is obviously the norm in pricier establishments.

WINE, BEER, AND SPIRITS

Walk down any side street with outdoor restaurant seating and you'll find gaggles of men socializing around an armada of empty green beer bottles. Beijing is a beer-drinking town, with Yanjing, Tsingtao, Beijing Beer, and Snow the local brands of choice. Chinese beer is not very strong (around 3% ABV) although usually very cheap. But while alcohol has long been a part of the Chinese social dining experience, bars solely for drinking in have only cropped up over the past few decades with the influx of Westerners. Nevertheless, they have been quickly adopted by a young generation of Chinese. Today, the wealth of bars around Sanlitun, Houhai, and Nanluguoxiang slinging obscure imported beers is a sign of the times. Beijing has even recently adopted microbrewing, with a spat of several excellent local labels and dedicated brewpubs now worth sampling.

However, drinking traditionally remains a big part of any meal. If you are invited to a banquet or special dinner by Chinese friends or colleagues, you may be in for a long night of gluttonous eating and imbibing. The spirit of choice for these occasions is *baijiu*, a noxious 56-proof rice wine that can sometimes taste of liquid blue cheese (better quality) or an old gasoline-soaked athletic sock (not so good quality). If your companions are a table of Chinese men, expect much machismo to accompany the festivities. When one of them yells "Ganbei!" you are expected to finish the entire shot. The best option for a nondrinker is to refuse any alcohol from the beginning and turn the shot glass upside down; or alternatively, if you drink, but don't think you can stomach the baijiu, have the waitress pour wine or beer into your shot glass. None of these actions are rude except backing down once you've started in on the baijiu shots.

▌ ELECTRICITY

The electrical current in China is 220 volts, 50 cycles alternating current (AC), so most American appliances can't be used without a transformer. A universal adapter is especially useful in China, as wall outlets come in a bewildering variety of configurations: two- and three-pronged round plugs, as well as two-pronged flat sockets.

Consider making a small investment in a universal adapter, which has several types of plugs in one lightweight, compact unit. Most laptops and cell-phone chargers are dual voltage (i.e., they operate equally well on 110 and 220 volts), so require only an adapter. These days the same is true of small appliances such as hair dryers. Always check labels and manufacturer instructions to be sure. Don't use 110-volt outlets marked "for shavers only" for high-wattage appliances such as hair dryers.

Contacts Steve Kropla's Help for World Traveler's. Steve Kropla's Help for World Traveler's has information on electrical and telephone plugs around the world. ⊕ *www.kropla.com.* **Walkabout Travel Gear.** Walkabout Travel Gear has a good coverage of electricity under "adapters." ⊕ *www.walkabouttravelgear.com.*

▌ EMERGENCIES

The best place to head in a medical emergency is the Beijing United Family Health Center, which has 24-hour emergency services. SOS is another international clinic with a good reputation; they also arrange Medivac.

Beijing has different numbers for each emergency service, though staff members often don't speak English. If in doubt, call the U.S. embassy first: staff members are available 24 hours a day to help handle emergencies and facilitate communication with local agencies.

Doctors and Dentists Beijing United Family Hospital and Clinics ✉ *No. 2 Jiangtai Lu, Chaoyang District* ☎ 010/5927–7000, 010/5927–7120 for emergencies ⊕ *www.ufh.com.cn/en.* **International SOS** ✉ *Suite 105, Wing 1, Kunsha Bldg., 16 Xinyuanli, Chaoyang District* ☎ 010/6462–9112 clinic, 010/6462–9100 24-hr hotline ⊕ *www.internationalsos.com.*

Contacts U.S. Embassy ✉ *55 Anjialou Lu, Chaoyang District* ☎ 010/8531–4000 🖷 010/8531–3300 ⊕ *beijing.usembassy-china.org.cn.*

General Emergency Contacts Fire ☏ 119. Police ☏ 110. Medical Emergency ☏ 120. Traffic Accident ☏ 122.

Hospitals and Clinics Beijing United Family Health and Wellness Centre ⊠ B1, *The St. Regis Residence, 21 Jianguomenwai Dajie, Chaoyang District* ☏ 010/8532–1221, 010/5927–7120 for emergencies ⊕ *www.ufh. com.cn/en/.* **China Academy of Medical Science (Peking Union Hospital)** ⊠ *1 Shui Fu Yuan, Dongcheng District* ☏ 010/6529–5284 ⊕ *english.pumch.cn.* **Hong Kong International Medical Clinic** ⊠ *Private Office Tower, 9th floor, Hong Kong Macau Center–Swissotel, 2 Chaoyangmen Bei Dajie, Chaoyang District* ☏ 010/6553–2288 ⊕ *www.hkclinic.com.* **Sino-Japanese Friendship Hospital** ⊠ *Public Ying Hua Donglu, Heping Li* ☏ 010/6422–2952. **SOS International** ⊠ *Private Bldg. C, BITIC Leasing Center, 1 North Rd., Xing Fu San Cun, Chaoyang District* ☏ 010/6462–9199 ⊕ *www.internationalsos.com.*

Pharmacies Beijing United Family Health Center ⊠ *Private, 2 Jiangtai Lu, near Lido Hotel, Chaoyang District* ☏ 010/5927–7000, 010/5927–7120 for emergencies ⊕ *www. unitedfamilyhospitals.com.* **International Medical Center (IMC)** ⊠ *Private Beijing Lufthansa Center, Room 106, 50 Liangmaqiao Lu, Chaoyang District* ☏ 010/6465–1561 ⊕ *www.imcclinics.com.* **Watsons.** Watsons can also be found in most large shopping centers. ⊠ *Holiday Inn Lido Hotel, Jichang Lu, Chaoyang District* ⊠ *Sanlitun Village South, No. 19 Sanlitun Lu, Chaoyang District* ⊕ *www.watsons.com.cn.*

∎ HEALTH

The most common types of illnesses are caused by contaminated food and water. Drink only bottled, boiled, or purified water and drinks; don't drink from public fountains or use ice. Make sure food has been thoroughly cooked and is served to you fresh and hot. If you have problems, mild cases of traveler's diarrhea may respond to Imodium (known generically as loperamide) or Pepto-Bismol.

Be sure to drink plenty of fluids; if you can't keep fluids down, seek medical help immediately. Tap water in Beijing is safe for brushing teeth, but you're better off buying bottled water to drink.

Infectious diseases can be airborne or passed via mosquitoes and ticks and through direct or indirect physical contact with animals or people. Some, including Norwalk-like viruses that affect your digestive tract, can be passed along through contaminated food. Condoms can help prevent most sexually transmitted diseases, but they aren't absolutely reliable and their quality varies from country to country. China is notorious for fake condoms, so it might be best to bring your own from home or get them from a health clinic. Speak with your physician and/or check the CDC or World Health Organization websites for health alerts, particularly if you're pregnant, traveling with children, or have a chronic illness.

SPECIFIC ISSUES IN BEIJING

Pneumonia and influenza are common among travelers returning from China— talk to your doctor about inoculations before you leave. If you need to buy prescription drugs, try to go to the pharmacies of reputable private hospitals like the Beijing United Family Medical Center. Do *not* buy them in streetside pharmacies as the quality control is unreliable.

OVER-THE-COUNTER REMEDIES

Most pharmacies carry over-the-counter Western medicines and traditional Chinese medicines. By and large, you need to ask for the generic name of the drug you're looking for, not a brand name.

SHOTS AND MEDICATIONS

No immunizations are required for entry into China, but it's a good idea to be immunized against typhoid and Hepatitis A and B before traveling to Beijing; also a good idea is to get routine shots for tetanus-diphtheria and measles. In winter, a flu vaccination is also smart.

Health Warnings National Centers for Disease Control & Prevention (*CDC*).

☎ 800/232–4636 ⊕ www.cdc.gov/travel.
World Health Organization (*WHO*).
⊕ www.who.int.

▌ HOURS OF OPERATION

Most offices are open between 9 and 6 on weekdays; most museums keep roughly the same hours six or seven days a week. Everything in China grinds to a halt for the first two or three days of Chinese New Year (sometime in mid-January through February, depending on the lunar calendar), and opening hours are often reduced for the rest of that season.

Banks and government offices are open weekdays 9 to 5, although some close for lunch (sometime between noon and 2). Bank branches and CTS tour desks in hotels often keep longer hours and are usually open Saturday (and occasionally even Sunday) mornings. Many hotel currency-exchange desks stay open 24 hours.

Pharmacies are open daily from 8:30 or 9 am to 6 or 7 pm. Some large pharmacies stay open until 9 pm or even later.

Shops and department stores are generally open daily 9 to 9; some stores stay open even later in summer, in popular tourist areas, or during peak tourist season.

HOLIDAYS

National holidays include New Year's Day (January 1); Spring Festival, aka Chinese New Year (mid-January/through February); Tomb-Sweeping Day (a spring festival when families sweep ancestors' graves; April 5); International Labor Day (May 1); Dragon Boat Festival (late May/early June); anniversary of the founding of the Communist Party of China (July 1); anniversary of the founding of the Chinese People's Liberation Army (August 1); Mid-Autumn Festival (mid- to late September) and National Day—founding of the People's Republic of China in 1949 (October 1).

▌ MAIL

Sending international mail from China is reliable. Airmail letters to any place in the world should take 5 to 14 days. Express Mail Service (EMS) is available to many international destinations. Letters within Beijing arrive the next day, and mail to the rest of China takes a day or two longer. Domestic mail can be subject to search, so don't send sensitive materials, such as religious or political literature, as you might cause the recipient trouble.

Service is more reliable if you mail letters from post offices rather than mailboxes. Buy envelopes here, too, as there are standardized sizes in China. You need to glue stamps onto envelopes as they're not self-adhesive. Most post offices are open daily between 8 and 7. Your hotel can usually send letters for you, too.

You can use the Roman alphabet to write an address. Do not use red ink, which has a negative connotation. You must also include a six-digit zip code for mail within China. The Beijing municipality is assigned the zip code 100000, and each neighboring county starts with 10. For example, the code for Fangshan, to the immediate southwest of Beijing proper, is 102400.

Sending airmail postcards costs Y4.20 and letters Y5.40 to Y6.50.

Main Branches International Post and Telecommunications Office ✉ *Jianguomenwai Dajie, Yabao Lu, 1,000 feet north of the Jianguomen overpass, Chaoyang District* ☎ *010/6512-8114* ⊕ *www.bipto.com.cn.*

SHIPPING PACKAGES

It's easy to ship packages home from China. Take what you want to send *unpacked* to the post office—everything will be sewn up officially into satisfying linen-bound packages, a service that costs a few yuan. You have to fill in lengthy forms, and enclosing a photocopy of receipts for the goods inside isn't a bad idea, as they may be opened by customs along the line. Large antiques stores often offer reliable shipping services that take care of customs in China. Large international couriers operating in Beijing include DHL, Federal Express, and UPS.

Express Services DHL. This German delivery giant also has express centers in the China World Trade Centre and COFCO Plaza. ⊠ 45 Xinyuan Jie, Chaoyang District ☎ 800/810–8000, 010/5860–1076 ⊕ www.cn.dhl.com. **FedEx.** Also has 24/7 counters in FedEx Kinko shops, which are located in Fortune Plaza, Oriental Plaza, Ocean Express, Focus Plaza, and more. ⊠ 3rd floor, Golden Land Bldg., 32 Liangmaqiao Lu, Chaoyang District ☎ 010/6464–8855, 800/988–1888 ⊕ www. fedex.com/cn_english. **UPS** ⊠ 1818, Bldg. 1, China World Trade Center, 1 Jianguomenwai Dajie, Chaoyang District ☎ 800/820–8388 ⊕ www.ups.com.

▌MONEY

The best places to convert your dollars into yuan are at your hotel's front desk or a branch of a major bank, such as Bank of China, CITIC, or HSBC. All these operate with standardized government rates—anything cheaper is illegal, and thus risky. You need to present your passport to change money.

Although credit cards are widespread in China, for day-to-day transactions cash is definitely king. Getting change for larger notes can be a problem in small shops and taxis, so try to stock up on 10s and 20s when you change money. ATMs are widespread; most accept Union Pay, Visa, MasterCard etc., hunt around and you're sure to find one that accepts your card.

ATMS AND BANKS

Your own bank will probably charge a fee for using ATMs abroad; the foreign bank you use may also charge a fee. Nevertheless, you'll usually get a better rate of exchange at an ATM than you will at a currency-exchange office or even when changing money in a bank. And extracting funds as you need them is a safer option than carrying around a large amount of cash.

Out of the Chinese banks, your best bets for ATMs is the Bank of China and ICBC, which accept most foreign cards. That said, machines frequently refuse to give cash for mysterious reasons. Move on and try another. Citibank and HSBC have lots of branches in Beijing, and accept all major cards. On-screen instructions appear automatically in English. Be sure to check all bills that you receive from the ATM; sometimes fake notes find their way into the system and it can be a nightmare to get the bank to exchange for real ones—especially if you leave the premises.

CREDIT CARDS

It's a good idea to inform your credit-card company before you travel, especially if you're going abroad and don't travel internationally very often. Otherwise, the credit-card company might put a hold on your card owing to unusual activity—not a good thing halfway through your trip. Record all your credit-card numbers—as well as the phone numbers to call if your cards are lost or stolen—in a safe place, so you're prepared should something go wrong. Both MasterCard and Visa have general numbers you can call (collect if you're abroad) if your card is lost, but you're better off calling the number of your issuing bank, since MasterCard and Visa usually just transfer you to your bank; your bank's number is usually printed on your card.

If you plan to use your credit card for cash advances, you'll need to apply for a PIN at least two weeks before your trip. Although it's usually cheaper (and safer) to use a credit card abroad for large purchases (so you can cancel payments or be reimbursed if there's a problem), note that some credit-card companies *and* the banks that issue them add substantial percentages to all foreign transactions, whether they're in a foreign currency or not. Check on these fees before leaving home, so there won't be any surprises when you get the bill.

TIP→ Before you charge something, ask the merchant whether or not he or she plans to do a dynamic currency conversion (DCC). In such a transaction the credit-card processor (shop, restaurant, or hotel, not Visa or MasterCard) converts the currency and charges you in dollars. In most cases you'll pay the merchant a 3% fee for this service in addition to any credit-card company and issuing-bank foreign-transaction surcharges.

Dynamic currency conversion programs are becoming increasingly widespread. Merchants who participate in them are supposed to ask whether you want to be charged in dollars or the local currency, but they don't always do so. And even if they do offer you a choice, they may well avoid mentioning the additional surcharges. The good news is that you *do* have a choice. And if this practice really gets your goat, you can avoid it entirely thanks to American Express; with its cards, DCC simply isn't an option.

In Beijing, American Express, MasterCard, and Visa are accepted at most major hotels and a growing number of upmarket stores and restaurants. Diners Club is accepted at many hotels and some restaurants.

Reporting Lost Cards American Express
☎ 800/528–4800 in the U.S., 336/393–1111 collect from abroad ⊕ www.americanexpress. com. **Diners Club** ☎ 800/234–6377 in the U.S., 514/881–3735 collect from abroad ⊕ www.dinersclub.com. **MasterCard** ☎ 800/627–8372 in the U.S., 636/722–7111 collect from abroad, 010/800–110–7309 in China, 010/800–711–7309 in China ⊕ www. mastercard.com. **Visa** ☎ 800/847–2911 in the U.S., 410/581–9994 collect from abroad, 010/800–711–2911 in China ⊕ www.visa.com.

CURRENCY AND EXCHANGE

The Chinese currency is officially called the yuan (Y), and is also known as *renminbi* (RMB), or "People's Money." You may also hear it called *kuai*, an informal expression like "buck." After being pegged to the dollar at around Y8 for years, it was allowed to float within a

small range starting in 2005. It appreciated quite a bit, especially between 2007 and the middle of 2008, then held firm again until mid-2010 when it was allowed to float again. As of this writing, the conversion was Y6.78 to $1.

Both old and new styles of bills circulate simultaneously in China, and many denominations have both coins and bills. The Bank of China issues bills in denominations of 1 (green), 5 (purple), 10 (turquoise), 20 (brown), 50 (blue-green), and 100 (red) yuan. There are Y1 coins, too. The yuan subdivides into 10-cent units called *jiao* or *mao*; these come in bills and coins of 1, 2, and 5. The smallest denomination is the *fen*, which comes in coins (and occasionally tiny notes) of 1, 2, and 5; these are largely useless in day-to-day exchanges and a relic of China's failure to revalue its own currency. Counterfeiting is rife here, and even small stores inspect notes with ultraviolet lamps. Change can also be a problem—don't expect much success paying for a Y3 purchase with a Y100 note, for example.

Exchange rates in China are fixed by the government daily, so it's equally good at branches of the Bank of China, at big department stores, or at your hotel's exchange desk, which has the added advantage of often being open 24 hours a day. Any lower rates are illegal, so you're exposing yourself to scams. A passport is required. Hold on to your exchange receipt, which you need to convert your extra yuan back into dollars.

▌ PACKING

Most Chinese people dress for comfort, and you can do the same. There's little risk of offending people with your dress; Westerners tend to attract attention regardless of attire and pretty much anything goes. Sturdy, comfortable, closed-toe walking shoes are a must. Summers are dusty and hot, so lightweight slacks, shorts, and short-sleeve shirts are great options. A light raincoat is useful in spring and fall.

Come winter, thermal long underwear is a lifesaver. A long overcoat, scarf, hat, and gloves will help keep icy winds at bay. That said, in Beijing you can arrive unprepared: the city is a shopper's paradise. If you can't fit a bulky jacket in your suitcase, buy a cheap one upon arrival. Scarves, gloves, and hats are also cheap and easy to find.

Carry packets of tissues and antibacterial hand wipes with you—toilet paper isn't common in Chinese public restrooms. A small flashlight with extra batteries is also useful. Chinese pharmacies can be limited, so take adequate stocks if you're picky about lotions and potions. Beijing is quite dry, so moisturizer is a must. Choice is also limited for feminine-hygiene products, so bring along extra or pay outrageous prices in the expat supermarkets.

If you're planning a longer trip or will be using local guides, bring a few items from your home country as gifts, such as candy, T-shirts, and small cosmetic items like lipstick and nail polish.

■TIP➔ If you're a U.S. citizen traveling abroad, consider registering online with the State Department (⊕ *travelregistration.state.gov/ibrs/ui*), so the government will know to look for you should a crisis occur in the country you're visiting.

PASSPORTS AND VISAS

All U.S. citizens, even infants, need a valid passport with a tourist visa stamped in it to enter China (except for Hong Kong, where you only need a valid passport). Getting a tourist visa (known as an "L" visa) in the United States is straightforward, but be sure to check the Chinese embassy website and call them to make sure you're bringing the correct documents. Visa regulations sometimes change on short notice. Standard visas are for single-entry stays of up to 30 days and are valid for 90 days from the day of issue (NOT the day of entry), so don't get your visa too far in advance. Costs range from $130 for a tourist visa issued within two to three working days to $160 for a same-day service.

As of 2013, U.S. travelers (and those of 44 other countries) transiting through Beijing Capital Airport and Shanghai's Hongqiao and Pudong airports can now stay for up to 72 hours visa-free, so long as you have proof of an onward ticket to or from a third country. Signs at the international arrivals area of the airport will direct you towards the appropriate channels.

Travel agents in Hong Kong can also issue visas to visit mainland China. ■TIP➔ The visa application will ask your occupation. The Chinese authorities don't look favorably upon those who work in publishing or the media. People in these professions routinely state "teacher" under "occupation."

Under no circumstances should you overstay your visa. To extend your visa, go to the Division of the Entry and Exit of Aliens of the Beijing Municipal Public Security Bureau a week before your visa expires. The office is also known as the Foreigner's Police; it's open weekdays 8 am to noon and 1:30 pm to 4 pm. Under normal circumstances it's generally no problem to get a month's extension on a tourist visa, but the rules change often. Bring your passport and a registration of temporary residency from your hotel. Keep in mind that you'll need to leave your passport there for five to seven days, so get a receipt and always keep a photocopy of your passport on you. If you're trying to extend a business visa, you'll need the above items as well as a letter from the business that originally invited you to China.

Info CIBT Visas. Formally known as Visa to Asia, CIBT Visas is a fast, efficient processer of all types of China visa requests. ☎ *800/929–2428 customer services* ⊕ *cibtvisas.com/china-visa.php.*

In the U.S. Chinese Consulate, New York ☎ *212/244–9456* ⊕ *www.nyconsulate.prchina.org.* **Visa Office of Chinese Embassy, Washington** ☎ *202/337–1956* ⊕ *www.china-embassy.org.*

Visa Extensions **Division of the Entry and Exit of Aliens, Beijing Municipal Public Security Bureau** ✉ *2 Andingmen Dongdajie* ☎ *010/8401–5300.*

▌RESTROOMS

Public restrooms abound in Beijing—the street, parks, restaurants, department stores, and major tourist attractions are all likely locations. Most charge a small fee (usually less than Y1), and seldom provide Western-style facilities or private booths. Instead, expect squat toilets, open troughs, and rusty spigots; "wc" signs at intersections point the way to these facilities. Toilet paper or tissues and antibacterial hand wipes are good things to have in your day pack. The restrooms in the newest shopping plazas, fast-food outlets, and deluxe restaurants catering to foreigners are generally on a par with American restrooms.

Find a Loo **The Bathroom Diaries.** The Bathroom Diaries is flush with unsanitized info on restrooms the world over—each one located, reviewed, and rated. ⊕ *www.thebathroomdiaries.com.*

▌SAFETY

There is little violent crime against tourists in China, partly because the penalties are severe for those who are caught—China's yearly death-sentence tolls run into the thousands. Single women can move about Beijing without too much hassle. Handbag snatching and pickpocketing do occur in markets and on crowded buses or trains—keep an eye open and your money safe and you should have no problems. Use the lockbox in your hotel room to store any valuables. You should always carry either your passport or a photocopy of the information page and the visa page of your passport with you for identification purposes.

Beijing is full of people looking to make a quick buck. The most common scam involves people persuading you to go with them for a tea ceremony, which is often so pleasant that you don't smell a rat until several hundred dollars appear on your credit-card bill. "Art students" who pressure you into buying work is another common scam. The same rules that apply to hostess bars worldwide are also true in Beijing. Avoiding such scams is as easy as refusing *all* unsolicited services—be it from taxi or pedicab drivers, tour guides, or potential "friends."

Beijing traffic is as manic as it looks, and survival of the fittest (or the biggest) is the main rule. Crossing streets can be an extreme sport. Drivers rarely give pedestrians the right-of-way and don't even look for pedestrians when making a right turn on a red light. Cyclists have less power but are just as aggressive.

Beijing's severely polluted air can bring on, or aggravate, respiratory problems. If you're a sufferer, take the cue from locals, who wear special pollution masks, or a scarf or bandana as protection.

▌TIP➡ Distribute your cash, credit cards, IDs, and other valuables between a deep front pocket, an inside jacket or vest pocket, and a hidden money pouch. Don't reach for the money pouch once you're in public.

Safety **Transportation Security Administration** (*TSA*) ⊕ *www.tsa.gov.*

▌TAXES

There is no sales tax in China. Hotels charge a 5% tax; bigger, joint-venture hotels also add a 10% to 15% service fee. Some restaurants charge a 10% service fee.

▌TIME

Beijing is 8 hours ahead of London, 13 hours ahead of New York, 14 hours ahead of Chicago, and 16 hours ahead of Los Angeles. There's no daylight saving time, so subtract an hour in summer.

Time Zones **Timeanddate.com.** Timeanddate. com can help you figure out the correct time anywhere in the world. ⊕ *www.timeanddate. com/worldclock.*

▮ TIPPING

Tipping is a tricky issue in China. It's officially forbidden by the government, and locals simply don't do it. In general, follow their lead without qualms. Nevertheless, the practice is beginning to catch on, especially among tour guides, who often expect Y10 a day. You don't need to tip in restaurants or in taxis—many drivers insist on handing over your change, however small.

▮ TOURS

SPECIAL-INTEREST TOURS

The likes of Bespoke Beijing, Stretch-a-Leg Travel, and WildChina specialize in taking visitors to off-the-beaten-track locations and can offer personalized tours.

Contacts Bespoke Beijing. ✉ B510, 107 Dongsi Beidajie, Dongcheng District ☎ 010/6400–0133 ✏ info@bespoke-beijing. com ⊕ www.bespoke-beijing.com ⊗ Office daily 9–5. **Stretch-A-Leg Travel.** ✉ 2 Qian'gulouyuan, Jiaodaokou, Dongcheng District ☎ 010/6401–8933 ✏ info@stretchaleg. com ⊕ www.stretchalegtravel.com ⊗ Office weekdays 10–6. **WildChina.** ✉ Room 803, Oriental Place, 9 E. Dongfang Lu, Chaoyang District ☎ 010/6465–6602, +1 888/902–8808 (US toll free) ✏ info@wildchina.com ⊕ www.wildchina.com ⊗ Office weekdays 9–6.

BIKING

Cycle China offers plenty of cycling trips in and around Beijing and beyond, such as the Great Wall. You can hire bikes from them, or take your own. Bike China Adventures organizes trips of varying length and difficulty all over China.

Contacts Bike China Adventures ☎ 800/818–1778 ⊕ www.bikechina.com. **Cycle China** ✉ 12 Jingshan Dongjie, Dongcheng District ☎ 139/1188–6524, 010/6402–5653 ⊕ www.cyclechina.com.

CULTURE

Local guides are often creative when it comes to showing you history and culture, so having an expert with you can make a big difference. Learning is the focus of Smithsonian Journeys' small-group tours, which are led by university professors. China experts also lead National Geographic's trips, but all that knowledge doesn't come cheap. WildChina is a local company with unusual trips: one of their cultural trips explores China's little-known Jewish history. The Hutong and the China Culture Center are also wonderful local resources for tours, classes, lectures, and other events in Beijing. The China Guide is a Beijing-based, American-managed travel agency offers tours that do *not* make shopping detours.

Contacts China Culture Center ✉ Room 4916, Liangma Antique Market, 27 Liangmaqiao Rd., Chaoyang District ☎ 010/6432–9341, 010/8420-0671 weekend number ⊕ www.chinaculturecenter.org. **The China Guide.** ✉ Room 81, 8th floor, Bldg. 7-1, Jianguomenwai Waijiaogongyu Diplomatic Compound ☎ 010/8532–1860 ✏ book@ thechinaguide.com ⊕ www.thechinaguide. com ⊗ Office weekdays 10–6. **National Geographic Expeditions** ☎ 888/966–8687 ⊕ www.nationalgeographicexpeditions.com. **Smithsonian Journeys** ☎ 855/330–1542 ⊕ www.smithsonianjourneys.org. **WildChina** ✉ Room 803, Oriental Place, No. 9 Dongfang Donglu, Dongsanhuan Beilu, Chaoyang District ☎ 888/902–8808 U.S. toll-free, 010/6465–6602 ✏ info@wildchina.com ⊕ www.wildchina.com.

CULINARY

Intrepid Travel is an Australian company offering a China Gourmet Traveler tour with market visits, cooking demonstrations, and plenty of good eats. Imperial Tours Culinary Tour combines sightseeing with cooking lectures and demonstrations, and lots of five-star dining.

Contacts Imperial Tours ☎ 888/888–1970 ⊕ www.imperialtours.net. **Intrepid Travel** ☎ 800/970-7299 ⊕ www.intrepidtravel.com.

HIKING

Beijing Hikers offer multiple hikes and camping stays on and around the Great Wall and always make sure that they leave no rubbish behind, unlike many other companies.

Contacts **Beijing Hikers** ✉ *Suite 4012, Bldg. A, 10 Jiuxianqiao Zhonglu* ☎ *010/6432–2786* ⊕ *www.beijinghikers.com.*

PEDICAB TOURS

Pedicabs (basically large tricycles with room for passengers behind a pedaling driver) were once the vehicles of choice for Beijingers laden with a week's worth of groceries or tourists eager for a street's-eye city tour. Today many residents are wealthy enough to bundle their purchases into taxis or their own cars, and the tourist trade has moved on to the tight schedules of air-conditioned buses. But pedicabs have made a big comeback in Beijing in recent years and can now be hired near major tourist sites. A ride through the hutong near Houhai is the most popular pedicab journey. ■TIP➜ Be absolutely sure to negotiate the fare in advance, clarifying which currency will be used (yuan or dollars), whether the fare is considered a one-way or round-trip (some drivers will demand payment for a round-trip whether or not you use the pedicab for the return journey), and whether it is for one person or two. Beginning in 2008, government-approved pedicab tours were supposed to be fixed at Y35 per hour, though the actual price is often higher. Feel free to tip your driver for good service on longer tours. Independent pedicabs for hutong tours can be found in the small plaza between the Drum Tower and the Bell Tower.

Beijing Hutong Tourist Agency. This agency was one of the first to offer guided pedicab tours of Beijing's back alleys, with glimpses of old courtyard houses and daily Beijing life. It offers trips ranging from 40 minutes to 2½ hours priced at Y80–Y220 per person (solo travlers pay extra). The longer tours will take you through what was once Beijing's most prestigious neighborhood (Houhai) and include a stop at the Drum and Bell towers as well as a visit to the home of a local family. ✉ *26 Di'anmen Xidajie, Dongcheng District* ☎ *010/6615–9097.*

▌ VISITOR INFORMATION

For general information, including advice on tours, insurance, and safety, call, or visit China National Tourist Office's website, as well as the website run by the Beijing Tourism Administration (BTA). ■TIP➜ The BTA maintains a 24-hour hotline for tourist inquiries and complaints, with operators fluent in English. BTA also runs Beijing Tourist Information Centers, whose staff can help you with free maps and directions in Beijing.

The two best-known Chinese travel agencies are China International Travel Service (CITS) and China Travel Service (CTS), both under the same government ministry. Although they have some tourist information, they are businesses, so don't expect endless resources if you're not booking through them.

China National Tourist Offices
United States ☎ *888/760–8218 New York, 800/670–2228 Los Angeles* ⊕ *www.cnto.org.*

Beijing Tourist Information
Beijing Tourism Administration ✍ *visitbeijingeng@163.com* ⊕ *english.visitbeijing.com.cn.* **Beijing Travel Hotline**. Beijing Travel Hotline ☎ *12301* ⊕ *www.english.visitbeijing. cn.* **BTG International Travel &Tours**. BTG International Travel & Tours ✉ *Beijing Tourism Bldg., 28 Jianguomenwai Dajie, Chaoyang District* ☎ *400-010-0808* ⊕ *www.btgtravel. com.cn.* **China International Travel Service** ☎ *010/6522–2991 CITS in Beijing* ⊕ *www.cits. com.cn* ☎ *626/568–8993 U.S.* ⊕ *www.citsusa. com.* **China Travel Service** ☎ *010/6462–2288 CTS Beijing Head Office, 800/899–8618 CTS New York* ⊕ *www.ctsho.com.*

ONLINE TRAVEL TOOLS

For a general overview of traveling in China, try the China National Tourism Office's website. The state-run travel agency, China Travel Services, is another helpful starting place.

All About Beijing Beijing Expat. Beijing Expat has pages and pages of advice and listings from foreigners living in Beijing. ⊕ *beijing.asiaxpat.com.* **Beijing International.** Beijing International, if slightly dry, is the comprehensive government guide to the city. ⊕ *www.ebeijing.gov.cn.* **Beijing Tourism Administration.** Beijing Tourism Administration offers well-organized information on sights and activities in Beijing, as well as hotel and restaurant information. ⊕ *english.visitbeijing.com. cn.* **Caixin.** English-language website for the popular business and economic paper. ⊕ *english.caixin.com.* **China Digital Times.** China Digital Times is an excellent Berkeley-run site tracking China-related news and culture, though you won't be able to access it from inside China. ⊕ *www. chinadigitaltimes.net.* **China National Tourism Office** ⊕ *www.cnto.org.* **China Travel Services** ⊕ *www.chinatravelservice.com.* **Chinese Government Portal** ⊕ *english.gov.cn.*

Business China Daily. Newspaper website with large business section. ⊕ *www. chinadaily.com.cn.* **Chinese Government Business Site.** Chinese Government Business Site offers news, links, and information on business-related legal issues from the Chinese government. ⊕ *english.gov. cn/business.htm.* **Global Times.** The best of the local newspapers. ⊕ *www.globaltimes. cn.* **NuiBBall.com.** has everything you ever wanted to know about Chinese basketball, plus schedules and ticket advice. ⊕ *www. niubball.com.* **Wild East Football.** looks at the weird world of Chinese soccer, with tips on how to get tickets and attend local games. ⊕ *wildeastfootball.net.*

Culture and Entertainment The Beijinger. The Beijinger has a weekly email newsletter about what's going on in the city. Their classifieds section is excellent, too. ⊕ *www.thebeijinger.com.* **Beijing Weekend.** Beijing Weekend is a weekly supplement from *China Daily* newspaper, with shopping, dining, and entertainment reviews. ⊕ *www.chinadaily.com.cn.* **Chinese Culture.** Chinese Culture has a detailed, searchable database with information on Chinese art, literature, film, and history. ⊕ *www. chinaculture.org.* **Smart Beijing.** has extensive listings, reviews, and offbeat articles on life in the city. ⊕ *www.smartbeijing. com.* **Time Out Beijing.** provides a great overview of all the major cultural (and noncultural) events in the city. ⊕ *www. timeoutbeijing.com/.*

INDEX

PHOTO CREDITS

Front cover: Guo Jian She/Redlink/Corbis [Beijing National Stadium]. 1, Boaz Rottem / age fotostock. 2-3, TAO IMAGES / age fotostock. 5, lu linsheng/iStockphoto. Chapter 1: Experience Beijing. 8-9, SuperStock/age fotostock. 10, Brian Jeffery Beggerly/Flickr. 11 (left), Fan Ping/Shutterstock. 11 (right), Wikimedia Commons. 14 (left), Ivan Walsh/Flickr. 14 (top center), claudio zaccherini/Shutterstock. 14, (bottom right), Jonathan Larsen/Shutterstock. 14 (top right), Ivan Walsh/ Flickr. 15 (top left), zhang bo/ iStockphoto. 15 (bottom left), fotohunter/Shutterstock. 15 (right), claudio zaccherini/Shutterstock.16, China National Tourist Office. 17 (left), Honza Soukup/Flickr. 17 (right), claudio zaccherini/Shutter-stock. 18, Holly Peabody, Fodors.com member. 19, Frans Schalekamp, Fodors.com member. 21 (left), yxm2008/Shutterstock. 21 (right), bbobo, Fodors.com member. 23 (left), Eastimages/Shutterstock. 23 (right), gary718/Shutterstock. 24, Artifan/Shutterstock. 25 (left), Hotel G Beijing. 25 (right), DK.samco/ Shutterstock. 26, Johann 'Jo' Guzman, Fodors.com member. 27, Steve Slawsky. 28, Gretchen Winters, Fodors.com member. 29, huang shengchun/iStockphoto. 32, Stefano Tronci/Shutterstock. 33, qinqing/ Shutterstock. 34 (left), Kowloonese/Wikimedia Commons. 34 (top right), Daniel Shichman & Yael Tauger/Wikimedia Commons. 34 (bottom right), wikipedia.org. 35 (left), Hung Chung Chih/Shutter-stock. 35 (right), rodho/Shutterstock. 36 (left), Chinneeb/ Wikimedia Commons. 36 (top right), B_cool/ Wikimedia Commons. 36 (bottom right), Imperial Painter/Wikimedia Commons. 37 (left), Wikimedia Commons. 37 (top right), Joe Brandt/iStockphoto. 37 (bottom right), 38 (all), and 39 (top left), Public Domain, via Wikimedia Commons. 39 (bottom left), ImagineChina. 39 (right), tomislav domes/Flickr. Chapter 2: Exploring. 41, TAO IMAGES / age fotostock. 42, fotohunter/Shutterstock. 44, lu linsheng/ iStockphoto. 45 (top), TAO IMAGES / age fotostock. 45 (bottom), Bob Balestri/iStockphoto. 46, Lance Lee | AsiaPhoto. com/iStockphoto. 47 (left), Jiping Lai/iStockphoto. 47 (top right), May Wong/Flickr. 47 (right, 2nd from top), William Perry/iStockphoto. 47 (right, 3rd from top), bing liu/iStockphoto. 47 (bottom right), William Perry/iStockphoto48 (top), Helena Lovincic/iStockphoto. 48 (bottom left and right), Wikipedia. 49 (top), rehoboth foto/Shutterstock. 49 (bottom left and right), Wikipedia. 50, Alexander Savin/Flickr. 53, shalunishka/Shutterstock. 54, claudio zaccherini/Shutterstock. 56, TAO IMAGES / age fotostock. 59, P. Narayan / age fotostock. 60, claudio zaccherini/Shutterstock. 61, Jose Fuste Raga / age fotostock. 63, claudio zaccherini/Shutterstock. 65, Lim Yong Hian/Shutterstock. 68, TAO IMAGES / age fotostock. 70, JTB Photo / age fotostock. 72, TAO IMAGES / age fotostock. 74, sanglei slei/iStockphoto.77, William Ju/Shutterstock. 78, Sylvain Grandadam/ age fotostock. 80 and 83, Daderot/Wikimedia Commons. 81, View Stock/age footstock. 85, TAO IMAGES / age foto-stock. Chapter 3: Where to Eat. 89, TAO IMAGES / age fotostock. 90, Frans Schalekamp, Fodors.com member. 98, beggs/Flickr. 99, FOTOSEARCH RM / age fotostock. 100 (bottom), Fotoos-VanRobin/ Wikimedia Commons. 100 (top), Chubykin Arkady/Shutterstock. 101(left), ImagineChina. 101 (top right), hywit dimyadi/iStockphoto. 101 (bottom right), Maria Ly/Flickr. 102 (bottom), Hannamariah/ Shutterstock. 102 (top), zkruger/iStockphoto. 103 (top left), Ritesh Man Tamrakar/Wikimedia Com-mons. 103 (center left), Rjanag/Wikimedia Commons. 103 (bottom left), Craig Lovell / Eagle Visions Photography / Alamy. 103 (right), Cephas Picture Library / Alamy. 104 (top left), Eneri LLC/iStock-photo. 104 (bottom left), Man Haan Chung/iStockphoto. 104 (top right), Holger Gogolin/iStockphoto. 104 (bottom right), Eneri LLC/iStockphoto. 108 Fumio Okada / age fotostock. 113, Thomas Roetting / age fotostock. 119, patrick frilet / age fotostock. Chapter 4: Where to Stay. 125, The Ritz-Carlton Bei-jing, Financial Street. 126, Hotel G Beijing. 134 (top), Red Capital Residence. 134 (bottom left), Hotel G Beijing. 134 (bottom right), Amanresorts. 144 (top), Hyatt Hotels. 144 (bottom), Starwood Hotels and Resorts. Chapter 5: Shopping. 149, Oote Boe / age fotostock. 150, fi repile/Flickr. 153, Renaud Visage / age fotostock. 160, TAO IMAGES / age fotostock. 164, Christian Kober / age fotostock. 166, TAO IMAGES / age fotostock.Chapter 6: Arts and Nightlife. 169, Peter Adams / age fotostock. 170, PhotoTalk/iStockphoto. 173, Werner Bachmeier / age fotostock. 175, FRILET Patrick / age fotostock. 180, TAO IMAGES / age fotostock. 182-83, Sylvain Grandadam / age fotostock. 186, J.D.Heaton / age fotostock. Chapter 7: Best Side Trips. 189, Sylvain Grandadam / age fotostock. 190, dspiel, Fodors.com member. 191 (left), chenyingphoto/Flickr. 191 (right), Lukas Kurtz/Wikimedia Commons. 192, Hung Chung Chih/Shutterstock. 196, John W. Warden/age fotostock. 197, Wikipedia.198-99, Liu Jianmin/ age fotostock. 202, Alan Crawford/iStockphoto. 203, Eugenia Kim/iStockphoto. 204, Jarno Gonzalez/ iStockphoto. 205, Chris Ronneseth/iStockphoto. 209, SuperStock/age fotostock. 210, JTB Photo / age fotostock. Back cover (from left to right): cozyta/Shutterstock; jaume/Shutterstock; Holly Peabody, Fodors.com member. Spine: testing/Shutterstock.

NOTES

NOTES

NOTES

ABOUT OUR WRITERS

Sky Canaves is a writer whose work has been focused on China since the late 90s, when she spent an academic year studying in Nanjing. She was reporter for The Wall Street Journal in Hong Kong and Beijing, where she covered the 2008 Summer Olympic Games and launched the publication's China Real Time blog. She has also written for various other news outlets including the *Financial Times* and *Bloomberg News*. After nine years in Asia, she recently returned to her hometown, New York City. For this edition, Sky updated the Exploring and Where to Eat chapters.

Gareth Clark has worked in magazines for nearly a decade, the bulk of which he spent writing for *Time Out* publications in the Middle East and Asia. In 2009 he moved to China, where he became the editor of local listings bible *Time Out Beijing* before going freelance. He loves nothing more than eating a hot baozi on a smoggy day. Gareth updated the Shopping and Side Trips chapters of this year's guide.

Born in Beijing, **Ami Li** grew up in the US. Luckily, her parents her to forced to go Chinese school every weekend for the first 15 years of her life because she ultimately parlayed her native-level Mandarin into her current job at Split Works, an independent music and festival promoter in China. Firmly ensconced back in the city of her birth, she spends most of her time checking out new bands, sipping craft cocktails in the *hutongs*, and riding her bike all over the city. Before finding her calling as a music promoter, Ami honed her translation skills by working for the *New York Times* Beijing Bureau and wrote for publications such as *City Weekend* and *China Music Radar*. Ami updated the Nightlife & Arts chapter.

Adrian Sandiford is a PTC and MDJA award-winning magazine journalist based in Beijing. Previously on staff at *Esquire* in London, he moved east in 2008 to become the editor of *Time Out Beijing*, the city's indispensable listings and entertainment guide, where he is now editor-at-large. He spent years uncovering the best that China's capital has to offer and his work has since covered everything from writing about trends in the local food scene for *The Times of London* to editing a series of books on contemporary Chinese art for leading critic and curator Karen Smith. He is also the author of the *Wallpaper* City Guide: Guangzhou* and *Wallpaper* City Guide: Beijing*. Adrian updated the Experience and Where Stay chapters.